THE BATTLE FOR GUADALCANAL

SAMUEL B. GRIFFITH II

UNIVERSITY OF ILLINOIS PRESS

Urbana and Chicago

FIRST ILLINOIS PAPERBACK, 2000

Maps drawn by John Carnes

Library of Congress Cataloging-in-Publication Data
Griffith, Samuel B.
The battle for Guadalcanal / Samuel B. Griffith II.
p. cm.
Originally published: Philadelphia : Lippincott, 1963, in series:
Great battles of history.
Includes bibliographical references and index.
ISBN 0-252-06891-2 (alk. paper)
1. Guadalcanal Island (Solomon Islands), Battle of, 1942–1943.
2. United States. Marine Corps—History—World War, 1939–1945.
I. Title.
D767.98.G7   2000
940.54'26—dc21   00-025905
CIP

P 5 4 3 2 1

UNIVERSITY OF ILLINOIS PRESS
1325 South Oak Street   Champaign, IL 61820-6903
WWW.PRESS.UILLINOIS.EDU

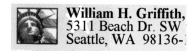
THE BATTLE FOR GUADALCANAL

"Long may the tale be told

in the great Republic."

—Winston S. Churchill,

Closing the Ring

CONTENTS

Book III

Book IV

PREFACE

In his *Marlborough,* Winston Spencer Churchill wrote of great battles, which, "won or lost, change the entire course of events, create new standards of values, new moods, new atmospheres in armies and in nations, to which all must conform." Such, in the Pacific in World War II, were the Battles of Midway, of Guadalcanal, and, later, of the Marianas.

To the recapture of the airfield on Guadalcanal, which was seized by American marines on August 7, 1942, the Japanese committed an army (the 17th) and a major proportion of the imperial navy's surface, air, and undersea strength. After six months of almost uninterrupted fighting, the defeated Japanese abandoned the island, and were denied further use of the surrounding seas, and of the air space above them. After this battle, decisive in both strategic and psychological terms, those Japanese able to face the future objectively knew that the treasure house of South East Asia, "the land of everlasting summer," would be taken away from them.

No book such as this can possibly be written without help from a great many people, and I have been most fortunate in securing the full co-operation of a number of Japanese who in 1942 were in positions of responsible authority. First among these is Colonel Susumu Nishiura, now Chief of the War History Division, Japanese Defense Agency. Thanks to his interest and good offices I was able to conduct a fruitful correspondence with former Lieutenant Generals Shuichi Miyazaki and Kumao Imoto, former Major Generals Tadashi Sumuyoshi and Toshinaro Shoji, and Colonel Kazuo Taguchi. To them all, I am much indebted.

Many American officers who served on Guadalcanal have given me information of the type not usually to be found in official records. Principal among these is General Alexander Archer Vandegrift, commander of the U. S. Marine Landing Forces which assaulted Guadalcanal–Tulagi–Gavutu–Tanambogo. General Vandegrift has considerately answered dozens of questions, some of which he no doubt considered impertinent.

His former chief of staff, now General Gerald C. Thomas, U.S.M.C. (retired), and his former operations officer, General Merrill B. Twining (now also retired), have shed light on a number of questions which are not clarified in reports. One of those who commanded the Allied Air Force on Guadalcanal, Lieutenant General Louis Woods, U.S.M.C. (retired), has, in long and pleasant conversations, been most patient and helpful. Major General Richard C. Mangrum, U.S.M.C. (then a major), who played such a vital part in the early phases of the campaign, labored twice through the first drafts of the manuscript, and his acute memory has saved me from many errors. As the original record (much of it handwritten) of Headquarters, First Marine Aircraft Wing, was lost, the contributions of these two officers proved to be uniquely essential to the story of the decisive struggle for control of the air.

Thanks for reading the manuscript, or portions of it, go also to Richard C. West, Professor of History, U. S. Naval Academy, to William Harbaugh, Professor of History, Bucknell University, to Rear Admiral Frank P. Mitchell, U.S.N. (retired), to Colonel Saville T. Clark and Colonel James E. Kerr, to Captain Robert Asprey, Colonel Robert D. Heinl, Doctor John Miller, Jr., and Henry I. Shaw, Jr. Not every aspiring military historian is blessed with friends so able and willing as were these to provide helpful criticism.

To Martin Clemens, who, with members of his Solomon Islands Constabulary, figures importantly in the narrative, I owe thanks for access to his private diary (as yet unpublished) of those eventful days.

Both Mr. Shaw, Head, Historical Branch, G-3, U.S.M.C., and

Doctor Miller, author of the U. S. Army's official history of the Guadalcanal campaign, sympathetically aided my researches in every conceivable way. At the World War II Records Division, National Archives, Mr. Wilbur J. Nigh and Mr. Joseph Avery did much mining for me, as did Mr. D. M. O'Quinlevan, Head, Records and Research Section, Historical Branch, U.S.M.C., and his staff. Mr. Lynn Delozier, Librarian, Marine Corps Schools, Quantico, Virginia, expeditiously responded to requests for books and periodicals. Mr. Dean Allard, Head, Operational Archives Branch, Naval History Division, and his staff were unfailingly helpful and courteous.

For translation of the Memoirs of Major General Kiyotaki Kawaguchi, I am indebted to Mr. Yukihisa Suzuki, at war's end in training as a kamikaze pilot, and now Librarian, The Asian Library, University of Michigan, Ann Arbor.

Rear Admiral William W. Wilbourne, U.S.N. (retired), who, as gunnery officer of cruiser *San Francisco,* participated in two night battles off Savo, has kindly given me, at length, his personal impressions of these ferocious encounters.

Mr. Clarke Kawakami and Mr. Roger Pineau put me on the track of several Japanese sources which I would otherwise no doubt have overlooked.

Fleet Admiral Chester W. Nimitz read the manuscript in its final form and made several valuable suggestions. My obligation to him, as to General Vandegrift, cannot well be repaid.

Any historian of World War II who has such an advisory editor as Hanson Baldwin is indeed fortunate.

The maps were prepared by Mr. John Carnes, and are based on those which earlier appeared in official histories. For permission to use these, I am indebted to the Chief, Office of Military History, U. S. Army, and to the Director, Historical Branch, G-3, U. S. Marine Corps.

It should be unnecessary to add that I alone am responsible for the facts as set forth in this book as well as for interpretation of them.

SAMUEL B. GRIFFITH II

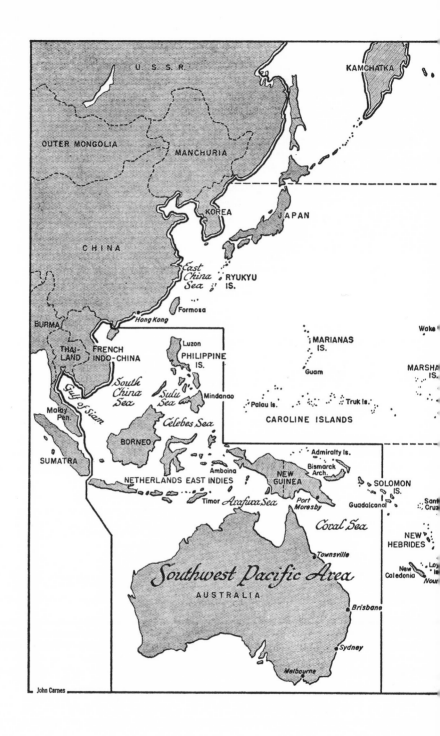

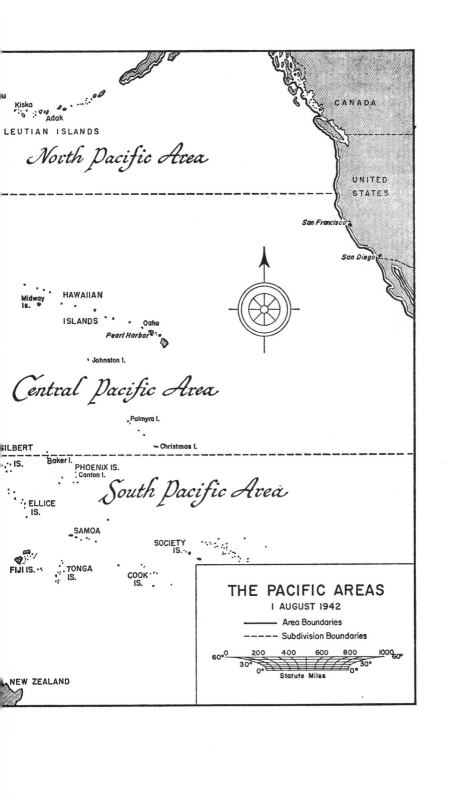

THE PACIFIC AREAS

I AUGUST 1942

——— Area Boundaries

- - - - Subdivision Boundaries

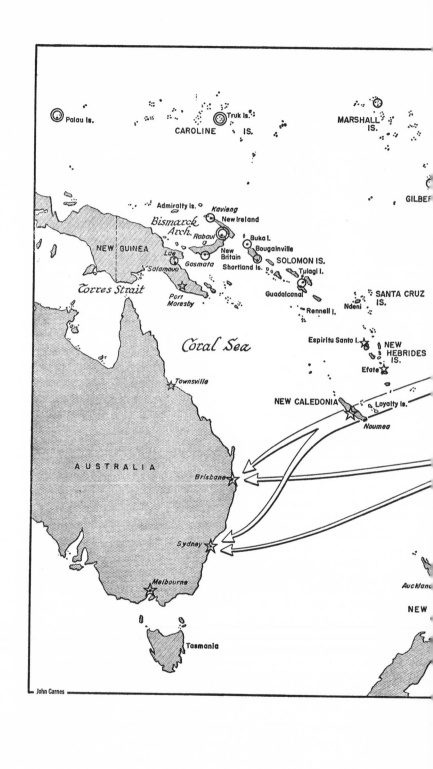

Palau Is.

Truk Is.

CAROLINE IS.

MARSHALL IS.

GILBER

Admiralty Is.

Kavieng

New Ireland

Bismarck Arch.

Rabaul

NEW GUINEA

Lae

Salamaua

Gosmata

New Britain

Buka I.

Bougainville

SOLOMON IS.

Shortland Is.

Tulagi I.

Guadalcanal

Rennell I.

Ndeni

SANTA CRUZ IS.

Espiritu Santo I.

NEW HEBRIDES IS.

Efate

Torres Strait

Port Moresby

Coral Sea

NEW CALEDONIA

Loyalty Is.

Noumea

Townsville

AUSTRALIA

Brisbane

Sydney

Auckland

NEW

Melbourne

Tasmania

John Carnes

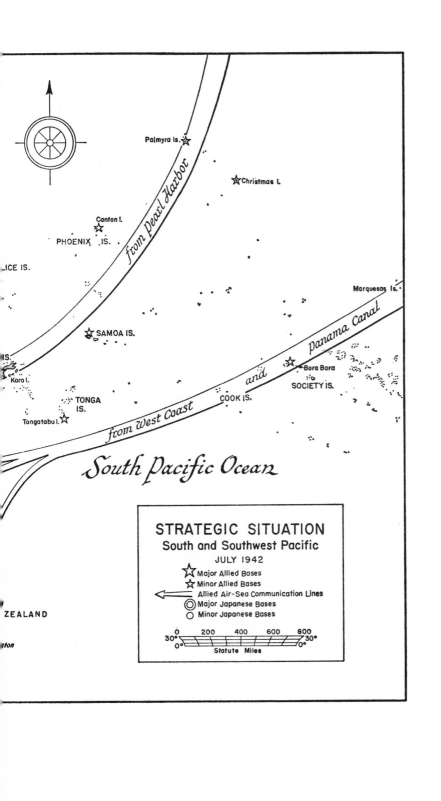

Palmyra Is. ☆

☆ Christmas I.

Canton I. ☆
PHOENIX IS.

ICE IS.

from Pearl Harbor

Marquesas Is.

☆ SAMOA IS.

IS.
Koro I.

Panama Canal

☆ Bora Bora
SOCIETY IS.

TONGA
IS.

COOK IS.

Tongatabu I. ☆

from West Coast

and

South Pacific Ocean

STRATEGIC SITUATION
South and Southwest Pacific
JULY 1942
☆ Major Allied Bases
☆ Minor Allied Bases
← Allied Air-Sea Communication Lines
◎ Major Japanese Bases
○ Minor Japanese Bases

0   200   400   600   800
30°   30°
0°   0°
Statute Miles

ZEALAND

ton

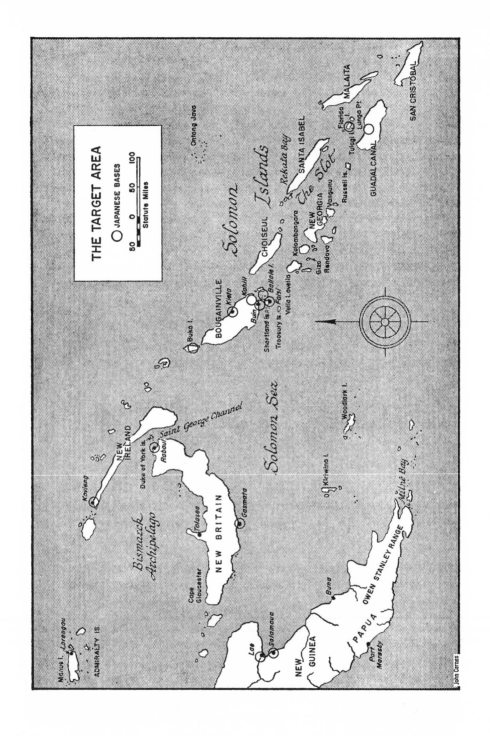

THE TARGET AREA

◯ JAPANESE BASES

50   0   50   100
Statute Miles

Bismarck Archipelago

ADMIRALTY IS.
Manus I.   Lorengau

Kavieng

NEW IRELAND

Saint George Channel

Duke of York Is.
Rabaul

NEW BRITAIN

Cape Gloucester

Talasea

Gasmata

Buka I.

BOUGAINVILLE
Kieta
Kahili
Buin
Shortland Is.
Treasury Is.   Faisi
Vella Lavella

Ontong Java

Solomon Islands

CHOISEUL

Rekata Bay

SANTA ISABEL

The Slot

Kolombangara
Gizo
Rendova
NEW GEORGIA
Vyagunu

Russell Is.

Tulagi
Florida I.
Lunga Pt.

MALAITA

SAN CRISTOBAL

GUADALCANAL

Solomon Sea

Woodlark I.

Kiriwina I.

Milne Bay

OWEN STANLEY RANGE

PAPUA

Buna

Port Moresby

NEW GUINEA

Lae
Salamaua

John Carnes

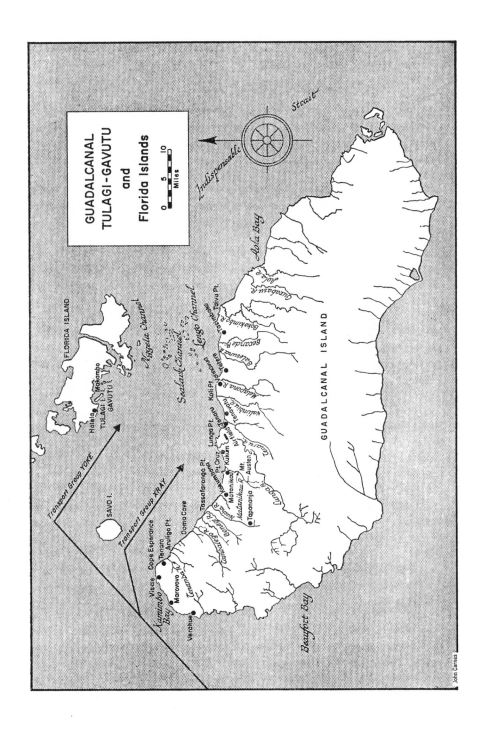

GUADALCANAL
TULAGI - GAVUTU
and
Florida Islands

0 5 10
Miles

Strait

Indispensable

FLORIDA ISLAND

Ngella Channel

Haleta
Makambo
TULAGI
GAVUTU I.

Transport Group YOKE

SAVO I.

Transport Group XRAY

Sealark Channel

Lengo Channel

Taivu Pt.

Koli Pt.

Lunga Pt.

Pt. Cruz
Kukum

Tenaro
Marovovo
Tassafaronga Pt.
Aruligo Pt.
Doma Cove
Matanikau R.
Mt. Austen
Tapananjo

Viscle
Cape Esperance
Teranbus
Verahue

Kamimbo Bay

Bexende R.

Aola Bay

Guadasu R.
Bokokimbo R.

Nalimbiu R.

Matanikau R.

Balesuna R.

Tenaru R.

Tenamba R.

GUADALCANAL ISLAND

Beaufort Bay

John Carnes

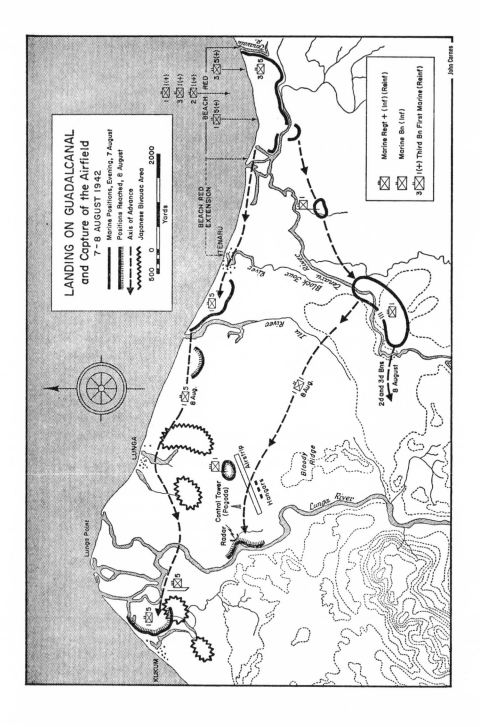

LANDING ON GUADALCANAL
and Capture of the Airfield
7–8 AUGUST 1942

Marine Positions, Evening, 7 August
Positions Reached, 8 August
Axis of Advance
Japanese Bivouac Area

Yards
500 0   2000

Marine Regt + (Inf) (Reinf)
Marine Bn (Inf)
3 ☒ I(+) Third Bn First Marine (Reinf)

BEACH RED EXTENSION
ITEMARU

BEACH RED

LUNGA

Lunga Point

KUKUM

Radar,
Control Tower
(Pagoda)

Airstrip

Bloody
Ridge

Lunga River

Tiu River

Black Bone River

Tenaru River

2d and 3d Bns
8 August

John Carnes

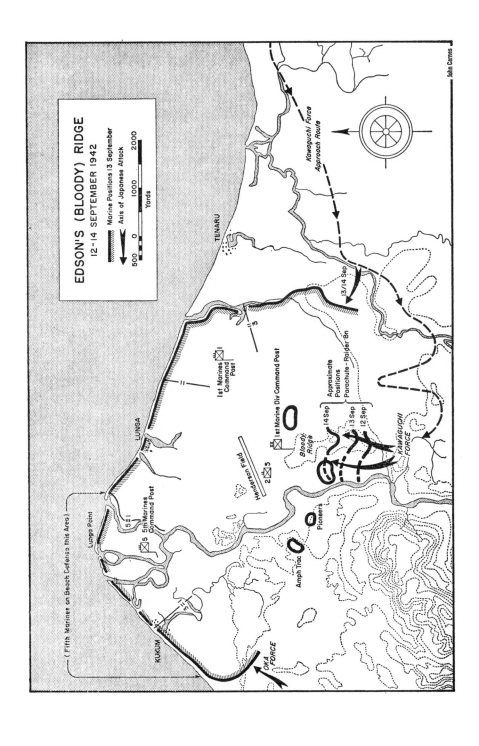

EDSON'S (BLOODY) RIDGE
12-14 SEPTEMBER 1942

Marine Positions 13 September
Axis of Japanese Attack

500 0   1000   2000
      Yards

Kawaguchi Force Approach Route

TENARU

13/14 Sep

1st Marines Command Post

1st Marine Div Command Post

LUNGA

Henderson Field

Bloody Ridge

Approximate Positions Parachute-Raider Bn

14 Sep
13 Sep
12 Sep

KAWAGUCHI FORCE

5th Marines Command Post

Lunga Point

(Fifth Marines on Beach Defense this Area)

Pioneers

Amph Trac

KUKUM

OKA FORCE

John Carnes

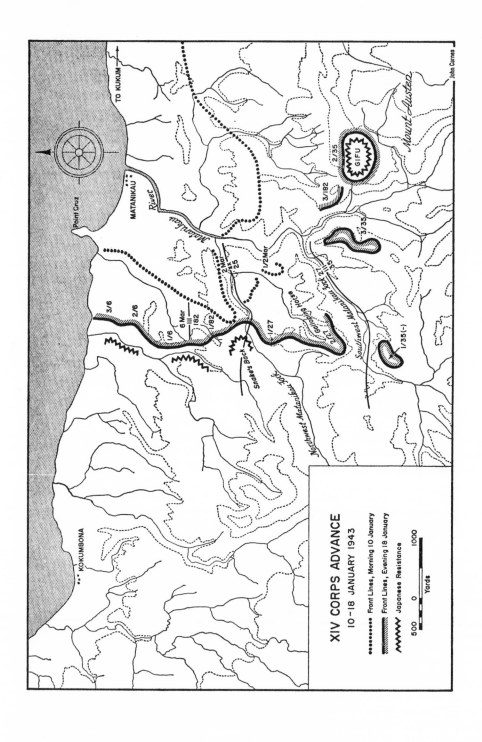

TO KUKUM

Point Cruz

MATANIKAU

Matanikau River

KOKUMBONA

GIFU

2/35

3/182

Mount Austen

3/35

III 3/35

Southwest Matanikau Fork

III 2/35

1/35(-)

Gallopin Horse

1/27

1/2 Mar

2 Mar
25

III 2
25

6 Mar
III
1/82

182

1/6

2/6

3/6

Snake's Back

Northwest Matanikau Fork

John Carnes

XIV CORPS ADVANCE

10–18 JANUARY 1943

•••••• Front Lines, Morning 10 January

━━━━━ Front Lines, Evening 18 January

⋀⋀⋀⋀ Japanese Resistance

Yards

500   0   1000

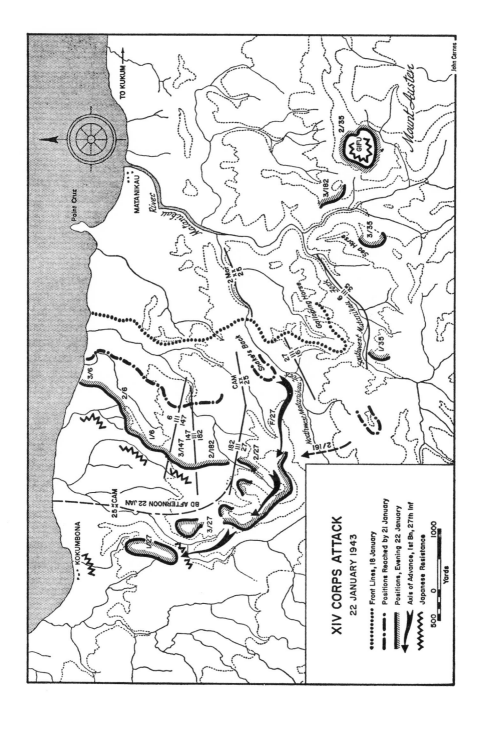

TO KUKUM

Point Cruz

MATANIKAU

Matanikau River

Mount Austen

GIFU
2/35

3/182

3/35

Sea Horse

2 Mar 25

Galloping Horse

35 Bde

Southwest Matanikau River

1/35

2/1

3/6

2/6

Snake's Back

CAM
XX
25

F/27

1/6

6
III
147

147
III
182

182
III
27

2/27

Northwest Matanikau River

3/147

2/182

191/2

KOKUMBONA

25 CAM

25 × CAM

Bd AFTERNOON 22 JAN

3/27

27

XIV CORPS ATTACK

22 JANUARY 1943

Front Lines, 18 January

Positions Reached by 21 January

Positions, Evening 22 January

Axis of Advance, 1st Bn, 27th Inf

Japanese Resistance

500   0   1000
            Yards

John Carnes

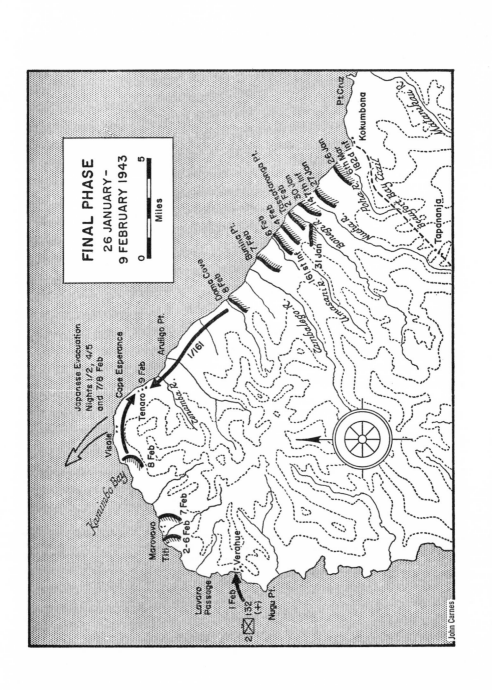

FINAL PHASE
26 JANUARY–
9 FEBRUARY 1943

0   5
Miles

Japanese Evacuation
Nights 1/2, 4/5
and 7/8 Feb

Cape Esperance

Visale

Tenaro – 9 Feb

8 Feb

Arutigo Pt.

1/161

Marovovo

Tifu

2–6 Feb   7 Feb

Verahue

Lavaro
Passage

1 Feb

Nugu Pt.

2   1/32
(+)

Kamimbo Bay

Tenamba R.

Doma Cove

Doma Pt.

8 Feb

7 Feb

Tassafaronga Pt.

6 Feb

5 Feb

2 Feb

30 Jan

31 Jan

1st/161st Inf.

Umasani R.

Bonegi R.

161st Inf.

147th Inf.

27 Jan

161st Inf.

26 Jan

182nd Inf.

6th Mar.

Kokumbona

Pt. Cruz

Nueha R.

Poha R.

Matanikau R.

Tapananja.

Binford Bay

John Carnes

BOOK I

"HE SHAVES WITH A BLOWTORCH"

1 As twilight settled over Tokyo on Sunday, November 30, 1941, Foreign Minister Shigenori Togo finished editing the draft of a dispatch to the Japanese ambassador in Berlin.[1]* This message contained information General Hiroshi Oshima had for some time expected to receive: There was "extreme danger" that war might "suddenly break out between the Anglo-Saxon nations and Japan through some clash of arms." Oshima was instructed to convey this news to the Nazi dictator "very secretly," and to add "that the time of the start of this war may be quicker than anyone dreams."[2]

On the following day, a formal State Council chaired by Premier General Hideki Tojo convened in the Imperial Presence. His Majesty Hirohito listened in silence as Tojo described with bitter brevity the obstructive and hostile attitudes of the American, Chinese, British, and Dutch Governments to "peaceful" expansion of the Japanese Empire on the Asiatic continent and into the rich tropical lands washed by the South Seas. The nation, he concluded, could be preserved only by force of arms.

Indeed, Tojo then knew (although the impassive Emperor did not) that the date for the first, sudden "clash of arms" had already been decided, the principal target selected, the Naval Striking Force secretly assembled. Already, Admiral Isoroku Yamamoto, Commander in Chief Combined Fleet, had made the signal "Ascend Mount Niitaka"; already Vice Admiral Chuichi Nagumo's six carriers, escorted by battleships, cruisers and destroyers, had slipped silently from lonely Tankan Bay in the remote Kuriles, and set a deceptive course into the slow-drifting fogs.[3]

The blow against the U. S. Pacific Fleet and its Pearl Harbor base was designed to delay American action and so gain time to seize and consolidate positions in the South Seas "Resources

* Superior figures refer to Notes at end of text.

Area." In a rapid series of synchronized operations, the Japanese hoped to immobilize the United States Navy and overrun the weakly garrisoned British, Dutch and American possessions in the Far East. These they would quickly absorb into the "Greater East Asia Co-Prosperity Sphere." Around the conquered territories they would constitute a defensive barrier, and make the Allies come to them. Eventually, they believed, the war-weary "Anglo-Saxons," frustrated by costly attacks on impregnable positions, would agree to a negotiated peace by the terms of which the empire would retain most of the loot.

The Japanese thus optimistically hoped to be allowed to conduct a war on their own terms, a war desirably limited in space and time. Experience in China should have suggested that it takes something more than the desires of one participant to limit a war in these, or indeed in any, terms.

Exactly one week after Japanese aircraft had made junk of "Battleship Row," Secretary of the Navy Frank Knox returned to Washington from a hurried trip to the Hawaiian base. Shocked and dismayed by what he saw and heard at Pearl Harbor, the Secretary had concluded during his homeward journey that he must make radical changes, and at once, in the upper levels of the command hierarchy over which he presided. On the day he arrived in the capital he forwarded his recommendations to the President. The most important of these concerned the future assignment of an admiral named King, an officer Roosevelt knew and admired.

On the afternoon of Tuesday, December 16, Knox was summoned to the White House. His companions were the Chief of Naval Operations, Admiral Harold R. Stark, and the Commander in Chief, Atlantic Fleet, Admiral Ernest J. King. All three were aware of the reason for the call they were about to pay: the Secretary had earlier informed the officers of Mr. Roosevelt's decision to resuscitate the post of Commander in Chief, United States Fleet, and to appoint King to fill it.

Admiral King, who had celebrated his sixty-third birthday three weeks previously, was far from being the most popular flag officer in the U. S. Navy, but he was one of the several most respected. A dedicated professional, King always expected those serving under him to meet his own exacting standards. The admiral was no martinet; during a career which spanned forty years, he had never learned to endure seniors whose preoccupation with detail left them little time to concentrate on any command function save unremitting harassment of their subordinates.

As an officer for four decades, King had acquired his own service reputation. A hard but fair, stern but just taskmaster, to some. Others described the admiral in terms less complimentary: "a stubborn crustacean," "so tough he shaves with a blowtorch," "unbending," "a driver." The trait the admiral's detractors described as "obduracy," others defined as "determination."[4]

King believed that a commander's first duty was to assign tasks and state the results expected; his second, to encourage full exercise of initiative in the execution of orders received. Those admirals of the past—Nelson, Tromp, Earl St. Vincent, Farragut—whose exploits inspired King, were all men in whom the offensive spirit predominated; men able to recognize fleeting opportunity and turn it to their advantage.

"Make the best of what you have" was one of the admiral's favorite admonitions:

> There must be no tendency to excuse incomplete readiness for war on the premise of future acquisition of trained personnel or modernized material . . . personnel shall be trained and rendered competent . . . existing material shall be maintained and utilized at its maximum effectiveness at all times.[5]

Within 48 hours of the interview at the White House, President Roosevelt signed Executive Order 9894. This prescribed that the Commander in Chief, United States Fleet, would exercise "supreme command of the operating forces comprising the several fleets of the United States Navy" and made him responsible for the preparation and execution of plans "for current war operations." On Saturday, December 20, King was designated Commander in Chief, United States Fleet (Cominch).[6] Ten days later, his flag was broken in U.S.S. *Vixen*, which lay at the Washington Navy Yard.

Cominch wasted little time composing his first directive, a dispatch to Chester W. Nimitz, who less than two weeks previously had assumed command of the Pacific Fleet. In this, King ordered the new "Cincpac" to cover and hold the "Hawaii–Midway line," protect communications with continental United States, and maintain the security of air and sea lines between the West Coast and Australia. The last-named task obviously postulated a chain of island bases. Ernest J. King had started the Navy's transoceanic march.

During the last week of December 1941, events in the Pacific moved with disconcerting speed. As senior British officers arrived in Washington for the "Arcadia" conference, the American flag was hauled down at Wake, American and Philippine troops began a planned retreat to Bataan, the Japanese landed on Sarawak, completed the conquest of Jolo in the Sulus, and pushed relentlessly south in Malaya. On Christmas Day, Hong Kong surrendered. The Allied position in the Far East was no longer under critical strain. It had fallen apart.

On the last day of this dismal month the conferees delineated a Pacific "ABDA" (Australian-British-Dutch-American) Area and nominated a British general—Sir Archibald Wavell—as supreme commander. Although this paper structure would soon disintegrate under the blows of the Japanese, there were at least two enduring products of "Arcadia." The principle of unity of command, vital to the eventual success of the Allied war effort in Europe, had been established, and the stamp of approval given to a concept of grand strategy, outlined in a document entitled "ABC-1."[7] This called for concentration of Allied effort against the European Axis, with a defensive attitude in the Pacific.

Under the terms of "ABC-1," King would become one of the principal executors of a strategy with which he was congenitally unsympathetic. For King's training and temperament would not permit him to accept the concept of a "holding" war in the Pacific. The admiral, to whom waiting was anathema, was thus faced with a dilemma. He had to support the grand strategic design. Indeed, had he failed to do so, Mr. Roosevelt would quickly have found another Commander in Chief, U. S. Fleet.

General Alan Brooke, Chief of the Imperial General Staff, frequently wished the President would do just that. He wrote later that nothing he or anyone could say "had much effect in weaning King away from the Pacific. This is where his heart was, and the bulk of his Naval Forces. The European war was just a great nuisance that kept him from waging his Pacific war undisturbed."[8]

Everywhere in the Far East the Japanese flood, seemingly irresistible, engulfed the desperate Allies. In Malaya, British General Sir Arthur E. Percival's beaten command, successively maneuvered out of one position after another, fell back almost intact into the dead end of Singapore. December and January produced only a monotonous record of Japanese triumphs and Allied reverses. With the exception of Wake Island, Allied leaders and their troops had demonstrated no particular inclination to fight with needed skill and determination. The theme was retreat, retreat, retreat. After less than eight weeks of war, no one could doubt that British, Dutch and American possessions in the Far East, together with their defenders, must be written off as a total loss.

This series of disasters confirmed King's opinion that immediate action must be taken to limit the Japanese advance. On January 29, U. S. Army troops had garrisoned the Fijis, one of the links in the tenuous chain of island bases which was to be forged between Hawaii and the west coast of Australia and New Zealand. But this did not satisfy King, who in mid-February wrote his colleague, General George C. Marshall, Chief of Staff of the Army, that it was essential "as rapidly as possible . . . to occupy several additional islands in the central and southwestern Pacific."[9] He named Tongatabu in the Tonga Islands, about four hundred miles southeast of the Fijis, and Efate in the New Hebrides.

The Chief of Staff did not reply to this letter for some time; when he did, he asked King to outline the concept of the operations proposed. On March 2, King did so. Essentially, he suggested that a series of "strong points" be established in the South Pacific, from which "a step-by-step" advance could be made, via the Solomons, upon the Japanese bastion at Rabaul.[10] Cominch did not yet realize it, but his finger was pointing to Guadalcanal.

Three days later, King concluded that his ideas for an offensive strategy in the Pacific would not get far in the War Department, and prepared a memorandum for the President. In this, he suggested a "useful" line for U. S. endeavor against the Japanese, and proposed an "integrated" plan of operations, which he summarized in nine words:

Hold Hawaii;
Support Australasia;
Drive northwestward from New Hebrides.[11]

The admiral's enthusiasm for a drive northwestward from the New Hebrides into the Solomons was not shared by Secretary of

War Henry L. Stimson or General Marshall, both of whom—in accordance with the strategic design approved by Roosevelt and Churchill—were intent on building up American strength in Britain for a cross-Channel assault they optimistically envisaged for late 1942 or early 1943. Under these circumstances, the high command of the Army was naturally inclined to view other proposals as diversionary and dangerously dispersive; Marshall lamented to Alan Brooke that King's constant demands were becoming more and more of a drain on slender military resources: the admiral was "continually calling for land forces to capture and hold land bases in the Pacific."[12]

Nevertheless, the Chief of Staff realized that the New Hebrides, a cluster of malarious islands lying four hundred miles north of New Caledonia, must be held if only to secure the line of communication from Hawaii to Australia. Accordingly, in mid-March he ordered Major General Alexander M. Patch, U.S.A., whose "Americal" Division had been hurriedly transported in increments to New Caledonia, to forward a reinforced infantry group to Efate, the southernmost island of the group. The Marine Corps contributed the 4th Defense Battalion, a conglomerate organization which consisted of both seacoast and antiaircraft artillery. This hastily organized task force, under command of the Army's Brigadier General Rose, arrived at Vila in late March and immediately set about clearing a site for an airfield.

While Rose's soldiers and marines hacked at the jungle, and Marshall confided his domestic problems to the Chief of the Imperial General Staff in London, King met in Washington with Vice Admiral Robert L. Ghormley, whom he had selected as prospective commander for the newly created South Pacific Force and Area. This extensive domain had been carved from the vast Pacific Ocean Area assigned to Nimitz by a recent JCS (Joint Chiefs of Staff) directive, and included New Zealand, New Caledonia, the New Hebrides, the lower Solomons, and the many island groups—Fijis, Tonga, Samoa, Phoenix, Society—known before the war principally to traders and missionaries. To the west of the SoPac Area lay the Southwest Pacific Area (SouWesPac), the realm allocated by the same directive to General Douglas MacArthur.

It is not entirely clear what prompted King to make this appointment. Some time previously, Ghormley had been Director of the War Plans Division in the office of the Chief of Naval Operations (CNO) where he had acquired a reputation as a brilliant strategist, but during the two years immediately preceding he had been special naval observer in London. There he was naturally immersed from day to day in a variety of problems unrelated to the area he was soon to command. The admiral was as ignorant of the South Pacific and the Japanese enemy he was to encounter there as everyone else in the Navy Department.

But Ghormley had one asset which distinctly qualified him for the new assignment: he was an accomplished diplomat—suave, gentle, patient, tactful. These qualities were to stand him in good stead, both in his dealings with the New Zealand Government, and in often frustrating negotiations with the volatile and recalcitrant Free French in New Caledonia. Still, the very qualities which were assets in a diplomatic role proved debits when the admiral assumed the executive burdens which devolve upon an area commander in war.

King's instructions to Ghormley were necessarily vague:

"You have been selected to command the South Pacific Force and South Pacific Area. You will have a large area under your command and a most difficult task. I do not have the tools to give you to carry out that task as it should be. You will establish your headquarters in Auckland, New Zealand, with an advanced base at Tongatabu. In time, possibly this fall (1942), we hope to start an offensive from the South Pacific. You will then probably find it necessary to shift the advanced base as the situation demands and move your headquarters to meet special situations. I would like for you to leave Washington in one week, if possible."[13]

In this brief interview, Cominch gave Ghormley no indication of possible target areas, nor could the prospective commander learn anything from King's subordinates, none of whom had even the slightest appreciation of the magitude of the task Vice Admiral Ghormley was about to face. Senior admirals in Washington had nothing to give their colleague but sympathy.

Sympathy was the one item Navy Bureau Chiefs could at the time freely dispense; Ghormley's repeated pleas for properly equipped base construction units ran into one bulkhead after another. Skilled personnel were simply not to be had; earth-moving machinery, pumps, pipes, valves, runway matting, cement, prefabricated steel sections for fuel storage tanks—these, and uncounted other essential items, were in short supply.

This information would have been no news to men working with picks and shovels on the Vila airfields, but in less than five weeks the soldiers and marines, now commanded by Brigadier General Neal C. Johnson, U.S.A., had their fighter strip, and on April 30, Vila was pronounced ready to receive light aircraft. No planes arrived for almost a month. Then, on May 27, a marine major, Harold W. Bauer, led in three Grummans of his Marine Fighter Squadron 212. Ten days later the remaining *Wildcats* landed.[14] In the months to come, scores of fighters, dive bombers and other planes of all types and descriptions would stage through this field en route to one from which many of their pilots, including Bauer, would not return.

In early June, elements of Johnson's force pushed north from Efate (code name: ROSES) to Espiritu Santo (code name: BUTTON) and began to build a bomber strip. Here a naval construction battalion, the "Seabees," appeared for the first time in the Pacific, and began to attack the jungle. The jungle fought back. By the end of June, over half the officers and men of the entire force were on their backs with malaria. Medical teams hastily flown from the States brought with them new medicines, including the suppressive atabrine, and the rampaging disease was gradually checked. But in the months to come, malaria would inflict more casualties on marines and soldiers than would Japanese shells, bombs and bullets.

The men who fought the jungles in the New Hebrides did not return to the United States as heroes, but they made it possible for others to do so. For occupation and development of the New Hebrides was the essential prelude to Guadalcanal. Without these islands, the operations projected by King could not possibly have been supported.

On June 18, Ghormley formally assumed command of the South Pacific Force and Area in Auckland, New Zealand. The domain over which he exercised control was vast, the threat of further Japanese encroachment imminent. Since late January the enemy had moved persistently, albeit remarkably slowly, to the southeast. It had become increasingly apparent to King that this advance, which threatened the Hebrides, must be checked abruptly. The man "so tough that he shaved with a blowtorch" was determined that the U. S. Navy would not sit idly by while the Japanese absorbed, one by one, the strategic islands of the South Pacific.[15]

2

BOXED ON THE NORTH by New Britain and the war club southern tip of New Ireland, on the west by New Guinea's forbidding Papuan peninsula, and on the east by the stringing Solomons, is the body of water known as the Solomon Sea. This treacherous expanse is actually the northern reach of the Coral Sea, which washes alike the coast of Australia from Cape York to Brisbane and the islands of the New Hebrides and New Caledonia lying a thousand miles to the east of the Great Barrier Reef.

A full month before Pearl Harbor, General Gen Sugiyama and Admiral Osami Nagano, respectively Chiefs of Army and Navy Sections of Imperial General Headquarters, had turned their attention to this area, and on November 10 had initialed an outline agreement for joint operations to seize "strategic points in the Bismarck Archipelago as soon as possible after the reduction of Guam."[1] Rabaul on New Britain and Kavieng on adjacent New Ireland were selected for development to buttress the south flank of the Palau–Truk line, and to provide bases from which to extend air and submarine reconnaissance southward into the Solomon and Coral Seas. But there was an additional dividend to be derived from occupation of the Bismarcks. For bases there would not only provide foci from which to interdict the sea areas northeast of Australia but would enable the Japanese to project their arms toward New Guinea and the continent it shields, as well as southeastward into the Solomons, the New Hebrides, the Fijis, Samoa and New Caledonia.

Under the terms of this Central Agreement, the army's South Seas Detachment (Major General Tomitaro Horii) and the navy's Fourth Fleet (Vice Admiral Shigeyoshi Inouye) were designated to seize Rabaul and Kavieng. But it was not until more than three weeks after the fall of Guam (December 10, 1941) that these commanders were alerted.[2]

Japanese estimates of Australian strength in the Bismarcks were accurate: defenses were undeveloped and defenders few. After a series of heavy air strikes flown from Vice Admiral Nagumo's big carriers, Major General Horii's troops landed at Rabaul at daybreak on January 23, 1942, against ineffective resistance. Simultaneously, the 500-man Second Maizuru Special Naval Landing Force (SNLF) seized Kavieng without firing a shot.

One week later nine *Zero* fighters flew in from Truk to Vunakanau, about twelve miles southwest of Rabaul, and christened the field from which most of the strikes against Guadalcanal later originated.[3] By the first day of March, pilots of the Fourth Naval Air Group (48 twin-engined *Betty* medium bombers, 48 *Zero* fighters, and 12 four-engined *Kawanishi Emily* flying boats) were toasting the latest conquests in hastily improvised officers' clubs at Vunakanau and Lakunai.[4]

These two established fields were not exactly primitive, but they naturally lacked blast pens, taxiways and installations essential to support combat air operations on a major scale. The Base Force set to work immediately to correct these deficiencies. An additional strip was fashioned out of two adjacent fairways of the local golf club, but after half a dozen planes cracked up trying to take off from its undulating surface it was abandoned. Ash from Vulcan, a nearby volcano, sifted down on Vunakanau, and vapors from semi-active Tavurvur ate into the skin of fuselages and wings of planes based on Lakunai.

One Japanese pilot who served at both fields later described them as either dust bowls or quagmires. Pilots, aircrews, and maintenance personnel were quartered in tents and hastily knocked-together shacks which lined the runways. But in spite of these conditions the morale of the Emperor's "sea eagles" was high. Many fighter pilots, aces who had flown in China and against the British over Malaya, were eager to come to grips now with the Australians and Americans.

With the almost bloodless occupation of the Bismarcks the Japanese had completed, at little cost to themselves, all operations planned for "Phase One." They had secured the sources of oil and rubber vital to sustain military operations and the rice they must have to keep a war economy going. But the navy had never been satisfied with the limited scope of the Bismarck operation as outlined in the Central Agreement of November 10. Indeed, as early as mid-September 1941, the Fourth

Fleet had war-gamed an offensive in the South Pacific and concluded that it was necessary to occupy Gasmata (on the southern coast of New Britain), Lae and Salamaua (eastern New Guinea) and Tulagi (in the southern Solomons) to effectively defend a Bismarck position and extend the range of air reconnaissance. Under constant prodding from Fourth Fleet, the Combined Fleet Staff, in late January, recommended immediate moves into the Solomons and New Caledonia.

The Army Section was reluctant to agree to further expansion in the southern area. Deeply committed in China, with a million men deployed against a Russian threat to Manchuria and Korea, and the conquered territories to police, the army's capabilities were already severely strained. Its general staff officers argued that Japan should now go over to the strategic defensive, integrate newly-won territories into the "Greater East Asia Co-Prosperity Sphere," and consolidate the "Resources Area" acquired at such little cost in blood, time and treasure. But navy planners were insistent; on January 29, 1942, the army capitulated, and the two staff sections issued complementary directives for a new forward move.

These provided for occupation by the navy of strategic points in the Solomon Islands with simultaneous seizure of positions in eastern New Guinea "in order to cut communications between these areas and the Australian mainland and to neutralize the waters north of eastern Australia."[5] Specifically, the plan prescribed joint invasion of the Lae–Salamaua area in New Guinea, while the seizure of Tulagi and its development as a naval air base was to be the navy's responsibility. After successfully completing these operations, the army and navy were to join in mounting an amphibious attack on Port Moresby on the south coast of the Papuan peninsula "if possible."

It was not, however, until February 16, over two weeks after receipt of their directives, that the prospective commanders finally met to organize the invasion of New Guinea. At this meeting, it was agreed that movement toward the Solomons would be postponed until after Lae and Salamaua had been taken. The first phase of this two-pronged operation was executed on March 8 against slight opposition, and four days later elements of the South Seas Detachment were relieved at Lae and Salamaua by Naval Landing Forces and embarked for Rabaul.

It was now mid-March. Since the occupation of Guam in early

December, the Japanese had conquered the oil-rich Indies and extended their control to include strategically vital territory from which they directly threatened the continent of Australia and posed a critical menace to Far Pacific lines of communication. But during this thirteen-week period, something like five precious weeks had been lost. Time is the essence in war, and while a defeat may be balanced by a battle won, days and hours—even minutes—frittered away can never be regained.

And now, with supporting carriers withdrawn for operations in the Indian Ocean, Fourth Fleet pressed for postponement of the Tulagi and Port Moresby invasions until Combined Fleet could once again allot flight decks. In the meantime, however, the Japanese occupied Buka Island, Kieta on Bougainville, and Ballale and Faisi in the Shortlands, an island group off Bougainville's southern tip. At Buka a fighter strip was surveyed and clearing begun.

Navy planners now exploded another bombshell. This was no less than a proposal to invade Australia, which one of Sugiyama's spokesmen described with admirable moderation as "ridiculous" and "reckless." Already the army had given way to the navy on the Bismarcks, on New Guinea, and on Tulagi; on April 28 it again surrendered to new navy demands. The result was a "Compromise Plan" which provided for the seizure of New Caledonia, the Fijis and Samoa as soon as possible after Port Moresby and Tulagi had been taken.

While Army and Navy Sections were arguing details of the Compromise Plan in Tokyo, Admiral Yamamoto's staff on the giant battleship *Yamato*, at anchor in the Inland Sea, was busy elaborating a project to draw the U. S. Fleet toward the western Pacific for decisive battle. This concept, expressed in the phrase *Yogeki Sakusen*, had dominated Japanese naval thinking for at least two decades; its principal proponent was Admiral Yamamoto.

Although receptive to new ideas—he had always personally encouraged younger officers who believed in the striking power of carrier air—Yamamoto was essentially a "battleship admiral" who had thoroughly digested Mahan. He held no brief for the amphibious concept; to him the arbitrament of war was to be sought in the classic engagement between ships of the line, just as it had been in Nelson's time, and later in Admiral Togo's.

When Yamamoto's representatives first went to Tokyo in early

April 1942 with an outline plan for the occupation of Midway—
Operation "MI"—they received no more than a polite hearing.
The naval general staff had expended considerable time and
energy in persuading the army to accept the New Caledonia–
Fiji–Samoa invasions (Operation "FS"), and was not in the
humor to entertain any such grandiose scheme as Operation
"MI." For its part, the army general staff violently opposed the
scheme as an uncertain gamble which, even if successful, would
produce no important strategic gain.

But Isoroku Yamamoto was a man of quiet determination and
inflexible will. He was the most highly respected flag officer in
the imperial navy; subordinates of all ranks have testified to his
inspirational leadership, his imaginative boldness, his capacity
for prolonged reflection, and the clarity of his guidance. Convinced that a victorious fleet action was the only way by which
Japan could gain the time necessary to consolidate her gains and
demonstrate to America the futility of further struggle, Yamamoto persisted in advocacy of the "MI" operation.

In Tokyo, navy general staff planners were playing "hard to
get," but on April 18 an event occurred which suddenly swung
opinion to full support of Yamamoto's project. This was the carrier-based raid led by Lieutenant Colonel James H. Doolittle of
the Army Air Force. Doolittle's daring attack on the Japanese
homeland, launched from a carrier force commanded by Vice
Admiral William F. Halsey, Jr., produced a psychological reaction out of all proportion to any material effect. The dramatic
gesture deeply affected Yamamoto, who considered it an affront
to the imperial navy, and deemed it necessary to apologize to the
Emperor for the navy's dereliction of duty. Yamamoto assured
His Imperial Majesty that there would be no repetition of such
presumptuous acts.

The wrangling between Army and Navy Sections over both
"FS" and "MI" was characteristic of their relationship, and it is
of more than passing interest to observe that the decision to
undertake the seizure of Midway only crystallized as the direct
result of the Tokyo raid. The weight of the admiral's argument
was now irresistible; the Compromise Plan was deferred until
mid-June, and on May 5 Imperial GHQ issued orders for Operation "MI," the seizure of Midway and selected points in the
Aleutian Islands. Sugiyama agreed to provide a regiment, the

Twenty-eighth Infantry, reinforced, to assault the Midway beaches.

While these projects were being developed in Tokyo, Vice Admiral Inouye, whose Fourth Fleet was based at Truk, had not been inactive. His efforts to get the long-delayed Port Moresby operation under way were rewarded in late April when the Sixth Cruiser Division (four heavy cruisers, one destroyer) plus light carrier (CVL) *Shoho* under command of Rear Admiral Aritomo Goto was assigned as a Support Force. At the same time, Heavy Carrier Division (Cardiv) 5 (*Zuikaku* and *Shokaku*) and Cruiser Division (Crudiv) 5 (heavies *Miyako* and *Haguro* plus seven destroyers), under command of Vice Admiral Takeo Takagi, were assigned as Covering Force.[6]

On April 25, Rabaul-based navy planes commenced the air assault on Port Moresby and northeast Australia; on the twenty-eighth, four-engined *Kawanishi* flying boats attacked Tulagi, Gavutu and Tanambogo. By the thirtieth, the scale of raids was perceptibly stepped up, and on the following day a dawn attack caught two Tulagi-based Australian *Catalina* boats riding on the water. Both were hit; one managed to flounder off clumsily to disappear forever; the other, badly damaged, was later towed to Aola on the north coast of Guadalcanal and destroyed.

Intermittent raids continued during the day, and in the drizzly grey light of the second day of May the Australian radio crew broadcasting from Tanambogo put on the air the prearranged signal reporting their imminent departure: "Staike and aiggs, goddamit! Staike and aiggs!"

The next morning Rear Admiral Goto's force slid down the long narrow seaway later to be known as "The Slot" and stood into the deserted harbor of Tulagi. There Goto landed the Third Kure SNLF, over 400 members of the Yokohama Air Group, a naval seaplane base unit, a four-gun heavy antiaircraft battery, a company of the Sixth Sasebo SNLF, and communications personnel necessary to install and operate a high-power radio station. Shortly thereafter, the first of twelve *Kawanishis* settled on the water and taxied to hastily anchored mooring buoys. Twelve float *Zero* fighters followed.

Throughout the day, Goto's transports methodically unloaded without molestation. The occupation of these tiny islands, whose names would three months later flare in the headlines of every

American newspaper, was uneventful. The Japanese took ashore a tremendous amount of radio and shop equipment, quantities of rice, cigarettes, aviation gas, lubricating oil, tinned sliced beef packed in soy sauce, thousands of bottles of beer, a good supply of *sake* in half-gallon flasks, hard candy, and cases of pineapple and crab meat. Later, some of these delicacies would be thankfully consumed by U. S. marines.

These activities had been observed with interest by reconnaissance pilots of Rear Admiral Frank Jack Fletcher's Carrier Task Force 17, then cruising in the Coral Sea 200 miles south of the central Solomons. At first light on May 4, fast carriers *Lexington* and *Yorktown* swung into the wind and launched aircraft. Target: Tulagi.

The strike caught the Japanese by surprise. A destroyer, two mine sweepers and a destroyer transport went to the bottom. On the same day Vice Admiral Inouye's impressive attack force, under tactical command of Rear Admiral Chiuchi Hara, sailed slowly out of Rabaul's spacious harbor, slipped through Saint George Channel and headed south toward the east tip of New Guinea. Target: Port Moresby.

The stage was set for the Battle of the Coral Sea.

This carrier battle of the seventh and eighth of May, a prelude to Midway, cost the United States the carrier *Lexington* plus fleet oiler *Neosho* and destroyer *Sims*. The Japanese lost light carrier *Shoho* (sunk); battle carrier *Shokaku*, gravely damaged, managed to stay afloat. And although battle carrier *Zuikaku* escaped without injury, over half the aircraft complement of the two big Japanese flattops was destroyed. The lost planes carried with them into the sea their irreplaceable pilots. At three o'clock in the afternoon, Hara broke off the action and turned north.

Tactically, the Coral Sea was a stand-off; strategically it was a decisive American victory. The attempt to seize Port Moresby by sea-borne invasion had been thwarted. And of even more importance, Admiral Nagumo's carrier force, now preparing to advance on Midway, had lost the services of *Shoho*, *Shokaku*, and *Zuikaku*. *Yorktown*, although damaged, survived to fight again.

The Coral Sea reverse did not perceptibly affect either Yamamoto's planning for Operation "MI" or the atmosphere of supreme confidence which pervaded Imperial GHQ. Here both Army and Navy Sections, with what must now appear to be amazing optimism, proceeded from day to day to develop details of the deferred Compromise Plan of April 28. As issued by the Navy Section of Imperial GHQ on May 18, an alerting order directed immediate preparations

> to carry out the invasion of New Caledonia and the Fiji and Samoan Islands, destroy the main enemy bases in those areas, establish operational bases at Suva and Noumea, gain control of the seas east of Australia and strive to cut communications between Australia and the United States.[7]

Tentative D days for this further advance to the southeast were set for early June. The Navy Section immediately assigned Combined Fleet and Eleventh Air Fleet in support, while the Army Section activated Seventeenth Army with headquarters at Rabaul, and ordered Lieutenant General Harukichi Hyakutake to assume command.

Coincidentally, on this eighteenth day of May, a Colonel Kiyanao Ichiki, commander of the elite regiment selected to assault the Midway beaches, boarded battleship *Yamato* at Kure with his staff for briefing. Both the lieutenant general and the colonel would fight on Guadalcanal. Hyakutake, one of the most promising "younger" generals, would lose a reputation there; Ichiki was destined to lose something a Japanese officer, perhaps correctly, held in less esteem—his life.

While the planners ground out paper in Tokyo and Truk, and the Combined Fleet made final preparations for its fatal voyage to Midway, Japanese on Gavutu and Tulagi enjoyed life. Patrols were sent to neighboring Savo and Florida Islands to barter for pigs, chickens and yams. *Kawanishis* slipped moorings at dawn and rose lazily to scour the Coral Sea. Spasmodic appearances of American B-17 *Fortress* bombers from distant Port Darwin inflicted slight damage and caused only minor inconvenience, but did serve to make shipping wary. Still, the invaders noticed a curious phenomenon: the natives avoided them as they would men stricken with the plague.

Not until May 28, almost four weeks after their arrival at Tulagi, did the Japanese cross to Guadalcanal; on this day patrols visited Lunga, Tenaru and Mamara plantations where they machine-gunned half a dozen grazing cattle, dressed the carcasses, and transported the meat to Tulagi. For the next three weeks they evinced no interest in Guadalcanal except as a source of meat and native labor for the base installations now nearing completion on the tiny islands which nestled closely to protecting Florida.

During the first week of June, tranquillity reigned in the Solomons. Construction units proceeded with leisurely development of base facilities in southeastern Bougainville. Although the Japanese were then unaware of the fact, their every move was watched and reported in detail to Allied headquarters in Australia.

The men who displayed such constant interest in Japanese activities were members of Commander Eric Feldt's Australian coastwatching organization, that unique intelligence network which proved an invaluable asset to the Allies in the South and Southwest Pacific Areas. Feldt's men, volunteers all, were not by profession soldiers or sailors, but islanders—traders, colonial officers, administrators and planters who had offered to stay behind should the Japanese occupy the chain of islands which shielded Australia. Each member of this pervasive net was assigned a strategic position he would occupy should the Japanese move in, and each was provided with a reliable "teleradio"—a transmitter, receiver and generator—together with simple but effective codes.

Feldt had personally recruited and instructed each of these men. A few minutes after the Japanese struck Pearl Harbor he alerted them, and as the enemy advanced southeast from island to island, each in turn "went bush." With him went loyal natives he knew and trusted. Without such help the coastwatchers could not possibly have survived. All, whites and natives alike, were fully aware of the acute discomfort and ever-present risks their action involved. If they were captured, the best they could hope was sudden, clean death.

From Guadalcanal, Martin Clemens, "Snowy" Rhoades, and a newly commissioned lieutenant in the Royal Australian Naval Volunteer Reserve, D. S. Macfarlan, all of whom stayed behind, had nothing particular to report except that Japanese foraging parties on Florida had appropriated the "episcopal pigs" left by Anglican Bishop Baddeley when he withdrew to Malaita. Unknown, of course, to these brave and lonely men, the storm of Midway—"the battle that doomed Japan"[8]—was making up far to the north.

Japanese losses at Midway—four carriers with aircraft, pilots and air crews—although successfully concealed by the navy from the hierarchy of the army, the Emperor, and of course the public, put a damper on plans to advance operational bases to the Fijis and New Caledonia, and on June 11 Operation "FS" was "temporarily postponed." For the time being the pendulum was at dead center.

In mid-June, Coastwatcher Rhoades sent out the following strategic information respecting Japanese activity in the lower Solomons:

> Japs at Savo with one machine gun and tin hats enquiring for whereabouts of white men on Guadalcanal. Said they would go there in two weeks' time. Japs also at Tenaru and Kukum joyriding on horses Friday last. Nearly caught police boy.[9]

Perhaps it was one of these unknown cowboys who conceived the idea that the flat coconut grove between Tenaru and Kukum was a promising site for an airfield. No one knows. But on June 19, the commander of the Tulagi base sent a survey party to Lunga plantation. A few days later, several bargeloads of Japanese arrived from Tulagi; during the following week, two water tanks were erected, and patrols visited coastal villages to hire or impress native labor gangs. But because of equipment shortages, work on the strip that later became one of the most famous airfields of World War II proceeded slowly. Coastwatcher Clemens reported these activities; there was no doubt of Japanese intentions.

At dawn on the first day of July, Dovu, a constabulary corporal in charge of Clemens's trusted scouts detailed to observe activities at Lunga, arrived at the coastwatcher's bush camp exhausted and breathless. After waking Clemens and gulping a cup of strong tea he blurted his information:

> "One thousand Jap-an come 'shore 'long Lunga 'long Monday." (29 June) "Altogether come 'shore 'long big fella launch-ich catch'm one hundred man, got'm big fella machine gun."
>
> "Which way you savvy altogether one thousand 'e stop 'long Lunga, Dovu? Which way you take'm long time for come tell'm me?"
>
> "Me fella sit down 'long scrub, catch'm ten fella stone 'long hand, and me count'm altogether come 'shore, got'm tin hat,

khaki boot, allsame pigpig got'm two toes and long fella bayonet. Me get'm sore leg, pain 'long belly b'long me."[10]

Two cruisers were indeed lying off Lunga discharging troops and equipment. During the next few days 400 men of the 81st and 84th Garrison Units dug slit trenches and emplaced machine guns near the beach. Advance echelons of the 11th and 13th Naval Construction Battalions of the 8th Base Force went to work on the airfield. Within a week the remainder of these battalions arrived, and the tempo of clearing perceptibly quickened as coconut trees fell by the hundreds. Progress was conscientiously reported by Macfarlan, Rhoades and Clemens, whose loyal scouts and police boys had infiltrated the impressed labor corps. They estimated that about 3000 Japanese were on Guadalcanal. This proved to be a remarkably accurate count.[11]

Clemens confided to his diary that the local situation was worsening daily, that there seemed little chance that anything would be done, and that he would soon be forced to move even deeper into the jungle. But the Japanese were not the only people interested in the level ground on the north coast of this island so many thousands of miles from Tokyo.

NIGHTMARE IN NEW ZEALAND; PESSIMISM

IN MELBOURNE; FIASCO IN THE FIJIS

3 On March 20, 1942, Brigadier General Alexander Archer Vandegrift, a handsome, soft-spoken, hard-jawed Virginia gentleman in his middle fifties, then assistant commander of the First Marine Division, received a telephone call from Lieutenant General Thomas Holcomb, the Commandant of the Marine Corps. Holcomb informed Vandegrift that he would assume command of the Division on March 23. On that date, Vandegrift was promoted major general, and at a brief ceremony in New River, North Carolina, his two-star flag was broken from a whitewashed pole in front of the rehabilitated farmhouse that would serve both as his residence and as a temporary headquarters.

The new Division commander, once a protégé of the flamboyant Major General Smedley Butler, had learned one important thing from that unique character: the most important element in war is man. Possibly by a process of osmosis, the younger officer had absorbed a share of Butler's amazing understanding of human nature. But Vandegrift was no extrovert. Those who met him even fleetingly carried away an impression that this was a man of quiet determination. Archer Vandegrift's patience and strength would be put to the test many times in the months to come.

Vandegrift did not inherit a going concern. The Division he took over was one in name only. It was then engaged (and for the third time in a year) in the simultaneous processes of planned disintegration and reorganization. Two days before he assumed command his predecessor had been ordered to ship out a regiment—the Seventh Marines—to garrison Samoa. To bring the reinforced Seventh up to war strength prior to sailing, all other elements were stripped of many of their most experienced officers, noncommissioned officers, and specialists. Vandegrift held little back. He expected the Seventh Marines to see combat; he gave them a disproportionate share of the best men, officers, arms and equipment available. The regiment, carrying with it the cream of the Division, sailed from Norfolk on April 10, 1942.

Five days later Vandegrift was verbally informed that his abbreviated command would begin to move to New Zealand on May 1, and that it would comprise the Landing Force of a South Pacific Amphibious Force.[1] The general received this news with mixed emotions; although he was elated at the prospect of moving the Division as an entity toward a front no doubt soon to be active, he was by no means satisfied with the situation in respect to unit training, or the status of equipment. Although its infantry battalions had trained rigorously during January, February and March (and by curious coincidence at Solomons Island at the mouth of the Patuxent River in Maryland) and the artillery was proficient, the Division had not, in its commander's words, "attained a satisfactory state of combat readiness." But Vandegrift was assured there would be ample time for further intensive training; he was informed by the commandant that he need not anticipate a combat mission prior to January, 1943. The commandant had received this information from a good source— Ernest J. King.

On April 29, 1942, King issued a formal directive for the establishment of a South Pacific Amphibious Force. "It is urgently necessary that an amphibious force be stationed in the South Pacific," he wrote.[2] The short title for this operation, chosen by Admiral King, was LONEWOLF.[3] King, who believed that he travels fastest who travels alone, was laying the groundwork for his great design: to drive northwest from the New Hebrides.

Headquarters Marine Corps now began pumping personnel into New River to bring Vandegrift's command to war strength; odd lots arrived almost daily. They were a motley bunch. Hundreds were young recruits only recently out of boot training at Parris Island. Others were older; first sergeants yanked off "planks" in Navy yards, sergeants from recruiting duty, gunnery sergeants who had fought in France, perennial privates with disciplinary records a yard long. These were the professionals, the "Old Breed" of United States Marines. Many had fought "Cacos" in Haiti, "bandidos" in Nicaragua, and French, English, Italian, and American soldiers and sailors in every bar in Shanghai, Manila, Tsingtao, Tientsin, and Peking.

They were inveterate gamblers and accomplished scroungers,

who drank hair tonic in preference to post exchange beer ("horse piss"), cursed with wonderful fluency, and never went to chapel ("the God-box") unless forced to. Many dipped snuff, smoked rank cigars or chewed tobacco (cigarettes were for women and children). They had little use for libraries or organized athletics and would not have known what to do with a career counsellor if they met one. They could live on jerked goat, the strong black coffee they called "boiler compound," and hash cooked in a tin hat.

Many wore expert badges with bars for proficiency in rifle, pistol, machine gun, hand grenade, auto-rifle, mortar and bayonet. They knew their weapons and they knew their tactics. They knew they were tough and they knew they were good. There were enough of them to leaven the Division and to impart to the thousands of younger men a share both of the unique spirit which animated them and the skills they possessed.

Simultaneously, an orgy of sorting, creating, boxing, marking and manifesting began. This continued until the last man of the advance echelon boarded *Wakefield* (formerly the liner *Manhattan*) at Norfolk, Virginia, on May 19.[4] At New Orleans, S.S. *del Brazil* loaded all categories of supplies required to stock a base depot which would be established in Wellington.[5] Meanwhile, a team of officers flew to New Zealand and selected a campsite in rugged bush country near Wellington. The second echelon, under command of Brigadier General William H. Rupertus, newly appointed assistant Division commander (ADC), entrained later for the West Coast and sortied in convoy from San Francisco.[6]

Neither echelon was "combat-loaded." The move was administrative, from camp to camp; its governing factor, speed. All ships were therefore commercially loaded. This cannot be viewed as an error of judgment on Vandegrift's part. His instructions had definitely precluded any possibility of early commitment to combat. And in any event there was not sufficient shipping to allow for carefully planned and regulated combat-loading, which in space required is most uneconomical.

On June 14 the advance echelon arrived in Wellington, and Vandegrift reported his presence to Admiral Ghormley by radio. Marines started to unload and to move to base camps. While they were still shaking down and meeting the New Zealand girls for the first time, Vandegrift decided to report progress to Ghormley at his headquarters in Auckland. As the Division commander and his senior staff officers boarded a plane on June 25, none realized that the visit was to be more than routine. None, in fact, if questioned that morning, would have known the precise location of Tulagi, Guadalcanal, or Gavutu. They were shortly to be enlightened.

Immediately after King began looking for an accessible chink in the enemy's armor, preliminary reports of Japanese losses at Midway were confirmed. But Douglas MacArthur had also scrutinized the Midway reports, and beat Admiral King to the punch. MacArthur's proposal to the Joint Chiefs was bold—and imprudent. The general suggested no less than the seizure of Rabaul, which he could accomplish, he said, with one amphibiously trained division supported by carrier aircraft. This meant committing fast carriers—and there were then only two in the Pacific—to the reef-littered Solomon Sea. Navy planners, who feared that MacArthur might regard the carriers as "expendable," had no intention of jeopardizing these precious ships so lightly.

Nor could the Navy undertake to support such an obvious gamble. Under the circumstances, King considered an amphibious assault on Rabaul to be about as sensible as ordering lead soldiers to storm a red-hot stove, and emphatically vetoed the idea. A few weeks earlier, with MacArthur's concurrence, he had turned down a plan presented by Nimitz, who had suggested that Lieutenant Colonel Merritt Edson's First Marine Raiders attack and gut Tulagi and withdraw. What King had in mind was an operation limited in scope, but designed to stop the Japanese rather than merely to delay or irritate them, and by mid-June he had satisfied himself that seizure of the "Tulagi area" and subsequent occupation of Ndeni in the Santa Cruz Islands could be accomplished with the means at hand.

The admiral's JCS colleagues proved difficult. General Marshall recognized the need for limited action in the Pacific, but correctly foresaw that operations up the chain of jungle-clad islands would inevitably draw resources from the European theater, to which joint strategy had given primacy. H. H. ("Hap") Arnold, Commanding General, Army Air Forces, agreed with Marshall that action in the Pacific must be defensive in nature until the build-up for invasion of Europe (BOLERO) was well under way. The President had made it clear enough to the Chief of Staff (but apparently not to Admiral King) that he did not want BOLERO slowed down. On the other hand, the Chiefs unanimously agreed that something must be done to check the Japanese. After some debate, they ratified King's proposal.

But there remained the thorny problem of command. Marshall wished MacArthur to conduct the march up the Solomons; King insisted that the first phase, or "Task" (code name WATCH-TOWER), be run by the Navy. The Chief of Staff stuck to his guns. King, after pointing out that the forces to be employed consisted entirely of naval and Marine elements, confronted Marshall with what amounted to an ultimatum: WATCH-TOWER would be under naval command or there would be no WATCHTOWER. To this arrangement, Marshall finally gave reluctant assent, and agreed to move the boundary of Ghormley's South Pacific Area, which originally passed through the west tip of Guadalcanal, one degree of longitude to the west.

Nimitz was therefore given responsibility for Task I and Mac-Arthur was named to execute Tasks II and III, the capture of the northern Solomons and seizure of Rabaul. He was directed to initiate these operations as soon as possible after successful conclusion of Task I. A warning order for the first phase of the offensive was issued on June 25. Prospective D day was set for August 1.

King had not previously intimated to his Pacific commanders that he or anyone else contemplated launching such an operation at this early date. Rear Admiral Richmond Kelly Turner, commander-designate of the Amphibious Force, South Pacific, had not even arrived in the area. "The first I knew of it," Ghormley later wrote,

> was in late June when I received orders to confer with General MacArthur in regard to the proposed seizure of the Guadalcanal-Tulagi area. Had I known this, our initial work in the South Pacific in planning operations and logistic support and collecting intelligence would have been pointed more directly towards the first objective.[7]

The first Vandegrift "knew of it" was when he walked into Admiral Ghormley's office in Auckland. Here he was told that his mission was to seize and defend Tulagi (code name RING-BOLT), the area on Guadalcanal (CACTUS) which embraced the airfield being industriously constructed by the Japanese, and Ndeni in the Santa Cruz Islands. His Landing Force would be augmented en route to the target area by the Second Marines (a reinforced regiment drawn from the Second Marine Division), the 1st Raider Battalion (then in New Caledonia), the 1st Parachute Battalion and the 3rd Defense Battalion.

Two pressing problems faced the Landing Force commander. The first was to acquire without delay that information of terrain and enemy which would enable him to formulate a basic scheme of maneuver ashore. On this depended the entire pattern of the landing. For until such a scheme had been prepared it was impossible to develop detailed plans for the ship-to-shore movement, for naval gunfire and air support, for supply organization of beaches, and for the complex communications network necessary to control and support an opposed landing. To collect the information on which to build his plan, the general immediately dispatched his intelligence officer, Lieutenant Colonel Frank B. Goettge, to Australia.

At the same time he recommended to Admiral Ghormley that a select group of officers, plus experienced communication personnel with their equipment, fly at once to Townsville, Australia, board a submarine there, and proceed to Guadalcanal to contact Coastwatcher Martin Clemens. The missions of this patrol would be to investigate tide and beach conditions, to observe Japanese activities on Guadalcanal, and to report enemy strengh and disposition. In view of the paucity of information, this request was both logical and reasonable. The suggestion was rejected by Admiral Ghormley as "too dangerous."[8]

Goettge, however, did fly to Melbourne, where MacArthur's staff and the Australian government rendered him all possible assistance. Commander Feldt instructed his coastwatchers to report every scrap of information relating to enemy ship and aircraft movements, enemy strength on Guadalcanal and Tulagi, the location of Japanese installations, and the daily routine of the garrison forces.

While MacArthur's intelligence people collated all information they had or could get, Goettge interviewed former colonial officers, planters, traders, island schooner captains, ex-missionaries and employees of Lever Brothers and Burns-Philp South Sea Traders, who knew the islands. Eight of them were hurriedly commissioned and assigned to Vandegrift's staff. With their help the intelligence section produced a rough map—a very rough map—of the north coast of Guadalcanal from Taivu to Kukum. A fragmentary uncontrolled air mosaic of this area provided a few terrain details. Daily coastwatcher reports amplified the scanty knowledge of enemy defenses, which appeared to be primitive and centered around Lunga and Kukum.

Vandegrift's other problem was equally acute. The second echelon of his Division was still at sea and was not due to arrive at Wellington until July 11, three weeks before scheduled D day. The commercially-loaded vessels carrying the First Marine Regiment, Division artillery, tanks, amphibian tractors, and most of the engineer equipment would have to be emptied and their cargo sorted on Aotea Quay before combat-loading could commence.

As the Navy had refused Vandegrift's request for his representatives to supervise outloading at ports of embarkation, the Division staff had at best a nebulous idea of what material was actually in each ship carrying the second echelon. This knot could be untangled later; the immediate task was to combat-load available ships with the units and equipment already at Tararua.

The excuse given New Zealanders for the unseemly haste with which the marines, having just arrived in their lovely islands, were now preparing to depart, was "amphibious exercises."

On July 2, Admiral King, acting as the Joint Chiefs' agent for Task I, issued a formal directive to Nimitz.[9] In this, the ultimate objective of the planned offensive operations was stated to be "seizure and occupation of the New Britain dash New Ireland dash New Guinea area"; their purpose, "to deny the area to Japan." The first Task was defined as "seizure and occupation of Santa Cruz Islands, Tulagi and adjacent positions." No mention was made of Guadalcanal or of a requirement for rapid airfield development there. Nor in his letter of July 9 to the Commander South Pacific Force and Area did Nimitz issue any instructions relative to airfield construction.[10]

The question which both the Joint Chiefs and Admiral Nimitz failed to clarify—or at least clarify to the satisfaction of Admiral Ghormley—was basic. Precisely what *was* the ultimate purpose of this lodgment? Was it defensive: to prevent the Japanese from moving into the Hebrides and New Caledonia and from these advanced positions severing the lines of communication to Australasia? This, Ghormley repeatedly averred, was his understanding:

to deny the area to Japanese arms. But the Chiefs had stated clearly that WATCHTOWER was the first step on the long road to Rabaul. And certainly this was the concept King had delineated in his March memorandum to the President. Nevertheless, the history of the campaign testifies that Admiral Ghormley was never sure just what use he was to make of "the Tulagi area" once he had grasped it. And in justice to the admiral, it must be said that he was not the only one who was confused.

WATCHTOWER was conceived, planned and launched on a crash basis in which the controlling element was time. The deliberate collection and evaluation of information, the allocation of balanced forces, the prolonged conferences and meticulous planning characteristic of future operations in the Pacific, were here distinguished by their absence. Thus, this first Allied offensive of World War II was destined to reveal a near-frantic and sometimes near-fatal series of improvisations. Such is the penalty inevitably exacted in war of those who for whatever reason neither make careful estimates nor lay comprehensive plans.

Several days before he received Nimitz's letter of July 9, Ghormley flew to Melbourne to confer with Douglas MacArthur. The admiral was pessimistic. He had concluded that WATCHTOWER was a dubious undertaking. The planned D day of August 1 was rushing toward him; the bulk of Vandegrift's Division was still at sea. The time factor did not allow for the detailed planning and execution of preparatory activities he deemed essential. Even elementary information respecting terrain, sea conditions, and weather in the target area was lacking. Available maps and charts were ancient, unreliable, and otherwise wholly unsatisfactory. Tide tables showed erratic rise and fall of a few feet, occurring with unpredictable irregularity. The only estimates of Japanese strength, arms and dispositions on Tulagi, Gavutu and Guadalcanal were those provided by coastwatchers buried deep in the jungle and were of questionable accuracy.

Japanese capabilities to respond to an invasion of the lower Solomons could not be assayed. Ghormley knew that MacArthur did not have the air strength required to neutralize Rabaul and Kavieng, much less that needed to interdict the sea approaches to the Guadalcanal–Tulagi area from the northwest. The forces assigned were, or so the admiral was convinced, insufficient and as yet not adequately trained. He saw small chance that the projected operation could be continuously supported.

Insofar as logistic planning was concerned, Ghormley had

perforce conducted his in a vacuum. To admirals in Washington, "logistics" was a term which described an esoteric science peculiar to the Army. "I don't know what the hell this 'logistics' is that Marshall is always talking about," King is said to have remarked in the early spring of 1942, "but I want some of it." So did Ghormley, but he didn't get any.

"*An outstanding failure*" in the Department was the fact that no one "*took proper cognizance of the time element in providing material for the construction work under various and adverse conditions.*" As a result of the Department's procrastination, the only airfield in the New Hebrides capable of supporting even limited operations was that at Vila, on Efate.[11]

Rear Admiral John S. McCain, Commander, Aircraft, South Pacific (ComAirSoPac), commanded all shore-based aircraft assigned Ghormley. But he was no more able than MacArthur to neutralize enemy air power in the objective area or to interdict the sea approaches to it. Most of the aircraft available to McCain were "short-legged." Without belly tanks (and there were none in the South Pacific) they could not, from present bases in New Caledonia and the New Hebrides, reach forward to operate over the lower Solomons. For distant reconnaissance, McCain could use B-17s, supplemented by two squadrons of tender-supported Consolidated *Catalina* flying boats.

His only long-range bombers were the same B-17s. Twenty-seven of these *Fortress* aircraft—the 11th Bombardment Group, commanded by a capable and courageous Army Air Force officer, Colonel LaVerne Saunders—had recently arrived in the area. Saunders's Group was split between Efate and New Caledonia. Even from Efate, the B-17s must fly 710 miles to reach the Solomons target area.

The conditions under which McCain and Saunders had to operate would have frustrated officers less determined. And although they made an aggressive team, no combination of will and skill could compensate for lack of airfields, of trained replacement pilots and air crews, shortage of planes and spare parts, and the primitive maintenance facilities available to the few mechanics.

This formidable bill of particulars was by no means exhaustive. The members of Ghormley's skeleton staff were as ignorant as he of the complexities of the amphibious assault. His chief of staff, Rear Admiral Daniel J. Callaghan, was a handsome and personable officer whose principal qualification for the demanding post he occupied was that he had been President Roosevelt's naval aide. As Air officer, Ghormley was sent a young aviator who was intelligent and industrious but junior in rank and unfamiliar with amphibious operations. The admiral had no suitably equipped headquarters from which to exercise command. Tactical communication facilities were limited, and there were not enough watch officers and operators to man properly those he did have. New Zealand could not provide the food items Washington planners kept assuring him were readily available. Rear-area hospitals were not yet completed. Construction of forward area harbor, dock, unloading and warehousing installations was still in the discussion stage. As Ghormley's plane approached Melbourne, he marshaled all these, and other, objections for presentation to his renowned colleague.

When the two men met, MacArthur hastened to express his opinion. The general went at once to the heart of the matter, which he correctly considered to be sustained air superiority, at least over the target area. No such operation, he stated, should be initiated unless there was positive assurance of adequate air cover and continuous air support. The Japanese were daily increasing air and surface strength at Rabaul and Kavieng. He confirmed Ghormley's suspicion, that from existing fields and with aircraft available to him, he could not neutralize these bases. The general pointed out that lack of shipping precluded the continuous flow of supplies and equipment required to insure the security of any lodgment on a hostile shore. He deemed successful accomplishment of WATCHTOWER "open to the gravest doubts." In any event, MacArthur concluded, the strategic concept left much to be desired. He conceived the three phases of the sweep from the lower Solomons to Rabaul as being accomplished in "a continuous movement," a roll-up which, once begun, would proceed northwest with snowballing momentum.

At the conclusion of their discussion, the two commanders drew up and signed an agreed dispatch to the JCS, recommending postponement of WATCHTOWER. The Chiefs, in a few well-chosen words, immediately rejected the advice tendered from Melbourne. They conceived it necessary to stop the Japanese and to stop them at once: they "did not desire to countermand the operations underway and the execution of Task I."[12]

While Admiral Ghormley conferred with his colleague in Melbourne, marines worked around the clock in Wellington, trying to clear the docks before the arrival of the Division's second echelon. With this echelon came the rains. Also came trouble with highly unionized New Zealand longshoremen whose bosses, oblivious to pleas from their government, refused to allow their men to work during "inclement" weather. This knot was not untangled—it was peremptorily cut. Outraged union leaders and their men were ordered off the docks by Wellington police. The marines worked steadily in eight-hour shifts and, when they could get to town, amused themselves by scrawling obscene references to New Zealand dock workers on the walls of hotel lavatories. "All wharfees is bastards" is possibly the most restrained of the recorded graffiti.

Aotea Quay made an indelible impression on those who saw it during this endless nightmare. Under the dim lights, drenched men wrestled with rainsoaked cartons of clothing, food, medicines, cigarettes and chocolate bars. The cheap cardboard containers containing Navy rations and Marine Corps supplies disintegrated; one officer remembers walking a hundred yards through a swamp of sodden cornflakes dotted with mushed Hershey bars, smashed cigar boxes, odd shoes and stained, soggy bundles of socks. Lack of time, restricted port facilities, terrible weather, improper packaging, and uncooperative labor combined to create what Vandegrift described, in language notable for moderation, as "an unparalleled logistical problem." Others in less elegant terminology described the dock area as "a mucked-up swamp."

As there were not enough ships available, individual and organization equipment was cut to the bone. All sea bags, bed rolls, tentage, suitcases and trunks were stored in Wellington. Post exchange supplies were limited to minimum quantities of soap, tobacco, matches, and razor blades. All bulk supplies—rations, fuel, lubricants—were reduced to 60 days; ammunition sliced from 15 to 10 days of fire for all weapons. In the words of the Division order, elements of the Landing Force would put on board the too few ships allotted only "items actually required to live and to fight."

Intelligence still left much to be desired, and on July 15 Lieutenant Colonel Merrill B. Twining, in company with another Marine officer, flew to Australia and thence to Port Moresby. There on July 17 the pair boarded a *Fortress* for a look at the target area. Over Guadalcanal the bomber was jumped by three float *Zeros*, and after flaming two, withdrew with the survivor on its tail. Twining was able to report only that the beaches were not obstructed and that the strip the Japanese were constructing seemed complete.

Some days previously Colonel Charles A. Willoughby, U.S.A., MacArthur's intelligence officer, had ordered thorough photo coverage of Guadalcanal and Tulagi as a "crash project," and by July 20 a controlled mosaic of the Lunga beaches had been prepared in Australia. The packages containing this invaluable photo-map were improperly addressed and were lost in Auckland.[13]

In the meantime—and even before Rear Admiral Turner had arrived in Wellington—Ghormley had accepted the basic landing plan presented by Vandegrift. His own plan, not formally issued until July 16, directed the "Expeditionary Force," on "Dog Day," to capture and occupy Tulagi and "nearby positions," *i.e.*, the islets of Gavutu and Tanambogo, and "an adjoining portion of Guadalcanal suitable for the construction of landing fields."[14] This construction was to be initiated "without delay." Thereafter, Turner would land a regiment of marines on undefended Ndeni in the Santa Cruz Islands, where additional fields would be prepared "without delay."[15]

But ComSoPac had no information as to what air units would operate from the field he expected the marines to capture. Aside from Bauer's *Wildcats*, now assigned to McCain, Ghormley had no more than a handful of Army Air Force fighters. Marine Air Group 23—two squadrons of fighters and two of dive bombers—commanded by Colonel William J. Wallace, was in Hawaii checking out in carrier landings and take-offs. As late as July 4, no specific plans existed for pushing land-based aircraft forward to man the field on Guadalcanal as soon as it was operational. On the morning of July 5, two Marine squadrons, one fighter and one dive bomber, were alerted. But no one seemed to know just how these short-legged planes were supposed to get across several thousand miles of ocean to the selected scene of action.

The manifold difficulties encountered in reloading, in collecting and evaluating current information, in preparing and coordinating complicated naval gunfire, air support, and communication plans, as well as the imperative necessity to rehearse, combined to prompt Ghormley to request a postponement of D day. The Joint Chiefs first deferred the date to August 4, then to August 7. King, now fully alerted to the enemy's progress on the Guadalcanal airfield, signaled in no uncertain terms that this concession was the last, and on July 22 the invasion fleet sortied from Wellington.

Leading the column was Turner's flagship, U.S.S. *McCawley*, soon to become famous in the South Pacific as "Wacky Mac." In midafternoon July 26, Turner's Task Force 62 rendezvoused with Vice Admiral Fletcher's Task Force 61 off Koro, a small, lonely island of the Fijis which had been selected as the rehearsal area. Here it was planned to exchange staff visits, perfect air and gunfire support plans, resolve difficulties affecting air-ground and ship-to-shore communications, conduct ground-controlled aerial bombing and ship's gunfire, and practice debarkation procedures.

The command arrangements for the first Allied offensive in the Pacific were not conducive to the successful execution of such a complicated and dangerous undertaking as WATCHTOWER. Ghormley was, of course, in over-all command, but had delegated execution of the operation to Vice Admiral Fletcher. Directly under Fletcher, Turner commanded the "Amphibious Force"— Task Force 62. Both Vandegrift, in command of the Landing Force, and the British Rear Admiral V. A. C. Crutchley, in command of the Escort Group (cruisers H.M.A.S. *Australia*, *Hobart*, *Canberra*, and U.S.S. *Chicago*, *San Juan*, plus nine destroyers), were under Turner. This organization was orthodox for amphibious operations as of that date.

But there was one very weak link. This was the anomalous position of Turner vis-à-vis Rear Admiral McCain, the shore-based air commander, who was responsible only to Ghormley. If, for example, Turner wanted distant reconnaissance or bombardment missions flown, he had to ask Fletcher to ask Ghormley to order McCain to execute them. The package of dynamite which would almost blow the operation apart, however, was concealed elsewhere than in the command structure.

The forces which assembled off Koro on July 26 had never before operated together. The Expeditionary Force commander, Vice Admiral Fletcher, had no previous experience in the type of operation he had been designated to execute. Admiral Ghormley had not issued a "Letter of Instruction" to Fletcher, nor had Fletcher (who had just returned to the South Pacific after a short stay at Pearl Harbor) submitted even a summary of his plan—if, indeed, he then had one—to Ghormley for scrutiny. The result was that the implementing commander arrived at Koro with a complete misconception of the nature of WATCHTOWER and of his responsibilities in connection with it.

These misunderstandings could have been dispelled had Ghormley come to Koro to preside over the conference called by Admiral Fletcher. But Ghormley was busy in Nouméa attending to multifarious vexing details he might better have entrusted to his staff. At this period of the war, most senior naval officers had no inkling of what a staff was for or how to use one, and Ghormley was no exception. Be that as it may, he failed to come to Koro, and this first, but not last, abdication of command responsibility set the stage for a series of tragic and near fatal events.

There are no minutes of the conference held on board *Saratoga* on July 26, but the impression which remained with both Turner and Vandegrift was that Fletcher conducted it in an arbitrary manner. Turner's later account of the proceedings not only substantiates this, but also sheds light on Fletcher's subsequent actions. At a previous meeting in Pearl Harbor "Vice Admiral Fletcher had been very much opposed to undertaking the attempt against Guadalcanal as he felt sure that it would be a failure." At Koro he "made many remarks against the execution of the plan" and "accused Rear Admiral Turner of instigating the project."

> At that time, Vice Admiral Fletcher asked Rear Admiral Turner as to how many days it would take to land troops. Rear Admiral Turner replied that it would take about five days. Vice Admiral Fletcher then stated that he would leave the vicinity of the Solomons after two days because of danger of air attacks against the carriers, and because of the fuel situation; and that if the troops could not be landed in two days then they should not be landed. In any case, he would depart at that time. . . . Rear Admiral Turner stated that the troops could not be landed in two days.[16]

Vandegrift, aghast at the prospect his Landing Force must inevitably face unless Fletcher's attitude could be modified, objected to this *diktat* as strenuously as had Turner. In vain he attempted to explain to Fletcher that WATCHTOWER was designed to gain a permanent lodgment in strength; that it was not "a ships' landing force maneuver but the landing of a division on a hostile shore" which required "air cover for a minimum of four days" in order to get personnel, their arms, equipment and supplies "ashore and established."[17]

Rear Admiral Callaghan, Ghormley's chief of staff, who had flown from Nouméa, took notes in silence. After announcing that he would entertain no further remonstrances, Fletcher closed the conference, if this gathering may accurately be so described. Thus, the record shows that Admiral Fletcher's reaction to WATCHTOWER was at least consistent: He was opposed to it.

This brings into sharp relief Admiral Nimitz's responsibilities in the circumstances. If at Pearl Harbor Fletcher expressed his opposition to WATCHTOWER in the unequivocal manner described by Turner, why did not Nimitz turn the job over to another commander? Or why did Fletcher, who lacked faith in the operation, not ask to be relieved?

The events of the following four days did nothing to alleviate the shock administered on *Saratoga*. The rehearsal was unsatisfactory—in Vandegrift's words "a fiasco"; "a complete bust." Coral heads prevented most units from landing on designated beaches, many boats broke down from mechanical failure, aerial dive-bombing was wild, and ship's gunfire inaccurate. Turner and Vandegrift were disappointed, but both optimistically embraced the theory that a poor dress rehearsal presaged a good performance, and neither was entirely depressed. Each separately took what measures he could to correct demonstrated errors in execution and rectify gaps revealed in planning; later, they concerted desirable modifications in debarkation procedure, established a boat pool, and made indicated adjustments in the ship-to-shore communication plan.

In late afternoon on the last day of July, ships of Fletcher's Task Forces assumed antisubmarine cruising disposition and set course west by south. This day the sun sank as a dull red disc which resembled a Japanese "meat-ball" battleflag, an augury which, according to some amateur soothsayers, boded ill for the expedition. Others speculated, however, that it portended success. Minutes later, the oppressive tropical night enveloped the Allied fleet.

BOOK II

4 AT FIRST LIGHT on August 7, Coastwatcher Martin Clemens awoke suddenly to dull reverberations of distant explosions. Without pausing to observe customary morning tea rites, he snatched up his field glasses and emerged from his thatched shack on the mountainside. Above Tulagi, where Marine units commanded by Brigadier General Rupertus were preparing to land, black smoke billowed. Although Lunga Point was hidden from him by ridges and towering jungle trees, Clemens enjoyed a panoramic view of a great fleet standing off the Guadalcanal beaches. This "city on the inconstant billows dancing" was the most powerful amphibious attack force until then ever assembled. Here in Lunga Roads, off Florida and Savo, "a fleet majestical"[1] —cruisers, destroyers, transports, supply ships—had gathered for the first of many such strikes against the inhospitable and unknown islands of the Far Pacific.

While the grey ships carrying the landing force moved deliberately to plotted positions, Admiral Crutchley disposed his cruisers and destroyers northeast and southwest of Savo Island to protect the transport areas from possible sudden incursion of enemy submarines and to thicken antiaircraft defense on the most likely avenue of approach. Previous Atlantic experiences had rendered this British admiral particularly susceptible to the submarine menace; he presumed that Japanese "I" boats were operating in the vicinity and anticipated speedy and violent air reaction.

One hundred miles south of Guadalcanal, Fletcher's Air Support maneuvered as carriers *Saratoga*, *Wasp* and *Enterprise*, shielded by combat air patrols (CAP), launched and recovered fighters and dive bombers with methodical precision. New, fast battleship *North Carolina* and six cruisers screened the flattops. Sixteen destroyers, sonars "pinging" and depth charge racks manned, were ready for underwater interlopers.

Clemens snapped on his radio: the air crackled with excited voice transmissions of airborne spotters adjusting ship's gunfire. As dive bombers released loads and pulled out, pilots exultantly reported hits on assigned targets and begged for new ones. In Tulagi harbor, seven moored *Kawanishis* were sinking, nine *Zero* float planes wrecked. Fuel storage tanks, riddled by incendiary bullets, spewed cascading clouds of oily smoke; a cluster of shacks roofed with corrugated iron sheeting was blown to bits; ramshackle dockside warehouses vomited flames.

Over Guadalcanal beaches, reconnaissance planes catapulted at dawn from cruiser *Astoria* skimmed the ordered ranks and files of coconut palms. Their rear-seat observers reported no sign of enemy activity. Division staff officers rightly regarded this information with considerable skepticism. But the negative reports were correct. The Americans had achieved what any commander should always seek: complete tactical surprise.

That Turner's fleet had closed the objective area without being discovered was due in part to careful planning. The approach course, calculated to reduce chance of detection by Japanese planes on routine searches over the Coral Sea, brought the Attack Force to a point well south of Guadalcanal and into a weather front on the afternoon of August 6. Under cover of rain and darkness, ships turned due north and ran at high speed to Cape Esperance, the northwest tip of the island. After rounding the cape, they swung 90 degrees east into the target area.

The Amphibious Force had been lucky: the driving rain that shielded the ships also washed out Japanese air searches from Rabaul toward the southeast on August 5 and again on the sixth. The operational record cryptically states: "Searches cancelled because of inclement weather." The routine search from Tulagi—three long-range *Kawanishis*—did go out on August 6, but within an hour all were forced back by lowering skies and squalls. Pilots reported visibility less than ten miles with ceilings as low as 100 feet: "Result of searches: Negative."

On Guadalcanal, the sleeping Japanese were not aware the enemy was upon them until shells from cruiser *Quincy* burst in the fronds that shaded their tents.

The date: August 7, 1942. The time: 6:41 A.M. As bombs splintered coconut trees and fragments of steel tore viciously into the earth, ships hove to off Red Beach and crews commenced to swing out and lower landing craft. Over the bull horns came the words so often to be repeated during the next two and a half years: "Land the landing force." Thousands of tense marines, grouped in 36-man "boat teams," began to move slowly and silently toward cargo nets suspended from the decks of the transports. The sea was calm; debarkation orderly and fast.

Loaded boats pulled away from the transports to assembly areas, formed there in "boat groups," and on signal moved toward the beach in regulated waves. All formations crossed the line of departure on time. Coxswains gunned engines, sweating marines squatted low. Strafing planes screamed twisting out of final runs; ships' gunfire lifted to inland targets.

At 9:09 A.M., one minute before "Zero Hour," hulls of first-wave boats jarred to a stop on the white sand, ramps splashed into warm greenish-blue water, and men finally released from the boredom of interminable waiting began wading slowly, their weapons held high, toward a quiet strip of beach backed by shattered coconut palms. These marines, Combat Group "A" (1st and 3rd Battalions, Fifth Marines) commanded by Colonel LeRoy P. Hunt, a much-decorated veteran of an earlier war, hit Red Beach against no opposition on a front of almost 2000 yards. Thus Vandegrift's hope—to land where the enemy was not—had been achieved.

This covering force was followed ashore by Combat Group "B"—the First Marines—commanded by Clifton B. Cates, another colonel who had gained a reputation in France. Cates's regiment landed in column of battalions, passed through the Fifth Marines, and began to push toward "Grassy Knoll" (Mount Austen), an eminence which dominated the airfield from the south. Shortly after landing, Cates realized that this key terrain feature, his first objective, was not—as faulty maps had indicated—less than two miles inland, but more nearly four. As his regiment moved toward it, the heat began to tell, and the advance slowed to an erratic crawl.

Until noon, debarkation continued without a hitch. "Unusually successful," Vandegrift wrote later; operations "proceeded with the smoothness and precision of a well-rehearsed peacetime drill." The boat pool organized at his insistence after the fiasco at Koro "functioned admirably." But soon this idyllic picture began to change. As artillery, tanks, jeeps, trucks and amphibian tractors moved inland, crated equipment, boxed supplies and drums of gasoline piled up alarmingly on Red Beach.

Untrained Navy coxswains brought boats loaded with rations to beach points marked to receive fuel; medical supplies were unceremoniously dumped with ammunition. Marines landed in late waves straggled about the beach awaiting the signal to move inland. Some went swimming; others cracked coconuts; others simply sat and watched the understrength shore party struggling to move precious cargo from boats to the shelter of the coconut groves. "Hell, Mac, we're combat troops. You unload the goddam stuff." These loafers were not combat troops yet. They soon would be.

But the casual assistance of idle spectators would scarcely have made a dent in the disordered piles. The plain fact was that there were not enough hands or enough wheels available to move hundreds of heavy cases from boats to dumps. What was congestion became chaos. In midafternoon, a hundred heavily laden boats bobbed in the gentle swell offshore as coxswains vainly sought a vacant stretch of sand to beach. Thus, although troop landings had been executed with a smoothness beyond expectation, progressively lagging logistic operations created a problem of monumental proportions and provided lucrative targets for enemy aircraft.

Vandegrift was fully aware of this situation, but was unable to ameliorate it. He had landed only five infantry battalions on Guadalcanal. Of these he necessarily held one in reserve. Assault troops were not yet closing the airfield, nor had its defenders revealed their strength or dispositions. The general had no choice but to keep his small Landing Force under tight control. To divert men who might be needed in a fight to resolve the growing problem at Red Beach would have meant taking not a calculated risk but a completely unjustifiable one.

As the first bombs exploded on Tulagi, Japanese transmitters there began crackling out the news that the island was under heavy attack from both air and sea, that a great fleet was assaulting Guadalcanal, and that hostile landings were imminent. At 8:05 A.M. Radio Tulagi signaled Rabaul that the Americans were coming ashore. "And so the last moving message was received, praying for a decisive battle to the last man and for permanent fortunes of war. Thereafter, communication ceased."[2]

Headquarters in Rabaul reacted immediately. As the commander of the navy's 25th Air Flotilla based at Vunakanau briefed his pilots, Vice Admiral Gunichi Mikawa, commanding the recently activated Eighth Fleet, radioed Rear Admiral Aritomo Goto, whose four heavy cruisers were at Kavieng, to sortie at once and proceed at flank speed to a rendezvous near Rabaul.[3] Meanwhile, he hastily threw together a composite group drawn from locally available units and ordered embarkation to commence without delay. This outfit, which included part of the Fifth Sasebo SNLF, boarded transports, of which the largest was the 5600-ton *Meiyo Maru*.[4]

While American landings proceeded, 25th Air Flotilla planes, earlier armed for a routine raid on Port Moresby, formed over Rabaul and swung southeast. This strike group was composed of 27 twin-engine *Betty* bombers covered by 18 *Zeros*. The sense of urgency conveyed in a dispatch from Admiral Yamamoto had so impressed the flotilla commander that he decided to push the planes off without changing their armament from bombs to torpedoes, a monumental stroke of luck as far as Turner's transports were concerned.

At 10:30 A.M. on August 7 the Japanese strike, ordered "to destroy the enemy invasion force with all its might," passed directly over Coastwatcher P. E. Mason, on station in the hills of southern Bougainville, and in less than ten minutes he was broadcasting on the "Bells" circuit: "From S T O. Twenty-four torpedo bombers headed yours."[5]

Landing of equipment and supplies ceased as Turner's cumbersome ships assumed antiaircraft disposition. When the raid came in 45 minutes later, the American ships, maneuvering at maximum speed, were ready. Thanks to Mason's early warning, a strong fighter CAP stacked over the island of Savo, some 20 miles northwest of the transport area, was ready to jump the Japanese, and the enemy, bombing wildly, inflicted only minor damage on destroyer *Mugford*. Very few *Bettys* escaped.

In midafternoon Mason reported a dozen unescorted dive bombers on the way; again ships were ready and fighters on station. Fletcher's pilots claimed they splashed four; ship's AA crews jubilantly claimed an equal number of "certains." Actually, three dive bombers were shot out of the air; six ran out of gas and ditched on the way back to base. Their pilots were not recovered.

Of 51 planes which left Rabaul that day, thirty did not return. Among the pilots who did was Saburo Sakai, Japan's greatest ace. His *Zero* was shot to pieces but still flew. Blinded in one eye and bleeding from multiple wounds, Sakai by a supreme effort of will made Vunakanau, skidded to a landing and fainted. It was his first and last combat over Guadalcanal.

The unexpected news from Tulagi did not unduly alarm Imperial GHQ, which estimated that not more than 2,000 Americans were involved and that the action was probably "a reconnaissance in force." GHQ speculated that even if a full-scale landing had been made it would be no trouble to recapture the positions. The Chief of Naval General Staff then donned dress uniform and proceeded to the Emperor's summer villa at Nikko to inform Hirohito that there was no cause for alarm.[6]

The erroneous assessment made by the army general staff was to a certain degree excusable. Not only had the navy kept secret from the army the full extent of the Midway disaster, but it had inflated American carrier and aircraft losses there to such an extent that the army hierarchy was convinced the U. S. Navy had been reduced to a condition of hopeless impotence. From the information supplied them by the navy, army planners had concluded that the Americans would not be able to mount a serious offensive in the Pacific prior to early 1943. The flurry in the Solomons did not suggest a need to revise this estimate.

Incredible as it may seem, the navy had never informed the army that it was building an airfield on Guadalcanal. When Colonel Takushiro Hattori, then Deputy Chief, Operations Division, Army General Staff, arrived at his office on August 7 he was astounded to learn that naval air-base construction units had for some time been working on "this insignificant island in the South Seas, inhabited only by natives."[7] The army's opinion that it was "inconceivable" for the American landings "to exceed the scope of a reconnaissance in force" thus derived partially from the fact that it had been misled by the navy. All the same, Army and Navy Sections agreed that the Americans must be ejected before they could put the practically completed air strip into operation, and General Sugiyama spent the morning of August 7 looking around for a suitable unit to send forward.

At the same time, Admiral Nagano sent urgent instructions to the Commander in Chief, Combined Fleet. Pursuant to these, Yamamoto constituted a Southeast Area Force, radioed Vice Admiral Nishizo Tsukahara, commanding Eleventh Air Fleet, with headquarters at Saipan, to fly at once to Rabaul to assume command, directed that first priority be given to the recapture of Guadalcanal, and ordered all available ships and planes to make ready for decisive counterattack.

By late afternoon the First Marines were still far short of Grassy Knoll, and Vandegrift ordered Cates to halt, consolidate, and dig in for the night. The halt was sorely needed. The men, who had been cooped up in the steaming holds of overcrowded transports for two weeks, were in deplorable physical condition. Burdened with excessively heavy packs and extra ammunition, blasted by the heat and stupefying humidity, short of water and salt tablets, they were in no condition to press forward, much less to fight. Fortunately, Cates's marines did not encounter any Japanese on their first afternoon ashore.

Nor was the progress of the Fifth Marines any more satisfactory. In spite of repeated exhortations from the regimental commander, his 1st Battalion advanced westward at an exasperatingly slow rate. By nightfall, this battalion had, however, reached its objective for the day: the east bank of Alligator Creek, a sluggish, semi-tidal stream about two miles west of Red Beach.

While on the first day of the first Pacific offensive, marines on Guadalcanal encountered no enemy, things were different on the Florida side. Here the most concentrated opposition was anticipated and here Vandegrift committed his most thoroughly trained and aggressive outfits, Edson's 1st Raiders to Tulagi, and Major Robert H. Williams's 1st Parachutists to the harbor islet of Gavutu.

To protect the left flank of the Raiders as they landed on Blue Beach at 8:00 A.M., Baker Company, 1st Battalion, Second Marines (Lieutenant Colonel Robert E. Hill) was previously to seize the Haleta promontory on neighboring Florida. To protect the Parachutists as they boated toward Gavutu for an 11:00 A.M. H hour, the remainder of Hill's battalion would before that time take a covering position on the tip of Halavo peninsula. This arrangement, not without complications, was phased to permit optimum use of naval gunfire and strike aircraft. Eight boats carrying Captain E. J. Crane's company beached at Haleta a few minutes before 8:00 A.M.; shortly thereafter the bulk of Hill's battalion seized the tip of Halavo. The first Americans to hit the beach in the Solomons landed without firing a shot. There were no Japanese in either place.

In the meantime, the 1st Raiders were debarking from the destroyer transports in which they had traveled from New Caledonia. They, too, had suffered from lack of exercise and crowded quarters, but unlike the troops who were to land on Guadalcanal an hour later, they were stripped down to minimum equipment for combat. Edson expected a tough fight. "Don't worry about the food," he had said to a company commander. "There's plenty there. Japs eat, too. All you have to do is get it."

At exactly eight o'clock two Raider companies—Baker and Dog—began wading ashore from Higgins boats grounded on coral shoals off Blue Beach, a landing area on the western end of the island selected in the hope that, because beaching seemed impossible, there would be no defenders. This hope was realized; no fire came from the jungle. As men struggled in waist-deep water to find footing on the slime-coated coral, many carrying heavy loads—mortar tubes, base plates and radio packs—went under. Yanked to their feet, they were propelled shoreward. Those who fell rose with hands bloodied by coral outcroppings, dungaree trousers ripped, and knees gory. Still, by 8:15, assault companies were ashore and the executive officer signaled Edson "Landing successful, no opposition." The remainder of the battalion followed quickly as first-wave boats returned to the APDs and embarked Companies Able and Cast.[8]

The Raiders climbed the silent steep ridge to their front, wheeled to the right, and began to move to the southwest along the spine and sharply sloping sides of the island. On their heels, Lieutenant Colonel Harold E. Rosecrans's 2nd Battalion, Fifth Marines, landed over Blue Beach, crossed Tulagi and swept its northwest half without encountering any sign of the enemy. Rosecrans then collected his battalion and moved into position to support Edson.

Resistance first developed in the former Chinese settlement which hugged the Burns-Philp docks on the north coast opposite tiny Makambo Island. Here, just before noon on August 7, marines suffered their first battle casualties of the South Pacific campaign. In attempting to render aid to three seriously wounded men, Lieutenant (j.g.) Samuel Miles, a young Navy doctor, was killed, and a company commander critically hit. As Raiders moved warily toward the flimsy shacks, the Japanese brought light mortars into action. Progress slowed, and late in the afternoon Edson called a halt to consolidate for the night.

The marines held a line generally along rising ground from

Carpenter's Wharf on the north to the spacious frame Residency in which the commissioner had lived until forced to flee the island in late April. On the south side of the Residency, a gently sloping finger fell off to a small golf club house near the beach. This defensive line was not organized; there was no time for that. Raiders dug shallow two- and three-man foxholes, and Rosecrans deployed his battalion to back up the forward positions.

The configuration of the ground favored the marines. The hogback they occupied sloped sharply down to a rectangular level area used in happier days for cricket matches and football games. The Japanese held positions on a rugged, rocky, brush-covered ridge which bounded the east side of the playing field. The afternoon's fighting had revealed that the defenders of Tulagi were liberally equipped with light mortars, grenade throwers, and heavy and light machine guns. The estimate was that there were between three and four hundred of them, and that they would attack during darkness.

They did—four times. But each assault was less impetuous than the one preceding, and all were repulsed. Some Japanese infiltrated; six crawled under the Residency porch and hid there. Just after first light on August 8 they killed three marines. Five minutes later they were grenaded to death.

In a foxhole in the center of the tenuous line he had done much to hold, Private First Class John Ahrens, an Able Company automatic rifleman, lay quietly, his eyes closed, breathing slowly. Ahrens was covered with blood. He was dying. Next to him lay a dead Japanese sergeant, and flung across his legs, a dead officer. Ahrens had been hit in the chest twice by bullets, and blood welled slowly from three deep puncture wounds inflicted by bayonets. Around this foxhole sprawled thirteen crumpled Japanese bodies. As Captain Lewis W. Walt gathered Ahrens into his arms to carry him to the Residency, the dying man, still clinging to his BAR, said, "Captain, they tried to come over me last night, but I don't think they made it."

"They didn't, Johnny," Walt replied softly. "They didn't."

The islet of Gavutu, connected to even smaller Tanambogo by a narrow causeway, proved a tougher D-day job than had Tulagi. Although defenders were fewer, so were the attacking Americans. Air bombardment of Gavutu, which measures about 500 yards in length and less than 300 in width, was brief and completely ineffective; hidden deep in reinforced dugouts and caves, the Japanese suffered only minor inconvenience, and set themselves to give the Parachutists a bloody reception.

As assault craft ran toward the shore, destroyers' guns neutralized defensive fire, but when boats grounded and marines scrambled out, this friendly fire ceased and the Japanese took charge. The Parachutists, momentarily disorganized by the hail of lead poured on them from invisible automatics, sought what cover they could find. There was not much. Before any progress had been made, Major Williams was hit; command devolved on Major Charles A. Miller. Men were dying on that thin strip of beach, but supporting destroyers, in uncharted waters, hesitated to close the range to deliver the pinpoint fire needed. The only escape was to move, and, in small groups, desperate men went toward the enemy. By midafternoon a squad gained the top of Hill 148, the highest point on the island. Here a marine broke the American flag. But a Rising Sun banner whipped defiantly above tiny Tanambogo, whose defenders were still very much alive. It was worth a man's life to expose himself near the causeway, periodically swept by bursts of automatic fire.

Obviously the Parachutists could not proceed with the capture of Tanambogo, originally assigned as their Phase Two objective. At the moment they were standing on top of a volcano which might erupt at any time, for under their feet some two dozen caves and dugouts harbored Japanese. These caves could be reduced only by explosive charges strapped to poles. Many were pushed into position by a huge, blond captain, Harry Torgerson. His trousers were ripped off by the first charge he detonated.

Thus, as the sun sank behind Savo, there remained the problem of Tanambogo. Rupertus called for air strikes on the islet, and directed Captain Crane, whose company had earlier withdrawn from undefended Haleta, to boat up and assault at dusk. The general's operations officer, Major William K. Enright, pointed out that this effort, concocted on the spur of the moment, promised small chance of success. Rupertus felt otherwise. As Enright had predicted, Crane's marines were met by murderous fire as the boats approached the landing point. Only one managed to beach; its occupants were shot to pieces. The other two, holed in half a dozen places, hastily withdrew to Gavutu.

This abortive attack did produce one lasting result, for it convinced Rupertus that he needed help. He appealed to Vandegrift, and at midnight Turner released Lieutenant Colonel Robert G.

Hunt's battalion of the Second Marines, slated in the basic plan to occupy Ndeni. Rupertus ordered Hunt to land on Gavutu at dawn, relieve the Parachutists, and capture Tanambogo.

Night and rain brought no surcease to Gavutu. Individual Japanese crawled from caves to throw grenades or fire spasmodic bursts from light machine guns. The marines had no choice but to endure these attacks and to wait for dawn.

On Guadalcanal, Americans should have passed their first night in comparative peace. But although no defenders disturbed them, rest was impossible. Trigger-happy sentries enlivened the long hours by discharging hundreds of rounds at imaginary targets. The uproar was noted by the Japanese beyond the Matanikau, who were quite unable to account for it. The marines were, of course, nervous and exhausted. All were apprehensive, and some were scared. They had landed expecting to find Japanese and to fight them, but the enemy had hidden. Surely he was there, somewhere in the impenetrable blackness. He was not, however, and at dawn the second day there was still no sign of him.

Before midnight on D day Vandegrift had issued new orders. In these, he directed Cates to forget Grassy Knoll, to swing west, push to the Lunga, and envelop the airfield from the south. At the same time, he ordered the Fifth Marines to move rapidly toward Lunga Point and continue to Kukum.

On Saturday morning, patrols moving hesitantly toward the airfield picked up a few Japanese and Korean laborers. The information they gave crystallized an opinion, to this point nebulous, that the enemy had withdrawn to the west, perhaps to Kukum, perhaps even farther. Division now urged Hunt to move to Kukum. But the Fifth Marines would not be hurried, and it was midafternoon before their dilatory patrols finally reached the abandoned Japanese camp area in the coconut groves near the north end of the strip.

A hasty survey of overrun billeting areas indicated that airfield construction personnel and their Naval Landing Force protectors had fled precipitately. Camp sites obviously abandoned in the haste induced by panic were found in a state of utter confusion. Uniforms, two-toed rubber-soled *tabi*, shirts, caps, helmets, blankets, mosquito netting, rifles, tea cups, chopsticks, rice bowls and their half-consumed contents littered the ground.

Scores of coconut trees, riven by bombs and shells, had collapsed, smashing small buildings and ripping tents. In temporary structures obviously used as offices, drafting equipment and papers were scattered about. When the marines came upon this scene the effect was eerie; here men had lived and worked until unexpected catastrophe suddenly struck their remote world.

In the meantime, less hesitant reconnaissance parties from the artillery (Eleventh Marines) had discovered the field clear of enemy. The artillery commander, Colonel Pedro A. del Valle, accompanied one of these. His report resulted in further proddings, and before dusk one of Cates's battalions crossed the strip and dug in for the night on the east bank of the Lunga.

Meanwhile, unloading at Red Beach continued in haphazard fashion. Total disorganization prevailed, and in an effort to disperse dangerously concentrated supplies, Vandegrift asked Turner to extend unloading to suitable beaches about a mile to the west of cluttered Red. Turner balked at this; he was afraid to move his ships into waters which might be mined. But Vandegrift insisted. After all, the admiral could see for himself that there was simply no space on Red Beach to land a fraction of the combat cargo still in ships' holds. And soon the boats began to disgorge near the mouth of Block Four River. To prevent a recurrence of the Red Beach shambles, some of the transports sent sailors ashore to reinforce the exhausted shore party.

While marines on the Guadalcanal side inspected abandoned camps, cracked coconuts, collected souvenirs, and sampled their first Japanese cigarettes, their brothers-in-arms on Tulagi and Gavutu were fighting, as they had the previous day.

When Edson's and Rosecrans's marines came out of the shallow foxholes at first light on Saturday, they for the first time saw in front of their lines the crumpled corpses of men who had a few hours earlier assaulted with a determination bordering on frenzy. For some, this first encounter with death by violence was a brutal shock. But it was one to which they perforce adjusted, and soon platoons and squads were moving against the caves in which the defenders had taken final refuge.

Neither dive bombers nor ships' gunfire could blast the enemy out of these rocky caverns. The marines had no Bangalore torpedoes, no flame throwers, no tanks. (The one tank put ashore on Tulagi threw a track and came to rest in a ditch.) They first tried hand grenades; the Japanese promptly picked them up and threw them back. In a very few minutes marines learned that to move in front of a cave was to die.

But fortunately the Raiders had a demolition section headed by Angus Gauss, a marine gunner who loved to blow up anything. To Gauss's ears, an explosion was the sweetest music conceivable. He and his crew spent the morning improvising pole charges, and around noon things began to happen to hidden Japanese. As two demolition men slid forward under cover of smoke grenades, supporting machine-gun fire poured into the dark mouths of the two adjacent caves selected to receive attention. In moments, muffled roars punctuated by screams signaled the successful completion of Gauss's first experiments. By midafternoon most caves were sealed. Two troublesome pockets and half a dozen snipers remained to be liquidated, but at sunset Rupertus was able to radio Vandegrift that Tulagi had been secured. The Raiders suffered 99 casualties—47 killed, 52 wounded; Rosecrans's battalion of the Fifth Marines, 56.[9]

Hunt's battalion, reluctantly released by Turner just before midnight Friday, began landing on Gavutu at 7:00 A.M. on Saturday, August 8, and by noon these fresh troops had the island under control. Hunt directed Miller to embark his Parachutists and proceed with them to Tulagi. Bloody Gavutu belonged to the Americans. The Parachutists had paid for it with 84 killed and wounded—a casualty rate of over 20 per cent.[10]

Hunt now signaled Rupertus that he was ready to attack Tanambogo, and asked for a preparatory air strike. Six carrier dive bombers, on station awaiting such a call, responded almost immediately. Their attack was much worse than useless: several bombs, released too soon, fell on Gavutu, blew three marines to bits, and seriously wounded nine others. Hunt profanely urged the flight leader to go back where he came from.

As the planes departed, cruiser San Juan stood into the harbor, shelled Tanambogo for a few minutes and withdrew. Shortly thereafter, a second carrier strike group appeared on the scene with the announced object of knocking down the Japanese flag still flying from the highest point on the island. Again, several bombs fell short and killed and wounded marines on Gavutu. The others hit the right island, but did not disturb the Rising Sun banner. After this exhibition, Hunt emphatically requested that air "support" be immediately discontinued.

At 4:00 P.M. Hunt, now hopeful that he no longer had to cope with both the Japanese and U. S. Navy dive bombers, called on destroyer *Buchanan* to fire at short range on Tanambogo. *Buchanan* boldly laid a course close inshore. Her brief bombardment was devastating, and five minutes after her guns opened, I Company (Captain W. B. Tinsley) landed on the island standing up. An hour later a sergeant pulled down the banner a dozen carrier pilots had failed to jostle.

Early this Saturday morning Coastwatcher Jack Read, on Bougainville, began the tiresome task of displacing his teleradio to a new position on top of a steep ridge, where he hoped to find better conditions for reception and transmission. As he and the sweating native carriers stumbled upward through the jungle, Reed heard the roar of low-flying aircraft. The *Bettys*, on course southeast, passed directly overhead in "V of Vees" with accompanying *Zeros* layered above and to their flanks. While two boys set up the aerial, Read counted the planes. In a few minutes he was on the air. "From J.E.R. Forty bombers heading yours." This message, picked up in Townsville, Australia, was relayed to Melbourne, thence to Pearl, and reached Fletcher and Turner forty minutes after Read had tapped it out.

Saratoga's fighter director center (FDC) again stacked *Wildcats* over Savo and again unloading ceased as transports and cargo ships got under way to repel air attack. But this time the Japanese, when 50 miles from Savo, swept off in an arc to the north and when the torpedo bombers thundered in, skimming treetops on Florida, the CAP was over Savo at altitudes of ten, fifteen and twenty-five thousand. With no resistance from the air, the Japanese anticipated a field day, but they had not calculated on the accuracy of Turner's gunners, whose many boring hours spent tracking low-flying aircraft now paid commensurate dividends.

At 20 to 40 feet above the water, the *Bettys* bored through flak toward their targets. This was the altitude prescribed by new torpedo doctrine, based on successful attacks against British ships. But American fire control systems were more advanced and their guns were built to depress. The *Bettys* bucked a storm of steel. One by one they flamed, blew up, disintegrated—some so close to the ships that pieces of wings and fuselages spattered against hulls and engines tore through top hamper. Sailors on one transport swept the legs, arms and torsos of Japanese airmen over the side that day.

The CAP, finally alerted, tangled inconclusively with escorting *Zeros*. Both sides were to make immoderate claims of ships sunk and planes shot down. Transport *George F. Elliott* was set afire by a bomber which crashed on her deck and exploded; destroyer *Jarvis* was heavily hit. Actual Japanese plane losses cannot to this day be determined. Carrier pilots claimed six *Zeros, Zero* pilots claimed six Americans. Shortly after noon, Read saw a lonely *Betty* flying northwest. The pilot of this plane, apparently the one survivor, landed in Rabaul and claimed he had sunk a battleship. No one there could dispute him.

Early Sunday morning, Hunt moved two companies to Tanambogo, and by noon his demolition sergeant was reducing cave positions. An unprejudiced observer—one of the regimental chaplains—reported this procedure tersely:

> Sergeant O. S. Bergner would coolly dig a deep hole above the cave, place a goodly dynamite charge therein, ignite the same, and blow up the cave, killing the occupants.[11]

Two light tanks commanded by Lieutenant R. J. Sweeney went ashore to assist in the reduction of caves. One got too far ahead of supporting infantry—or perhaps the platoon moved too slowly—and came to grief:

> The Japanese rushed out of their dugouts and caves and stalled it by inserting a large iron bar into the track. In attempting to free this bar the tank backed into the stump of a coconut tree and became lodged thereon, thus preventing any forward or rearward movement of the tank. The Japanese threw Molotov cocktails and other inflammables which killed the entire crew with the exception of one man who managed to escape.[12]

In midafternoon of Sunday, August 9, Rupertus informed the Division commander that the Northern Landing Force had taken all objectives. Marines buried over six hundred Japanese and sealed approximately one hundred more in caves. Possibly seventy or eighty escaped to adjacent Florida. Two hundred and ninety-five Americans were killed or wounded.

All attempts to induce the defenders to surrender had been answered with lead; the Japanese refused to ask for quarter. Vandegrift described Tulagi–Gavutu–Tanambogo as

> . . . a storming operation . . . unremitting and relentless . . . decided by the extermination of one or another of the adversaries engaged. Soldierly behavior was manifest wherever the enemy was encountered . . . and there was an unflinching willingness to accept the . . . hazards of close and sanguinary combat. . . .[13]

The Solomons landings had proved that amphibious doctrine to which many Marine and a few naval officers had made signal contributions during the previous decade was basically sound. True, several critical technical problems remained to be solved, the most pressing of which was how to speed and control unloading. Marines on Guadalcanal were not aware that tank landing ships (LSTs) existed, and indeed, in August 1942, very few did. Although the amphibian tractor—a vehicle the Marine Corps had sponsored, and which Vandegrift in a personal letter to General Holcomb described as "our life savers," had demonstrated its versatility, that efficient hybrid, the DUKW, was still only in the experimental stage.[14]

The exacting requirements of coordinated combat by land, sea and air revealed many weaknesses in planning, in equipment, and in training. Vandegrift was particularly concerned with the wretched performance of patrols, the lack of liaison between units, and the abominable standard of fire discipline. Communication material, he wrote the Commandant, was "rotten." The sets would simply "not do the job, and it is not the fault of the personnel."[15]

Serious deficiencies were revealed in leadership at all levels from regiment to platoon. On Guadalcanal, there was entirely too much hesitation. Vandegrift would shortly effect changes in his staff and in regimental and battalion commands to insure more forceful and imaginative direction.

Medium calibre naval guns had clearly established that area fire against a defensive system of caves and dugouts amounted to little more than a waste of ammunition. Such targets could be destroyed only if exactly located and attacked by flat trajectory direct fire at short range. Marine Corps naval gunfire experts had been trying to tell admirals this for some time, but with small success. Later, "Close-in" Connolly would show more cautious naval commanders just how effective naval gunfire support could be.

Strategically, the operation promised to accomplish all that King had hoped. The Allies had gone over to the offensive and stopped the Japanese tide at its critical crest. They had (at least temporarily) saved the Santa Cruz Islands and the New Hebrides and established a position from which to interdict Japanese operations in the Solomon and Coral Seas. A vast sigh of relief arose from Australia. But jubilation in Washington, Melbourne and Honolulu was destined to be short-lived.

5

IN EARLY AFTERNOON of Saturday, August 8, with assigned objectives taken or their capture imminent, Turner and Vandegrift had only one outstanding problem—or so they thought. This was to hasten unloading. The invasion fleet had weathered three vicious air attacks in 24 hours. Turner knew—he had been told in quite definite terms at Koro—that he could expect air cover for no more than another 18 hours. He also knew that he could not possibly empty his ships in that time. He had followed the progress, or lack of it, of unloading, and was aware that practically no heavy equipment had yet been put ashore. As he surveyed the scene from the flag bridge of *McCawley*, Turner was a worried man. During dinner, an orderly handed him a piece of paper calculated further to diminish his extraordinary stock of optimism and to induce one of the bursts of colorful profanity for which he was justly celebrated.

This, an intercept of an operational priority dispatch from Fletcher to Ghormley, contained information the Amphibious Force commander found, in his own uncompromising word, "unbelievable." In his message, Fletcher reported a large number of enemy torpedo and bomber planes in the area; his fighter strength reduced from 99 to 78; his fuel critically low. He recommended immediate withdrawal of the carriers. The Expeditionary Force commander took this "most unfortunate" decision without reference either to Turner or Vandegrift.[1]

Although Fletcher could hope that his ships had not been detected, he could not be sure, and apparently surmised that they had been, or soon would be. We know now that neither enemy submarines nor aerial snoopers had spotted Task Force 61, that Fletcher's bunkers held oil adequate to operate in the area for at least two more days before he needed to proceed to a fueling rendezvous, that he had over twice the fighter strength available to the Japanese on fields in the Bismarcks, and that he actually began to pull out 12 hours before he received Ghormley's authority to do so. His "desertion of the vital parts of the force," as Turner later described the withdrawal, continued despite the information, of which Fletcher was aware within two hours after he had originated his request to retire, that a Japanese surface force was advancing toward the lower Solomons.[2] Ghormley was loath to leave Turner and Crutchley without air cover, but did not feel that he could direct Fletcher to remain. After all, ComSoPac could not read the fuel logs in Fletcher's ships.[3]

The decision left Turner no alternative. He must withdraw his vulnerable and valuable amphibious ships, the only such west of Hawaii, and as quickly as possible. He forthwith summoned Vandegrift and Crutchley to the "Wacky Mac."

At the time the American carriers turned toward the southeast, Vice Admiral Gunichi Mikawa's column of five heavy and two light cruisers and a destroyer, with *Chokai* in the lead, was boring down The Slot north of New Georgia Island. On the bridge of this flagship was a man not afflicted with doubts and fearsome apprehensions; Mikawa moved boldly to the sound of the guns. He knew exactly what he was going to do: destroy the Anglo-American invasion force in a night attack.

Morning reconnaissance by cruiser float planes gave Mikawa a reasonably accurate assessment of Allied strength; based on his observers' reports, the admiral drew up his battle plan. This provided for high-speed "rush-in" south of Savo, immediate attack on Allied cruisers and transports off Guadalcanal, destruction of shipping lying off Tulagi, and withdrawal to the north of Savo. The simplicity and audacity of this conception would have commended it to Horatio Nelson. At about 2:20 P.M. Mikawa signaled his instructions. These were brief and to the point:

> We will penetrate south of Savo Island and torpedo the enemy main force at Guadalcanal. Thence we will move toward the forward area and strike with torpedoes and gunfire, after which we will withdraw to the north of Savo Island.[4]

Even though the Japanese ships had never operated together, Mikawa deemed amplification of his orders unnecessary. Night battle doctrine was highly developed in the imperial navy, the captains were skilled veterans, the crews superbly trained. And in their high-speed, oxygen-powered, 24-inch "Long Lance" torpedoes, the Japanese possessed a lethal weapon in which they reposed a confidence events of the immediate future would fully justify.

Two hours later, all topside flammable materials were thrown into the sea, and, as the sun sank behind his ships, Mikawa sent a visual signal:

> In the finest tradition of the Imperial Navy we shall engage the enemy in night battle. Every man is expected to do his best.[5]

Mikawa counted on surprise, and he was to achieve it, despite the fact that his force had been detected and shadowed on August 8 by two reconnaissance planes of the Royal Australian Air Force. One pilot did not even bother to stay with the contact long enough to develop it accurately, and with incredible insouciance, reported sighting enemy ships only after he had completed his patrol, landed, and enjoyed afternoon tea. His colleague, less remiss, made an incomplete report. For a variety of reasons, the information was not processed promptly; transmission of both reports was inexcusably delayed, and it was not until 7:00 P.M. (or about an hour after Turner's communicators had intercepted and decoded Fletcher's priority to Ghormley) that one of these messages reached Turner. He relayed it to the ships of his command. Possibly bcause of ambiguous wording—"Three cruisers, three destroyers, two seaplane tenders or gunboats course 120°, speed 15 knots"—both Turner and Crutchley (who at Turner's behest had hastened from his position in the screen to McCawley in flagship Australia) jumped to the conclusion that the Japanese were no doubt en route to Gizo Bay to establish a seaplane base. Here was no attempt to assess enemy capabilities, but rather an unimaginative, crude guess as to his intentions.

Had Fletcher remained, and sent planes to conduct pre-dusk searches toward the northwest, an elementary security measure obviously dictated by the situation, Mikawa's column might have been detected. Or had all sighting reports (there were, in fact, a total of four) been collated, compared and evaluated. . . .[6] Or had Saunders's B-17s not been grounded on the 8th by weather. . . . Or had a supplemental search up The Slot earlier requested by Turner of Admiral McCain been executed. . . .[7]

One error piled on another, bad luck, poor judgment and pure negligence, ingredients to be seasoned all too soon with dashes of

Mikawa's audacity and the skill of his crews, were combining to produce a brew which Australian and American sailors manning the ships screening the northwest approaches to the transport areas would soon choke down to the ultimate dregs.

It was now something after 9:00 P.M., and while Crutchley and Vandegrift (who had boated out from his command post near Lunga) conferred with Turner on board darkened *McCawley*, officers and men in Mikawa's cruisers, only 100 miles northwest of Savo, prepared for the rush-in. On ships of the screen, cruising slowly and methodically north and south of Savo, all was serene. None of their captains seemed conscious that the report earlier sent by Turner could connote danger. None except Bode in *Chicago*, temporarily in command, was even aware that Crutchley had withdrawn *Australia* from the screen and was now 20 miles to the east. Bode did not bother to pass this information to anyone. The British admiral had issued vague instructions but no specific night battle orders, and none of the captains had asked for them. Although there had been opportunity at Koro to call a conference at which the possibilities of a night surface action might have been explored and the admiral might have outlined a desirable operating procedure, Crutchley had neglected to summon his captains to the flagship.

To be sure, his geometrical dispositions looked satisfactory—on a chart. South of Savo, with orders to patrol between that island and Cape Esperance, were three cruisers: *Australia*, *Canberra* and *Chicago*, with two destroyers. Cruisers *Vincennes*, *Astoria* and *Quincy*, also with two destroyers, blocked the northern approach between Savo and Florida. Additionally, one radar-equipped destroyer was posted on sentry beat some six to eight miles west of each of Crutchley's two Savo groups. To the east of the transport area, in Lengo Channel, Rear Admiral Norman Scott patrolled in *San Juan*. Australian cruiser *Hobart* and destroyers *Monssen* and *Buchanan* were under his command. This was an unhappy arrangement, for of the eight cruisers and eight destroyers available to Crutchley, only *San Juan* had new surface search (SG) radars.[8]

One need not be an expert naval tactician to observe that the British admiral had divided his force in such a way as to place each element in a position to be struck and annihilated separately. By prescribing a "box" patrol north of Savo he had, as well, deprived the cruisers there of the ability to "cross the T"—that is, to be constantly able to place themselves speedily in such formation that their main battery and broadside guns could rake the length of an intruding column. All destroyers were equipped with torpedoes, but no orders respecting their use were issued.

That neither Crutchley nor his immediate superior seriously considered the possibility of enemy surface attack is not an excuse, but a damning indictment. Some 2000 years earlier, the Chinese military philosopher Sun Tzu had warned: "In war, do not presume that the enemy will not come, but prepare to meet him."[9] The Japanese were coming, and coming fast, and neither the Allied ships nor their crews were ready to meet them.

Some 40 minutes before midnight, the Japanese admiral again launched float planes with orders to reconnoiter the waters east of Savo, locate enemy ships, report continuously to him, and illuminate with flares as ordered. These planes, nonchalantly showing red and green running lights, arrived over Mikawa's prospective victims at midnight and buzzed around for 30 minutes inspecting the invasion fleet, dimly but adequately silhouetted by the beached and still burning *Elliott*. The aircraft were heard and their lights observed. They were assumed to be "friendly." Mikawa was in the fortunate position of the stalker whose prey is not only utterly oblivious to his presence but too insensate to heed clear warning of impending destruction.

At 12:40, lookouts on *Chokai* sighted the southern picket destroyer, U.S.S. *Blue*, approaching from starboard. The distance was 10,000 meters. So much for the ignorant prejudice which held the Japanese race to be endowed with inferior eyesight.

Blue's radar did not pick up the Japanese column, nor, as she approached, did her myopic lookouts see the enemy. On the flag bridge of *Chokai* the admiral and his staff froze. Mikawa murmured an order: "Left rudder. Slow to 22 knots." He was not interested in destroyers.

Still *Blue* closed the range:

From her deliberate, unconcerned progress it was plain that she was unaware of us—or of being watched—and of the fact that every gun in our force was trained directly on her. Seconds strained by while we waited for the inevitable moment when she must sight us—and then the enemy destroyer reversed course![10]

This was a minute heavily charged with fate; before the Japanese "could fully appreciate" their "good fortune," another lookout reported a ship 20 degrees on the port bow. This was *Ralph Talbot*. She was steaming north—away from the column. The door was open.

Mikawa at once jumped the speed of advance to 30 knots, and at 1:37, exactly four minutes after sighting cruisers on the starboard hand (*Canberra* and *Chicago*), *Chokai* launched her terrible fish. With range closing at an incredible half-a-mile a minute, the cruisers in the flagship's wake now opened fire. By 1:46 *Canberra*, listing and ablaze, was finished.

The Japanese now turned the fury of guns and torpedoes on *Chicago*; 60 seconds later she, too, was knocked out, her bow blown off. Punch-drunk, she staggered erratically off into the blackness. She was harmless; Mikawa let her survive. He had eyes on new game. He had disposed of two of five Allied cruisers in slightly less than ten minutes from the moment of opening fire. This Japanese admiral wasted no time, and luck attended his boldness.

As *Chicago* wallowed ineptly toward Cape Esperance, *Chokai*, followed by *Aoba*, *Kako* and *Kinugasa*, swung northeast. At approximately the same time, the last three cruisers in the column— *Furutaka*, *Tenryu* and *Yubari*—executed successive 90-degree turns to the left and formed column heading almost due north. They were now on a course roughly parallel to Mikawa's, but about two miles west of his track, echeloned slightly to his left rear. The three remaining American cruisers—*Astoria*, *Quincy* and *Vincennes*—were still steaming sleepily at ten knots. In minutes, in seconds now, Mikawa's iron arms, the arms of death, would embrace, in turn, each unsuspecting victim.

At 1:49 flares blossomed over the American ships, remorseless searchlights picked them out, and less than two minutes later the first 8-inch salvos splashed around them. Within six minutes *Astoria*, hit by torpedoes, was burning. Japanese gunners pumped hundreds of rounds into the flaming ship as she staggered off to the southeast. But mangled *Astoria* still fought; her last salvo smashed a turret on *Chokai*.

About this time, *Aoba*'s searchlight beams fell full on *Quincy* and revealed her with turrents trained fore and aft. Seconds later, an 8-inch salvo blew one of her cruiser planes off its catapult. Flames leaped, and the Japanese "continued the battle very easy-minded, without any worries."[11] *Quincy*, now engulfed in fire, was deluged with shells from both sides. Nevertheless, her guns—or some of them—were manned and firing. But not for long. A torpedo ploughed into number 4 fireroom, a turret exploded, the bridge was wrecked, and her captain killed. In a few minutes she was down by the bow, and at 2:35 A.M. she capsized and sank.

Meanwhile *Kako* had illuminated *Vincennes*. Again, one of the first Japanese salvos hit aft, where scout planes rested on catapults. Again flames leaped into the air, and again shells and torpedoes found their targets. At least three, possibly four, torpedoes plunged into the cruiser and ripped her vitals. She was in her final agony at 2:15 when the Japanese ceased fire. Half an hour later *Vincennes*, too, went down.

This round had lasted a few minutes longer than the first, but the results were identical: the Americans were surprised and smashed before they had a chance to respond. A few salvos hit Japanese ships: fortunately for WATCHTOWER, one of the few fired by *Quincy*'s main battery landed near the flag bridge of *Chokai*, destroyed her operations room, and killed 30 officers and men whose presence was essential to the conduct of the battle.

It was at this time that Mikawa made his decision to break off the action and retire. At 2:23 *Chokai* blinkered "All forces withdraw," and immediately, "Force in line ahead, course 320, speed 30 knots." As the ships headed out, they sighted and engaged *Ralph Talbot*. In succession, the turrets and broadside guns of *Furutaka*, *Tenryu* and *Yubari* lay on her. But the Japanese were committed now to a speedy retirement and their fire was neither sustained nor accurate. The game destroyer, hit by half a dozen shells, returned the fire and launched torpedoes. Happily, a heavy rainstorm suddenly enveloped her. When it passed, *Ralph Talbot* was dead in the water, but the Japanese had gone.[12]

First light of August 9 revealed over 1000 oil-covered sailors, many burned, others seriously wounded, clinging desperately to empty shell cases, life rafts, orange crates, or to any flotsam or jetsam which would hold their heads above water. Trails of blood attracted sharks; during the long night men had occasionally disappeared with appalling suddenness. Rescue operations inaugurated at dawn proceeded during the morning. In five hours more than 700 wounded were saved. A dozen sharks were killed by sailors who shot them with rifles from the rescue craft and decks of destroyers.

Until occasional boats began in early morning to deliver oil-soaked and half-clad men to the beach, no one ashore was aware of the result of the sea fight. Incoherent accounts of exhausted survivors suggested that the vicious action had perhaps been a stand-off, an inference confirmed by the presence of the transports, some of which were discharging. That the Navy was still around—or that its amphibious ships were—was a propitious omen.

But their commander was now a man in a hurry. Before 6:00 A.M., Turner had enough firsthand information to enable him to comprehend the extent of the tragedy of the night before; indeed, at 5:00 o'clock the admiral ordered *Canberra* either to join him at once or be abandoned. As the ship was listing heavily and could neither steam nor steer, there was no choice, and *Patterson* and *Blue* closed her to take off the crew. Two hours later she was torpedoed by another American destroyer. *Astoria* was still afloat, but efforts to save her were to no avail. She went down a few minutes after noon.

Although at Savo Mikawa's ships sustained only superficial damage and their crews suffered but few casualties, they were not all destined to return to safe haven in the Bismarcks. As his victorious cruisers retired up The Slot, Mikawa signaled Goto to break off with *Aoba*, *Furutaka*, *Kinugasa* and *Kako* and proceed to Kavieng. The admiral, in *Chokai*, set course for Rabaul, accompanied by *Tenryu*, *Yubari* and destroyer *Yunagi*. Each group proceeded toward the harbor assigned at comfortable speed for the remainder of the day. Early Monday morning the four Kavieng-bound cruisers, now covered by an aircraft on anti-submarine patrol, swung 90 degrees left and headed for the port less than 70 miles distant where a deserved welcome awaited them.

Kako, last in column, would not enjoy it. At 8:00 A.M. her life expectancy was exactly 13 minutes, for at that moment Lieutenant Commander John R. Moore in submarine *S-44* selected her as a target. For several minutes Moore tracked her; then, at a range of 700 yards, fired bow tubes. At 8:08 four torpedoes ripped into *Kako* and in five minutes she had disappeared. In the uproar, *S-44* slipped quietly away.

Nor for the Allied side was the balance sheet of this battle yet complete. Destroyer *Jarvis*, heavily hit in Saturday's air raid, had shortly thereafter commenced withdrawing slowly to the west. She somehow miraculously passed through the melee off Savo without injury. Sighted by one of Fletcher's scout planes south of Cape Esperance just after sunrise Sunday, *Jarvis* was moving laboriously to the southwest, down by the bow and trailing oil. This was the last news of her. She was assumed to have sunk with all hands.[13] Loss of *Jarvis* added 247 names to the tally of Savo. Almost 1300 Allied sailors died; another 700 were burned or wounded. Japanese casualties were considerably less than one-tenth of this number.

In his radio report to the Commander in Chief, Combined Fleet, Mikawa listed five heavy cruisers and four destroyers sunk, and other ships damaged. He stated that two cruisers had withdrawn. This somewhat exaggerated the toll exacted, but Mikawa and his men nevertheless deserved the congratulatory message awaiting them at Rabaul:

> Appreciate the courageous and hard fighting of every man in your organization. I expect you to expand your exploits and you will make every effort to support the land forces of the Imperial Army which are now engaged in a desperate struggle.[14]
>
> (*signed*) Yamamoto Isoroku.

In Japan, press and radio were justifiably jubilant. Huge headlines and excited commentators announced "great war results . . . unrivalled in world history." Mass victory parades were held in every city; in Tokyo, rejoicing crowds thronged the streets. As a result of Savo, proclaimed Radio Tokyo, Australia had "absolutely become an orphan of the southwest Pacific." Twenty-four warships and eleven transports "filled to capacity with Marines" had been sunk!

The House of Peers directed that a certificate of gratitude be at once inscribed and delivered to the Minister of the Navy. In an English language broadcast on August 15, the audience (which included marines on Guadalcanal and Tulagi) was informed that the U. S. Navy now had no operational carriers: all had been "blown to bits at the Coral Sea and Midway." The commentator added that the Pacific Ocean was now under Japan's control. The marines in the Solomons were dismissed as "summer insects which have dropped into the fire by themselves." Where it really mattered, this bombast was greeted with jeers.

As Tokyo propagandists increased the toll of Allied losses, further tributes were paid the navy, whose "power, so deep and uncomprehensible [*sic*] to the enemy" had annihilated the Anglo-American "remnants" and isolated Australia. Marine listeners were assured of "certain death" which would not be long in coming, and the U. S. Navy was warned that there was still "plenty of room at the bottom of the Pacific for more American Fleet, ha! ha!"[15]

The Japanese admiral's decision to withdraw when he did has been severely criticized. He was, in fact, privately and politely reprimanded by Admiral Yamamoto. He should, it is said, have gone after the transports. But over him there hung this night the threat of Fletcher's carrier aircraft. He was well aware that if American pilots attacked his naked column with the accuracy and determination they had displayed at Midway, his ships would be destroyed, his victory utterly nullified. What he could not know was that Fletcher was already long gone, "departed," as Turner said, "to other regions."[16] Mikawa's action must be judged in the light of the information available to him at the moment he made his vital decision. For indeed, it was vital. Had he plunged in among the transports, he would no doubt have destroyed them. But no more than most of his contemporaries of high rank in the Japanese Army and Navy did Mikawa *at this time* visualize the threat to Guadalcanal as a serious one. The Americans were few in number, beneath contempt as fighters, and would be attended to in due course by the imperial army. Further, the doctrine of decisive surface action, *Yogeki Sakusen*, dominated this admiral's thinking. The proper targets for combat ships were combat ships. This was dogma.

In Pearl Harbor and Washington, official reaction was numbed silence. First sketchy reports suggested defeat; amplifying details indicated near-disaster. It was clear that nothing could be divulged to the press, and King's spokesman confined himself to the laconic statement that operations were "proceeding." Unable to pry specific information from the reluctant Department, *Time* magazine finally decided to expand the Navy's exploits even if its Commander in Chief would not, and on August 24 revealed that on the night of August 8

Japanese cruisers and destroyers tried to smash the invasion fleet. Then came what U. S. tars had long prayed for: the first real gun-to-gun test of U. S. and Japanese surface sea power. Result: a licking for the Japs.[17]

For the first time, but not the last, Tokyo Rose was purveying more authentic information than the weekly newsmagazine.

An official and complete report of this debacle was withhheld from the American people for weeks. King knew that to release specific details would serve only to depress morale, plaster a monumental black eye on his Navy, and give aid and comfort to the enemy. And he knew, too, that when Allied naval losses were finally revealed, the inevitable hunt for a scapegoat would begin. To one segment of the American press, Rear Admiral Crutchley was tailor-made for the role. Certainly this feckless admiral must bear his share, but many others, too, must carry theirs.

Although his screen disposition invited defeat in detail, Crutchley's plan had been examined and approved by Turner.[18] Unfortunately, neither he nor his British subordinate was familiar with the capabilities and limitations of the search radars in the two picket destroyers, which had been assigned such positions that adjacent land masses rendered radar plots meaningless.

Passage of information was faulty in the extreme; Turner's assessment of it was disastrous. Communications were execrable. This aspect of the situation has been well summarized:

> The physical system faltered, which is understandable considering the equipment then available in the fleet, but the more serious fault was the human one of failure to communicate to others the knowledge each commander had. The night was replete with tragic breaks in the chain of intelligence. Admiral Crutchley did not tell the Northern or Eastern Forces of cruisers he was leaving the scene, nor did he tell Admiral Turner that he was not resuming his place in the screen. The Southern Force failed to inform the Northern Force that it was under enemy attack, for minutes of warning that were vital. Admirals Turner and Crutchley gave neither group an appreciation of the situation as known to them by midnight, the most damaging omission being the news that the carriers had withdrawn. Had this been known, any planes overhead might instantly have been assumed to be enemy. Each commander lay down on a blanket of assumptions, each his

own and a little different from the others', and all of them wrong, and each awoke in a shattering nightmare of death.[19]

Ships' captains and crews had no appreciation of the difficulties and hazards of night combat. Both *Quincy* and *Vincennes* were recent transfers from the Atlantic Fleet, where during the preceding fifteen months neither ship had encountered the enemy, engaged in night battle exercises, or conducted night battle practice.[20]

Later, Turner interviewed many survivors of Savo. He found very few of them to have any awareness of the stresses battle entails. A number of people who were paid to be awake were asleep. Only a minority were psychologically prepared; none of the ships they crewed was materially prepared. All ships were in an extremely bad condition in respect to fire hazard.[21] Careless topside stowage of high-octane aviation gasoline and other flammables cost several ships and hundreds of lives. Officers and men repeatedly proved their courage at Savo, but valor alone could not suffice.

The Navy's top command faced a most unsavory predicament. The Expeditionary Force commander had displayed a monumental lack of judgment, to say the least. Nor had the Area commander, who had absented himself from the crucial Koro conference and had failed to empower his chief of staff to speak there in his name and with the full support of his authority, particularly distinguished himself. Again, however, we must try to view the situation in the light of information then available to King and Nimitz. It was weeks before a coherent report of Savo was available to either of them. By the time they had sufficient knowledge to act objectively, Savo had been overtaken by exploding events. Perhaps it was in essence a question of "least said, soonest mended."

At noon on the day following this near catastrophe, Turner's transports and cargo vessels began to call in and hoist boats and in late afternoon the last of his ships, accompanied by *Australia*, *Hobart*, *San Juan* and wallowing *Chicago*, disappeared eastward through Lengo Channel.

The marines were on their own.

6   At 9:00 A.M. on this Sunday, Vandegrift called a conference of his staff and regimental commanders. After speculat-
ing pessimistically on the outcome of the naval battle, the general
directed that:

1) Further ground operations be restricted to vigorous patrolling,

2) Defenses be immediately organized to repel attack from
the sea,

3) Supplies be moved to dispersed dumps, and

4) The field be prepared to support air operations at the
earliest possible moment.

Assigned groups went to work on these four projects, and by
evening a rudimentary cordon beach defense stretching from the
Ilu (Tenaru) to the west around Lunga and thence to a point
about 1000 yards west and south of Kukum was established.[1]
This lightly manned screen was reinforced with dug-in 37-mm.
and .50-calibre antiboat guns sited to break up the counterlanding
the general was convinced was imminent.

Vandegrift moved one battalion to a central location as Landing Force reserve; he retained control of tanks and half-tracked
75-mm. guns. During the day, Colonel Robert H. Pepper, commanding 3rd Defense Battalion, sited his mobile 90-mm. AA guns
near the airfield.[2] All this involved a prodigious amount of labor,
but by Monday evening Vandegrift felt his arrangements had
progressed sufficiently to guarantee a hot welcome to attackers
from the sea.

Unfortunately, only 18 spools of barbed wire had been landed;
the holds of ships returning to Nouméa held thousands of sand-
bags, as well as all squad, platoon, and company tools: axes,
saws, post-hole diggers, shovels, spades, machetes, picks. Neither

antitank nor antipersonnel mines were available, and while there was no substitute for these, the woven straw rice bags left by the Japanese proved better than an acceptable replacement for the "bags comma sand" now en route to New Caledonia.

Inventory of captured equipment revealed a rich haul which alleviated to some degree the shortage of engineer equipment needed for completion of the strip. Four heavy-duty tractors, six road rollers, two gasoline locomotives with hopper cars, and a dozen Chevrolet trucks undamaged by bombs and naval shells were speedily put to work. The engineers faced a difficult problem. The Japanese had worked from both ends of the field toward the middle; there a depression almost 200 feet long required an estimated 7000 cubic yards of fill. Power shovels, dump trucks, patrollers and graders were in the holds of the ships. However, one precious item of engineer equipment had been landed in an earlier wave. This was a medium bulldozer which, with its experienced operator, was under the circumstances worth a great deal more than its weight in gold.

Other shortages were critical. Search radars, ground-to-air radio equipment, sirens to warn of imminent air raids, surveying, mapping and reproduction sets—all these were now on the way south. But the Japanese had thoughtfully hooked up an effective air-raid warning system and left behind a remarkable assortment of high-quality drafting instruments.

On August 9, most marines on Guadalcanal moved supplies and dug foxholes. Others went on patrols. One of these, a 12-man reconnaissance party, set out to investigate the Matanikau, an unfordable and forbidding river a mile and a half west of Kukum. The marines reached the east bank without incident, but as the point waded in ankle-deep water over the sand bar at the river's mouth, it was taken under fire. One officer was killed and several enlisted men wounded. On the following day a platoon-strength combat patrol forced a crossing, but was chased back to the east bank. As forays to the east and up the Lunga flushed no enemy, surmises that the Japanese had fled to the west now appeared substantially verified. Korean laborers—"termites" to their captors—provided confirming testimony. One Japanese seaman, a surly fellow wearing a white uniform with blue collar and cuffs, was captured on August 12. After lengthy interrogation, which included a few shots of medicinal brandy, he reluctantly admitted that hundreds of his comrades, starving in the jungle, were eager to surrender.

This not unlikely story substantiated a curious report the intelligence officer had received the day previously, when a patrol had seen a "white flag" displayed on the west bank of the Matanikau. It was enough for Lt. Col. Goettge, who then and there decided to investigate the situation personally.

As he ate cold beans that evening with Vandegrift, Goettge submitted his proposal. The general was not enthusiastic. But his G-2 was persistent, and the Division commander finally agreed that Goettge might personally lead a patrol to the area where the white flag had been seen. The colonel immediately assembled 25 men, most of them from his intelligence section. Shortly before midnight they embarked in a Higgins boat at Kukum.

Complete details of the tragedy which overtook this ill-advised expedition will never be known. The three survivors agreed that the patrol landed just west of the Matanikau about midnight, that it was at once discovered by the Japanese, and practically annihilated in a fire fight lasting less than five minutes. The three who escaped did so by swimming, crawling and wading to the east. They reached the outposts at dawn, their hands and knees deeply lacerated by coral, and sick of exhaustion. Nothing more was ever learned of the fate of Goettge or those who presumably perished with him.

Just before the G-2 set forth on the mission from which he did not return, a *Catalina* piloted by Rear Admiral "Slew" McCain's aide landed on the strip soon to be named "Henderson Field" in honor of a marine dive-bomber pilot killed in the Battle of Midway. This was the first aircraft to use the runway which had just been completed by marine engineers. The unmatted strip, still only 2600 feet long, as yet lacked taxi-ways, revetted hard stands, and a drainage system. But McCain's aide pronounced it suitable for fighter operation.

Bad weather had grounded Rabaul's "eagles" on August 9, but on each of the three following days they pounded the primitive field vigorously. The moment the all clear sounded, the engineers, with equal vigor, filled the craters. And, by August 12, Pepper's antiaircraft guns were beginning to talk. Several days later, Eleventh Air Fleet reported to Tokyo that in the day's raid five *Bettys* had been seriously damaged: "Enemy AA guns are proving rather accurate." The bombers, duly warned, escalated from ten to twenty-five thousand feet, with consequent loss of accuracy.

Arrival of promised marine aircraft was now eagerly anticipated. Daily the engineers extended the runway. With Japanese dynamite they cleared obstructing trees from the north end, and with three earth tampers operated by Japanese air compressors laboriously packed new fill excavated by marine-powered Japanese picks and shovels, and brought to the site in Japanese trucks fueled with Japanese gasoline.

Meanwhile, the pioneers used Japanese girders to construct bridges, and Japanese pier material to repair Japanese jetties damaged in the D day bombardment. Cooks prepared meals on field stoves burning Japanese kerosene. Marines queued up to use latrines built of Japanese lumber and protected from flies by Japanese screen. When the Japanese siren announced the approach of Japanese planes, marines dove into holes dug and roofed by the Japanese. All hands smoked Japanese cigarettes, drank Japanese beer, and listened to Tokyo Rose.

Some varied their emergency rations with canned Japanese seaweed eaten from Japanese bowls with Japanese chopsticks; a fortunate few stuffed themselves with Japanese crab meat and delicious tinned sliced beef packed in soy sauce, which they topped off with Japanese hard candy and *sake* quaffed from delicate Japanese cups. Many wrote letters on Japanese rice paper, counted the number of days until their enlistments expired on a Japanese abacus, and used Japanese occupation money to buy Japanese souvenirs. One gunnery sergeant opened a small class in Japanese flower arrangement; his text a beautifully illustrated book on the subject recently published in Tokyo.

On Tulagi, Merritt Edson spent a few hours daily reading in English translation a "Short History of Japan"; a company commander, who had liberated a Victrola and a collection of Japanese records from a warehouse on Carpenter's Wharf, provided suitable dinner music for the colonel's mess. In those days the suggestion was frequently made that marines might with advantage swap the quartermaster of the corps for his opposite number in Tokyo. "The men are fine, in good spirits and, thank God, still in good health," their general reported to the Commandant.[3]

Marines talked happily of returning to New Zealand in three weeks. As soon as Army "garrison forces" arrived, the heroes of the Solomons would embark and sail over azure seas to the south, there to meet exciting and possibly complaisant young women, to breakfast on steak and eggs, and beat up the bars in Wellington and Auckland. But some viewed the situation more objectively.

One who did so was Major General Millard F. Harmon, the senior Army officer in Ghormley's area. Under ComSoPac, Harmon commanded all United States Army and Air Force units in the South Pacific. Both he and his chief of staff, Brigadier General Nathan B. Twining (elder brother of Vandegrift's assistant operations officer), were clear-headed realists, and both were skeptical of the Navy's ability to support the position won. On August 11, Harmon penned his worries to General Marshall in a personal note:

> The thing that impresses me more than anything else in connection with the Solomon action is that we are not prepared "to follow-up". . . . Can the Marines hold it? There is considerable room for doubt.[4]

Harmon was not being pessimistic; there was indeed considerable room for doubt. Happily, this gloomy letter did not fall into the hands of the American press, whose Washington representatives were now avid for any crumb of information.

And in mid-August 1942, crumbs were their daily diet—at least as far as the Navy was concerned. For weeks after Savo, Admiral King deigned to drop very few from his table. During this period, the admiral's public information officer repeatedly asked him what to tell reporters who badgered him every day for news from the Solomons. "Tell them nothing," the exasperated King snapped. "When it's over, tell them who won."

Within a few days after Savo the Japanese had concluded that the U. S. Navy was no longer a threat to the waters between Guadalcanal and Tulagi, and daily from August 11 a cruiser or several destroyers paraded insolently up and down just out of reach of Colonel Pepper's old 5-inch naval guns. Occasionally a submarine brazenly surfaced to shell Tulagi lazily and chase Higgins boats passing to and fro. Watchers on Tulagi first witnessed one of these "cops and robbers" affairs on the morning of August 12. About ten o'clock an observation post reported two Higgins boats two miles offshore. No one paid much attention; this was the first run of what was expected to become a routine mail and passenger service.

But in moments it became evident to each of the spectators that he was witness to the most dramatic of all imaginable scenes: a literal race between life and death. For 3000 yards west of the unsuspecting Higgins boats, a black shape rose slowly from the choppy waters. As the submarine turned toward the boats, white-clad figures sprawled out of her conning tower, and ran to man her forward gun. Men in the Higgins boats saw her then, and the spray began flying from their bows as coxswains gunned engines. Suddenly, blue smoke rose from one boat, and she slowed.

"Jesus, her engine's conked out!" a marine said in a choking voice. He was crying. As the helpless men on shore cursed and prayed, the lead boat throttled down to a crawl, the second slid alongside, and her crew and passengers piled out of their craft into the other, which leaped ahead. A 30-foot geyser spouted 100 yards behind the packed boat, a second an equal distance ahead. The submarine then overshot. She had closed the range to less than a mile; the Higgins boat had a mile to go to reach the safety of Tulagi harbor.

At this juncture, four water spouts drenched the Japanese manning the deck gun. Thus did one battery of marine pack artillery first demonstrate that proficiency which was to become a byword in the Pacific. One shell of a second bracketing salvo appeared to strike the submarine. The gun crew piled into the conning tower hatch and the Japanese captain took his boat down. Within minutes the Higgins boat swung alongside Carpenter's Wharf and tied up.[5]

Three days later American ships appeared off Lunga for the first time since Turner had left the same waters a week previously. These were destroyer transports *Little*, *McKean* and *Gregory*. They brought in a small Marine Air operations detachment headed by Major Charles H. Hayes, 400 drums of aviation gas, almost 300 bombs, belted aircraft ammunition, tools and spare parts. Other important passengers were Ensign George W. Polk and a group of men attached to "CUB One," a naval air base maintenance unit. "CUBs" were then strange to marines, but they soon learned to cherish Ensign Polk's.

This sortie gave Admiral King's public information officer something to talk about; on the following day the *New York Times* headlined the news that marines were "TIGHTENING THEIR

GRIP" on the Solomons "AS NAVY KEEPS SUPPLIES FLOWING IN."
According to that eminently reliable newspaper's financial correspondent, official confirmation that the U. S. Navy had the
situation firmly under control generated considerable enthusiasm
in Wall Street, where prices "were enhanced 1 to 2 points." The
Herald Tribune's man on the financial front displayed a marked
skepticism and confined himself to the temperate observation
that "professional traders were disposed to keep to the sidelines
pending the outcome of the Solomon Islands invasion." The
"professionals" were destined to be on the sidelines for a considerable time.

Japanese records of the period reveal a curious blend of mys-
tification and growing satisfaction with the situation. Why were
not the quiescent Americans reinforced? If they were indeed
abandoned on this "insignificant island" they obviously could be
liquidated at no great cost. But first it was desirable to establish
contact with the hungry elements west of the Matanikau. Thus,
on August 16, destroyer *Oite* landed supplies in daylight and
put ashore a 200-man advance echelon of the Fifth Sasebo SNLF.
The previous day, transport planes had dropped woven baskets
containing food, small arms ammunition, medicines, and exhortations to be of good cheer. Many containers fell within marine
lines; in one, an ominous message was discovered: "Help is on
the way! Banzai!"

Possibly this influenced Vandegrift to order Rupertus to ship
the 2nd Battalion, Fifth Marines, Raiders, and Parachutists from
Tulagi to Guadalcanal as soon as transportation was available.

And now a new problem, one which threatened seriously to
debilitate the fighting strength of the Division, suddenly became
urgent. Laxness in sanitary discipline promoted the rapid spread
of an acute form of dysentery which took pounds off a man between sunrise and sunset. Hundreds of sufferers visited latrines
twenty to thirty times a day, and by mid-August one man of five
was so weak he could scarcely drag himself to these stinking
boxes. Many had to be assisted to take their trousers down and
to pull them up.

The Division surgeon took steps: the incidence of dysentery
began to fall slowly, but as it was brought under control, fungus
infections, particularly of the feet, became common. Men who
knew they might have to dive into a hole any hour of the
twenty-four naturally hesitated to remove shoes, socks and

trousers. Most marines were unbelievably filthy. A bath in the Lunga, an experience to be coveted, was one very few enjoyed.

On August 17 and 18, Tulagi and Guadalcanal were shelled from the sea, and on both days *Bettys* dumped delayed-action bombs which burst sporadically under the runway and complicated the task of the engineers, who suffered casualties after each raid as they repaired the strip to receive the planes that were to come. But when?

Tension gradually became palpable; there was now little of the banter common during the first few days. With no Japanese on whom to vent their aggravation and growing frustration, the marines poured full measure of scornful invective on the "swab-jockeys" who had "hauled ass"; on the Army, "the dog-faces sitting on their butts in New Caledonia"; on "Dug-out Doug" MacArthur. Vandegrift's marines were more than ready for a fight. They were aching for one.

Since the destruction of Goettge's patrol, Vandegrift had been thinking of a limited operation to clean out the west bank of the Matanikau and so free his position from the threat existing in that quarter. This threat was, indeed, more potential than real; nevertheless the Japanese entrenched there were too close for comfort, and their presence cast a shadow over the beachhead. Thus, on August 17, the general decided to crack the enemy simultaneously from three directions.

Love Company, 5th Marines (Captain Lyman D. Spurlock) would proceed overland to a point about 1000 yards upstream of the river mouth, cross, wheel to the right and attack toward the sea. Baker Company (Captain William L. Hawkins), as distracting force, would from positions on the east bank engage the Japanese by fire and cross the sand bar if possible. A third company (Captain Bert W. Hardy, Jr.) would proceed by boat to a point several miles west of the river, disembark, overrun the village of Kokumbona, and attack to the east. This coordinated operation was to be preceded by artillery concentrations on likely enemy positions.

Spurlock jumped off from his inland bivouac, reached the night before, at 9:00 A.M., August 19, and advanced north toward the small coastal village of Matanikau. Almost immediately he encountered difficulties, both with the unknown terrain and the Japanese. Two platoon leaders were killed and several men wounded by automatic fire, but he continued to push toward the seacoast. Meanwhile, Hawkins, pinned to the east bank of the river by accurate machine-gun fire, was unable to move from his position, much less to cross the bar.

Hardy's company, supposed to close in from the west after landing, had not arrived on the scene of action when Spurlock's scouts stopped at the edge of the jungle which fringed the collection of deserted palm-thatched huts known as Matanikau village. Here the advance guard was taken under fire, which they returned vigorously.

The Japanese hurriedly collected themselves, and before Spurlock's men knew what was happening, they were on the receiving end of the first daylight banzai bayonet charge of the Pacific war. In less than ten minutes it was all over—for the Japanese. From front and flanks half-a-dozen Browning automatics sliced into the attackers; the few Japanese who had not joined in the assault fired a few rounds, and fled toward Point Cruz. Sixty-five enemy dead were counted; four marines were killed and 11 wounded.

About this time Hardy's company landed from Higgins boats in the vicinity of Kokumbona village. Their journey had been adventurous. Shelled first by a submarine and later by two destroyers, the captain had been accountably delayed. But his landing was successful, and the routed defenders of Kokumbona ran into the jungle. Spurlock, meanwhile, surveyed the field, collected weapons, diaries and other papers, and withdrew by boat to Kukum.

That this engagement culminated in a minor success was due entirely to the coolness, determination and vigilance of Captain Spurlock and his men. And although it had no influence on the campaign, the skirmish held its own lessons. Communications had failed, as usual. Voice radios again proved completely useless under existing terrain conditions. Coordination of the movements of widely separated units broke down completely. Spurlock's march indicated clearly how much time and energy were required to move a column of no more than company strength through the jungle. On August 19 he had spent an exhausting four hours negotiating less than a mile.

On the same day, Roosevelt cabled Stalin: "We have gained, I believe, a toe hold in the Southwest Pacific from which the Japanese will find it very difficult to dislodge us. We have had substantial naval losses there, but the advantage gained was worth the sacrifice and we are going to maintain hard pressure on the enemy."

Possibly the Chief Executive had not yet read Ghormley's messages of August 16 and 17 to King and Nimitz. In these, ComSoPac warned his superiors that the Japanese might recapture Guadalcanal unless more carrier support and reinforcements were made available. Ghormley would have been surprised, to say the least, had he seen a copy of the President's message to the Soviet Marshal. At this time, neither the Japanese nor the Americans had in the South Pacific the means to apply much pressure. But in Tokyo and Rabaul, planners had already designed a scheme to crack down harshly and as soon as possible on American toes.

7 DURING THE MORNING of August 10, Imperial GHQ received a message which confirmed the earlier estimate that American landings in the Solomons were insignificant. This dispatch described the invaders as a force of several thousand troops whose morale was low, and whose mission was only to destroy the airfield and withdraw. The source of this misinformation was the Japanese military attaché in Moscow. The imperial navy was thus no longer alone in bamboozling the army; even the Russians got into the act.

On the same afternoon, Admiral Nagano met with General Sugiyama. The product of their conversation was a new Central Agreement which outlined future operations in eastern New Guinea and the Solomons "in accordance with the changed situation."[2] This paper stressed the importance of continued pressure against Port Moresby and directed Hyakutake to recapture Tulagi and Guadalcanal immediately with forces to be made available. The Army Section of Imperial GHQ hurriedly assigned the 35th Infantry Brigade plus two reinforced regiments to the order of battle of the Seventeenth Army.

Actually, this paper assist did not greatly improve General Hyakutake's situation. The 35th Brigade was in the Palaus and one of the infantry regiments in the Philippines. The unit nearest the scene of action, Colonel Kiyanao Ichiki's Twenty-eighth Infantry, was at Guam, preparing to return to Japan. Ichiki's regiment had not, after all, stormed the Midway beaches.

Two days later (August 12), Vice Chief of Army General Staff Lieutenant General Moritake Tanabe undertook to resolve Hyakutake's problem:

> The scope of operations for the recapture of strategic points in the Solomon Islands will be decided by the Army Commander on the basis of his estimate of the enemy situation. General Headquarters believes that it is feasible to use the 35th

Infantry Brigade and Aoba Detachment if the situation demands. However, since tactical opportunity is a primary consideration under existing conditions, it is considered preferable, if possible, to recapture these areas promptly, using only the Ichiki Detachment and Special Naval Landing Forces.[3]

This dispatch is important for two reasons. First, because it reflects the atmosphere of incredible overconfidence which then enveloped Imperial GHQ; second, because it foreshadows the policy of piecemeal commitment which contributed decisively to the series of defeats Japan suffered on Guadalcanal.

Some at Imperial GHQ vigorously opposed commitment of "only the Ichiki Detachment and Special Naval Landing Forces." One of these officers (formerly Tojo's staff secretary, and currently Chief of the Administrative Division, Army Section, IGHQ) was Colonel Susumu Nishiura. When he heard of the plan, he recalled "what had happened so often before; at Nomanhan, where we fought the Russians, and later, time after time in China, when we had committed forces inadequate to the task."

So perturbed was Nishiura at the prospect that he called Premier and Defense Minister Tojo at his residence on a scrambler telephone. "But he (Tojo) replied that he could do nothing; that the decision was General Sugiyama's; that he would not interfere." Nishiura then sought an audience with his chief. Sugiyama listened quietly, and said: "The orders have been issued. They cannot now be rescinded." The colonel returned to his office. "Nothing more could be done. Would it not have been better to wait a few days to collect a larger force, and thus not repeat our previous mistake? Still, I could but hope for the success of Colonel Ichiki."[4]

The army element designated for Operation "KA," the annihilation of American troops and the "prompt recapture of strategic points in the Solomon Islands," embarked at Guam without delay and sailed immediately for Truk. There, several days later, the regimental commander was briefed by a staff officer flown from Hyakutake's headquarters. The orders Colonel Ichiki received read:

Headquarters, 17th Army 1530 hr. 13 August. Rabaul.

a. The strength of the enemy who landed in the Solomon area

is still unknown, but there is no enemy activity as we had expected. Even to this day, 13 August, it is certain they are not utilizing the airfield there.

b. The Army will cooperate with the Navy and quickly attack and destroy the enemy in the Solomons while the enemy is endeavoring to complete the occupation. It will recapture and maintain these vital places.

c. The Ichiki Detachment will cooperate with the Navy and quickly recapture and maintain the airfields at Guadalcanal.

d. If this is not possible, this detachment will occupy a part of Guadalcanal and await the arrival of troops in its rear. For this purpose a spearhead unit of approximately 900 troops will be organized and loaded on six destroyers that are near at hand and will advance towards Guadalcanal by a direct route.

The advance echelon would land at Taivu Point, about 22 air miles east of the American position, shortly after midnight on August 18. A detachment of a Naval Landing Force (about 250 officers and men) would land near deserted Kokumbona, in a distracting move. The remainder of Colonel Ichiki's regiment, totaling almost 1500, was to debark at Taivu within the week.[5]

Admiral Mikawa protested assignment to this mission of an army unit which had previously been told that it would return to the homeland. He feared morale would be impaired by the unexpected change of orders. He had readily available in Rabaul three Landing Force units he felt were better suited to do the job than Colonel Ichiki's command. Also, the admiral observed, the Tulagi–Guadalcanal area was one for which the navy was primarily responsible. His suggestions were not accepted.

Responsibility for safe delivery of this "spearhead unit" was assigned to Commander Reinforcement Force, Rear Admiral Raizo Tanaka, a man whose name rightly belongs with those of the top commanders of either side. Tanaka viewed his orders with misgiving at the time, and later wrote:

> With no regard for my opinion . . . this order called for the most difficult operation in war—a landing in the face of the enemy—to be carried out by mixed units which had no opportunity for rehearsal or even preliminary study. . . . In military

strategy, expedience sometimes takes precedence over prudence, but this order was utterly unreasonable.

I could see that there must be great confusion in Headquarters of Eighth Fleet.[6]

The order Tanaka received was not "utterly unreasonable." Nor was that handed Ichiki at Truk. But Ichiki's orders were based on very sketchy and totally unreliable information. Ichiki had been told that there were approximately 2000 Americans in this "jungle beachhead," that their morale was low, that some were fleeing from Guadalcanal to Tulagi, and that all seemed anxious to escape from an island "under control of the Japanese Naval Air Force."

Ichiki was a distinguished officer with an outstanding record. He was known in the Japanese Army as a brave and resolute man and an expert in infantry tactics. In China, he had commanded battalions for several years. As he read his orders and reflected on the information he had received at Truk, he must have reached the conclusion that one of his battalions could do the job without waiting for the remainder of the regiment. For it is perfectly clear that the colonel paid little attention to Hyakutake's instructions. A more circumspect man would not have acted with the impetuous haste which was to doom Ichiki.

A few minutes before midnight of August 18, marines on listening posts heard the beach wash created by ships passing close inshore at high speed; at about three o'clock, they again reported wash. By dawn, rumors of a night landing to the east were circulating freely, and the G-3, Colonel Gerald C. Thomas, took immediate steps to find out what was happening. The man he called on was the former British Colonial officer, Martin Clemens. After drinking a cup of tepid tea and eating a stack of "starched" pancakes, Clemens (who had walked into marine lines four days previously with a dozen scouts) ordered Sergeant Major Vouza to lead a native patrol from east to west around the marine position.

Vouza, an ex-constable of Island Police, was an old hand at bushwhacking on Guadalcanal. Through its jungles he had tracked murderers, pig rustlers, chicken thieves, and disturbers of His Britannic Majesty's peace. In 1939, after twenty-five years' honorable service, Vouza had retired to Malaita to raise yams, but when the Japanese came to Guadalcanal he hastened back in a canoe and requested assignment to active duty. This experienced, intelligent, and loyal native was to prove himself a man of uncommon valor and indomitable will.

Even before Vouza and his scouts set out, Captain Charles Brush, accompanied by Corporal Daniel Pule and three other native police, had crossed the Ilu at the head of a strong combat patrol from Able Company, First Marines, and headed east along the government track. At noon, Brush was in the vicinity of Koli Point. There his advance guard reported a group of Japanese moving toward them through the coconuts between the trail and the beach. Brush deployed immediately and held fire until the Japanese were within a hundred yards. Then he struck.

While the bulk of his patrol pinned the Japanese, his executive officer, Lieutenant Joseph Jachym, swept rapidly off to the right with a squad and took position to the left rear of the enemy. Converging automatic fire poured on the Japanese and, of 34, only three escaped. The marines suffered six casualties. After his victory, Brush "tightened his helmet strings," posted security to the east and south, contacted regimental headquarters by radio, and personally searched the bodies.

The helmets of the dead Japanese bore the star of the imperial army, not the chrysanthemum of the navy. Four were officers carrying swords and field glasses, wearing polished boots, and dressed in pressed uniforms complete with rows of varicolored ribbons. Brush wasted no time rifling their map cases, and returned in early afternoon with precious documents. These were immediately delivered to Captain "Pappy" Moran, the one-man Japanese language section of Division intelligence. His hurried perusal of them indicated that the marines were in for plenty of trouble: the captured maps showed an amazingly accurate picture of artillery dispositions in the vicinity of the airfield. (How the enemy procured this information remained a mystery for some time; only later was it discovered that a Japanese observation post on Grassy Knoll had been transmitting daily reports of activity around the airfield. Low-level aerial photographs had provided amplifying detail; no camouflage materials had been landed).

Vandegrift now faced the first of many critical decisions which only he could make. The diaries Brush brought in revealed that the enemy force to the east consisted of part of a regimental detachment of the imperial army that had sailed from Guam. But, unfortunately, the industrious diarists had neglected to record such interesting details as their strength and armament, present location, or intentions. Vandegrift considered, and properly rejected, a suggestion that one battalion be sent eastward. Without a reserve he would be completely hamstrung if simultaneously attacked from one or both flanks and the sea. There was nothing for it but to intensify defensive measures, to reinforce outposts and, above all, to be constantly vigilant.

Accordingly, tanks were alerted, 37-mm. antitank guns provided with an extra allotment of antipersonnel canister ammunition, hundreds of empty Japanese rice bags filled with sand, and wire from plantation fences hastily strung along the Ilu (Tenaru) position. Forward observers from del Valle's Eleventh Marines joined the defenders of the river line and after test of wire and radio communications a battalion of 75-mm. pack howitzers and the short-barreled 105s registered on its east bank and the sandspit at its mouth.

And important help was on the way. During the afternoon of August 20, escort carrier *Long Island*, lately improvised from S.S. *Mormacmail*, reached a position southeast of San Cristobal and launched the first plane of Major Richard C. Mangrum's Squadron 232. Captain John L. Smith's Squadron 223, nineteen pot-bellied Grumman *Wildcat* fighters, followed Mangrum's twelve *Dauntless* dive bombers into the air.

An hour later, in the gentle glow of early evening, Mangrum found the strip, dragged it once, and was brought in by Major Charles H. ("Fog") Hayes, a former carrier "landing-signal" officer. In moments, the SBDs and *Wildcats* tailing Mangrum bounced down on the runway and bumped awkwardly to the parking areas that flanked it. Hundreds of officers and men in soiled dungarees greeted the advance echelon of MAG 23. One spectator, perhaps a bit too elated, clapped his hands as he jumped and shouted, "*Now* let the bastards come!"

A few hours later they began to come.

Just after midnight, listeners posted in the coconut grove on the east bank of the Ilu reported unidentifiable "clanking noises," whispers, and other ominous sounds, and Lieutenant Colonel Edwin A. Pollock, commanding 2nd Battalion, First Marines, withdrew them to safety. A heavy silence, punctuated only by occasional rustling of palm fronds, enveloped the river banks; the warm sea washed monotonously against the sand at its mouth.

At 2:40 A.M. the Japanese hit. Machine guns and light automatic weapons played their distinctive threnodies, and as mortar shells exploded in marine positions, the ghastly green light shed by flares revealed a closely-packed body of Japanese hurrying through the shallows.[7] The defenders were ready. At point-blank range 37-mm. guns pumped canister into the attackers' ranks. Banzais changed suddenly to screams; the few Japanese who survived this blasting fire crawled over the mangled bodies of their dead and dying comrades to the east bank.

Ichiki's first attempt had failed, but he reorganized and tried again. After drenching marine positions with cannon and mortar fire, he sent a reinforced company through the surf to seaward of the sandspit to assault with the bayonet. At 5:00 A.M. these Japanese hit Pollock's lightly wired-in beach position. The attackers, faltering at the wire, were enfiladed by beach machine guns emplaced to the west. A few seconds later, called artillery concentrations erupted in the sand and enveloped the beach in flame and death.

With grey first light came a welcome lull. At ranges of over 200 yards some of Pollock's riflemen picked off Japanese who flitted about indistinctly under the coconut fronds. "Line 'em up and squeeze 'em off," Pollock adjured these marksmen, in best Marine Corps rifle range tradition. "It was like 'record day' at Quantico," a wounded machine gunner said. "Jesus, anybody could have sliced them dumb bastards. They stood up, for Chrisake, they didn't have enough sense to crawl. Who the hell told those shit-heads they were soldiers?"

Just before sunrise a gravely wounded native dragged himself into marine lines. This was Sergeant Major Vouza. Marines assisted him to Pollock's command post; when Clemens arrived, Vouza was near death:

> . . . he was in an awful mess, not able to sit up. I could hardly bear to look at him. We dragged him behind a jeep, and he told me his story as best he could in spite of the gaping wound in his throat.

> He had gone out on his patrol, taking with him a miniature American flag, which had been given him as a souvenir. Going to hide it in a house at Volonavua, he had walked slap into

three or four platoons of Japs. They were dispersed all round the village and he had no chance of escaping with his American flag. He was caught red-handed and hauled before the Commanding Officer. The man Yishimoto was there, the Jap who had been in the Solomons in peace time and who could speak English. He could not deny that he had been with the Americans. They tried to get information out of him and, failing completely, they got angry and tied him to a tree with straw ropes. After hitting him with rifle butts they jabbed him with fixed bayonets until he passed out. He had seven wounds in his chest and the biggest of all in his throat. When dusk fell they left him for dead and moved into position for the attack.

Many hours later he had come to, and had managed to bite through his ropes; he set off to try and contact the Marines, but after a bit he became so weak that he had to crawl on all fours. He must have crawled nearly three miles, right through the whole battle. This was merely what had happened to him. As if this wasn't enough, he also insisted in spluttering out a very valuable description of what the Jap force had consisted, its numbers and weapons. All this was passed on immediately. A bullet hit the jeep as I was telephoning.

Vouza had lost pints of blood and was in terrible shape. He fully expected to die and before he passed out again he gave me a long dying message for his wife and children. Once he had done his duty, the terrific strain told, and he collapsed. We carried him back and got the doctors working on him. He was operated on, pumped full of new blood, and it was expected that he would live, that was, if the hospital was not disturbed by air-raids. What loyalty the man had, and what amazing vitality. I felt immensely proud.[8]

Vouza rallied, and lived to lead many jungle patrols.

The marines had thrown back two desperate attacks; hundreds of silent bodies sprawled on the sand testified to the serious wound inflicted on a persistent enemy. But how gravely was the Jap hurt? The sporadic chatter of *Nambu* light machine guns, the slower and more methodical bup-bup-bup of hidden heavies, furtive movement in the shadows of the coconut palms across the river—all suggested to Thomas that in spite of the battering he had absorbed, the Jap was very much alive. "We aren't going to let those people lie-up there all day," he said, and proposed immediate envelopment of the enemy position. Vandegrift concurred and released Division reserve, the 1st Battalion of Cates's First Marines, commanded by Lieutenant Colonel Lenard B. Cresswell.

Thomas explained the scheme of maneuver: Cresswell would cross the river upstream of the Japanese as soon as possible, turn 90 degrees north, fan out and drive toward the sea, while from the west bank Pollock's battalion pinned the enemy. Shortly after noon, Cresswell's battalion completed its concealed deployment to the rear of a line of departure along the edge of the jungle which enclosed the coconut grove to the south. When the attack jumped off, it moved slowly but steadily. Caught in a hail of cross fire, and with artillery shells bursting in the palms above them, the Japanese abandoned their foxholes and ran desperately in every direction.

But there was no escape. While three companies relentlessly compressed them, a fourth cut off retreat to the east. Artillery fire crashed down on what was left of Colonel Ichiki's pocketed 1st Battalion; the newly-arrived planes made repeated bombing and strafing runs. At three o'clock a platoon of light tanks rolled across the sandspit belching canister, their steel treads mangling and crushing alike the living, the dying and the dead. Vandegrift, in describing this final phase of the battle, wrote "the rear of the tanks looked like meat grinders."[9]

The battle of the "Tenaru" was history. The "divine influence" of the imperial army's "devil-subduing sharp bayonets" had been nullified.[10] Almost 800 Japanese had been killed, 15 wounded prisoners taken. About 30 of the demoralized survivors crawled off into the jungle; some, grievously wounded, lived only to starve to death; a mere handful, including Ichiki, managed to return to Taivu to join the signal group there. Pollock's battalion sustained 69 casualties; Cresswell's but 20.

Most of the wounded resisted marines who were now trying to help rather than kill them. Several souvenir hunters were shot by prostrate and apparently dead Japanese, and Lt. Cols. Twining, Pollock and Cresswell, who were surveying the carnage, were momentarily discomposed by a dying noncommissioned officer who discharged an automatic pistol in their faces and then blew off the top of his own head. One officer, Captain

Takao Tamioka, survived the holocaust. Colonel Ichiki, who after defeat had hurried to Taivu with the color bearer, reverently tore his regiment's color to shreds, poured oil on the scraps, set a flame to them, and committed hara-kiri.

At a total cost of 99 casualties, including 43 killed, the marines had eliminated one of the elite storm detachments of the Japanese Army.[11] But in truth they had accomplished much more. The myth of Japanese invincibility, fractured at Tulagi and Gavutu, was shattered at the "Tenaru." Here, in the words of the Japanese report, "the detachment commander gradually poured in his entire strength but there was no development in the battle situation. . . . The greater part of the 1st echelon . . . now without any advantages, died heroically."[12]

A few days later, Vandegrift found time to write Holcomb:

> General, I have never heard or read of this kind of fighting. These people refuse to surrender. The wounded will wait until men come up to examine them . . . and blow themselves and the other fellow to pieces with a hand grenade.[13]

These bloody 12 hours posed their own perplexing questions. Why, after his patrol was nearly annihilated, had Ichiki not deduced that the Americans were aware of his intentions? Why had he attacked so hastily? Why had he not reconnoitered the river line a mile inland? Had he done so, he could have crossed the bulk of his force there, turned north and taken the Ilu position in the rear. Why had he launched a second attack in the same manner as the disastrous first? What twisted and obscure reasoning produced this self-induced holocaust?

Part of the answer is, of course, that the colonel's information was faulty. But of more importance were his arrogant denial of reality, his obstinacy, his incredible tactical inflexibility. And part can perhaps be traced to the willingness of the Japanese in the moment of desperation to embrace with stoicism what fate has clearly ordained. To die gloriously for the Emperor in the face of insurmountable odds was the ineluctable duty and indeed the subconscious desire of many Japanese soldiers. What had emerged, first on Tulagi and Gavutu, and again on the banks of the sluggish river the marines called the "Tenaru," was the pattern of total resistance: resistance to the last breath of the last man.

Later, Admiral Tanaka would say:

> I knew Colonel Ichiki from the Midway operation and was well aware of his magnificent leadership and indomitable fighting spirit. But this episode made it abundantly clear that infantrymen armed with rifles and bayonets had no chance against an enemy equipped with modern heavy arms. This tragedy should have taught the hopelessness of "bamboo spear" tactics.[14]

But there was something more fundamental involved here than action taken on the basis of poor information, a reckless and stupid colonel, dedicated soldiers, and a disparity in weapons. This was "face." Once he committed his sword, Ichiki must conquer with it or die. This was the code of the Samurai, "The Way of the Warrior": *Bushido.*

For their part, the marines had learned one lesson they would not forget. From this morning until the last days of Okinawa, over two and a half years later, they fought a "no quarter" war. They asked none for themselves. They gave none to the Japanese.

8 WHILE COLONEL ICHIKI advanced from Taivu to destroy the presumptuous Americans "at one stroke," Imperial GHQ passed control of operations on Guadalcanal from the navy to the Seventeenth Army, and General Hyakutake ordered Major General Kiyotaki Kawaguchi, commanding the 35th Infantry Brigade at Truk, to make ready to proceed to Guadalcanal with his Borneo veterans, assume command of all army and navy units there, and finish off any Americans who might elude Ichiki. The general put his brigade on immediate embarkation alert.

Simultaneously, Rear Admiral Tanaka, whose night-running destroyers (the celebrated "Tokyo Express") were soon to become more a dagger than a thorn in the side of the U. S. Marines, embarked the Yokosuka 5th Special Naval Landing Force and the balance of Ichiki's regiment at Truk in transport *Kinryu Maru* and four converted destroyers.

With these preliminary measures under way, Yamamoto ordered Kondo's Second Fleet battleships and Nagumo's Third Fleet carriers to sortie from Truk. Mission: to locate and destroy American carriers reported in the area between the New Hebrides and San Cristobal, to smash the newly commissioned airfield on Guadalcanal, to bombard marine positions, and to cover and support the landing of the Fifth Yokosuka SNLF and the remainder of the Twenty-eighth Infantry. To optimists on his staff—and there were many—it appeared that Fleet Admiral Yamamoto was using a sledgehammer to crack a walnut. But Yamamoto had learned a lesson from Midway: he had developed a healthy respect for U. S. carrier air.

News that Combined Fleet had sailed from its base and was standing toward the Solomons reached General Vandegrift just before noon on August 22; a few hours later a sighting report forwarded to Guadalcanal placed several units of the enemy fleet within range of Henderson. The decision to attack was pondered carefully. Was the risk of committing the few available planes justified? Vandegrift thought so, and ordered his air commander, Colonel Charles L. Fike, to locate and hit the Japanese ships.

Mangrum led the strike group, his dive bombers covered by Captain Smith's fighters, on what many thought was a desperate mission. In thickening weather the formation headed due north over Tulagi and Florida toward the passage between Santa Isabel and Malaita. Here they ran into a solid front. Driving rain misted windscreens, and in conditions approaching zero visibility the strike turned back. When the disappointed flyers returned, they found General Vandegrift pacing the muddied wooden floor of the pagodalike structure from which the Japanese had planned to conduct their own air operations. "He was calm, comforting, to a bunch of frustrated aviators, but deeply distressed by the discouraging outlook."[1]

Others, too, were distressed. In Nouméa, Major General Harmon took pen in hand to address a personal note to "Hap" Arnold. In this, he expressed his opinion that payment would be exacted of the marines in the Solomons because WATCH-TOWER had been hastily conceived and planned, and no adequate logistic "back-up" scheduled. The campaign "had been viewed by its planners as [an] amphibious operation supported by air, not as a means of establishing strong land-based air action."[2]

As Harmon wrote this letter, Kondo's Covering Force and Nagumo's Striking Force were cruising about 200 miles north of the southern Solomons. Fletcher's *Saratoga*, *Enterprise*, and *Wasp*, operating as three task groups in waters now heavily seeded with Japanese submarines, lay 300 miles to the southeast. In midmorning, *Saratoga* picked up a sighting report from one of Admiral McCain's long-range *Catalinas:* an enemy transport group about 300 miles north of Guadalcanal heading due south at 17 knots. This information was also received at Henderson, where strike aircraft were armed and pilots briefed. On Fletcher's flagship a similar exercise was being conducted.

The object of this shared interest and activity was Rear Admiral Tanaka, whose transport force was sighted well to the west of Nagumo's carriers. In flagship *Jintsu*, the admiral, scheduled to land embarked troops on the following night, was not unaware that he had been spotted. He had immediately reported the snooping *Catalina* to Rabaul, and as the big flying boat lumbered off into leaden clouds, Commander Eighth Fleet radioed Tanaka to turn his convoy north.

This evasive tactic paid off: strikes launched from Henderson Field and *Saratoga* were unable to pierce the obscuring mists. The ordeal of air attack on his naked transports was thus at least postponed, but Tanaka did not enjoy an afternoon free of harassment. After lunch a messenger handed him a radio from headquarters, Southeast Area Force. He was to turn around, proceed south again, and execute landings as planned. The time element made this impossible, and his conflicting orders caused Tanaka to wonder what was going on at Rabaul.

At this point both Nagumo and Fletcher felt sure the other's carriers were around. But where? Fletcher determined to get the answer, and in early afternoon launched a search-and-strike group from *Saratoga*. Commander Harry D. Felt sought in vain for targets, and with needles on fuel gauges rapidly wavering toward zero, brought "*Sara*'s" group to Henderson. Here his pilots spent the night. The following morning, in exchange for hospitality and the fuel Felt needed to return his planes to *Saratoga*, marines detached the 1000-pound bombs cradled under his SBDs. These were the first "half-tonners" to reach the island.

In the meantime, the American admiral, always anxious to fuel to capacity, chose this interlude to send the *Wasp* group south to top off. By this unfortunate decision, Fletcher deprived himself of the marginal superiority which might well have changed the final score in the battle now making up.[3]

On the morning of August 24, Kondo, aware of Fletcher's general position, detached carrier *Ryujo*, cruiser *Tone*, and two destroyers from Nagumo's Striking Force and ordered them to proceed on a southerly course to bait the Americans. This they succeeded in doing. *Ryujo* was discovered, fiercely attacked, and left burning and listing. But the sacrifice gave Nagumo what he wanted—a clear crack at Fletcher's two flight decks. *Enterprise* began to catch it at 41 minutes past four o'clock; four minutes later she had absorbed three direct hits from successive attacks of over 30 dive bombers. But "The Big E," a tough and well-crewed ship, survived. *Saratoga*, as well as Nagumo's *Shokaku* and *Zuikaku*, was undamaged. Twilight deepened as Fletcher broke off the battle, turned south, and headed for a fueling rendezvous.

One *Enterprise* strike of 11 SBDs and 12 torpedo planes (TBFs) was still airborne and looking for the Japanese. But luck did not attend their search; the dive bombers, with fuel dangerously low, had no choice but to jettison loads and try for Henderson Field. As Lieutenant Turner F. Caldwell's "Flight 300"—a mixed group of dive bombers from "Scouting Five" and "Bombing Six"— received a vociferous greeting from pilots of the depleted Cactus Air Force, the longer-ranged TBFs were successfully recovered by wounded *Enterprise*. Next morning the carrier left the area for repairs and bequeathed "Flight 300" to Henderson. This unexpected and welcome addition to Vandegrift's air component was ashore for over a month, and contributed mightily to the toll levied upon Japanese shipping.

Nagumo, Kondo and Fletcher may have thought the action later known as "The Battle of the Eastern Solomons" was over, but they were wrong. There remained the persistent Admiral Tanaka, who had pushed his ill-assorted Transport Group southward on August 24, while the carriers slugged it out to the east. By the following morning he had advanced to a point only 100 miles north of Guadalcanal.

Here was fresh meat, and at 8:30 A.M. a mixed flight of Mangrum's SBDs and Caldwell's "Flight 300" lifted off Henderson and went after it. Tanaka proved hard to locate. Finally, Smith passed the disconcerting news to Mangrum over voice radio that covering *Wildcats*, now at extreme range, must return to base, and two minutes later the fighters turned back. The unprotected SBDs swung to a westering leg, then wheeled to a southern course and started home. And suddenly, under them, were Tanaka's ships.

The first bomb scored on light cruiser *Jintsu* just forward of her bridge. The explosion buckled plates, started fires, floored everyone on the bridge and knocked out communications. Tanaka, momentarily unconscious, came to in a hurry, shifted his flag to destroyer *Kagero* and appeared on her bridge just in time to see 9000-ton transport *Kinryu Maru* catch a 1000-pounder delivered by Ensign Fink, lately of *Enterprise*. The admiral ordered destroyers *Mitsuki* and *Yayoi* to stand by the transport for rescue work. Henderson flyers, bombs expended, surveyed the scene from a safe distance, formed up, and flew off.

But Tanaka's travail was by no means over. No sooner had the SBDs disappeared to the south than a flight of "Blondie" Saunders's Hebrides-based B-17s arrived on the scene and let go a pattern. *Mitsuki* went down: *Yayoi*, her plates started by a near miss, stayed precariously afloat. As *Jintsu* limped away, Tanaka received orders to retire to the Shortlands with what was left of his force.

The first major attempt to retake Guadalcanal by direct assault from the sea had failed.

While the burned and soaked survivors of the deceased Colonel Ichiki's second echelon proceeded in destroyers to the Shortlands, new plans to liquidate the Americans were formulated. These called for steady build-up of strength on Guadalcanal by stealthy night landings from destroyers. Area headquarters directed Tanaka to plan the first of such runs—aptly designated "Rat" Operations—for the night of August 27. The admiral speedily loaded a battalion of Ichiki's regiment on three destroyers and pushed them off toward Guadalcanal. Two hours after the ships had cleared Shortlands harbor and were well on the way, Eighth Fleet directed him to issue an immediate recall; the landing was postponed for 24 hours.

The admiral was now frustrated and furious. For the second time in three days he had received orders from Area headquarters which contradicted those received from Admiral Mikawa:

> I had again received contradictory and conflicting orders from the Area Commander and my immediate superior and was at a loss what to do. If such circumstances continue, I thought, how can we possibly win a battle? It occurred to me again that the operation gave no evidence of careful, deliberate study; everything seemed to be completely haphazard. As commander of the Reinforcement Force this put me in a very difficult position.[4]

Here the admiral put his finger on a key issue: there was little coordination at Rabaul. The Area commander and his nominal subordinate, the Eighth Fleet commander, operated from separate and apparently rival headquarters. Each read what he wished into available intelligence reports, and devised his separate projects. The inevitable result was impetuous action and confusion.

After recalling the destroyers, Tanaka calmed down sufficiently to lay plans for "Rat Two," a four-ship run on the following night. Again higher headquarters, by insisting on a too early departure, threw a wrench into the machinery. The schedule Rabaul prescribed brought the four "cans" within range of Henderson-based aircraft just before dusk on August 28. They were promptly hit by Mangrum's dive bombers. *Asagiri* took one 500-pounder in her vitals and blew up. *Shirakumo* was left dead in the water; *Yugiri* limped off, badly hurt. When this discouraging news was received in the Shortlands, Admiral Tanaka boiled over; in commendably restrained language he later wrote that these precious destroyers were needlessly lost; was it not "sheer recklessness" to attempt a landing operation without "preliminary neutralization of enemy air power?"[5]

Although only one usable ship now remained of Destroyer Division 20's complement of four, the admiral derived some solace from the fact that Division 24, which had left the Shortlands later on the same day, put troops ashore successfully at midnight. "Rat One" had been recalled and "Rat Two" blown apart, but "Rat Three" had redeemed the situation to a degree. Tanaka passed this news to Rabaul and composed himself for a few hours' needed rest.

Commander Reinforcement Force was not allowed much time to relax. Shortly after breakfast the next morning his orderly announced the arrival in the flagship of Major General Kawaguchi and his staff. The general had just come south in troop transport *Sado Maru* and was anxious to follow his first echelon to Guadalcanal with the bulk of his brigade as soon as possible. This, the admiral assured him, would be no problem. "Rat" runs were swift and, if properly planned, entirely reliable: the Japanese Navy owned the waters surrounding Guadalcanal from dusk until dawn. Further, the "sea eagles" were now in a position to render some air cover. The strip on Buka was operational; 29 *Zeros* had advanced to it from Rabaul on August 28.

Kawaguchi listened politely. When Tanaka had stopped talking, the general let it be known he would have nothing to do with "Rat" transportation. He recalled that because of space limitations on destroyers, Colonel Ichiki had landed with reduced rations and an unsatisfactory amount of equipment: only two mountain guns, not enough heavy mortars, inadequate ammunition, no field telephones, and only one radio. The Kawaguchi brigade would proceed by large and small barges, and with the equipment necessary to support its punitive operations against the Americans, or it would not go. Such, the general concluded, were his orders from Seventeenth Army. Such were his intentions.

Tanaka was equally adamant. *His* orders were to send the 35th Brigade by destroyers. There were but few barges available.

Kawaguchi would go by destroyer or he couldn't go. Already, the admiral went on, a thousand troops were on board Captain Murakami's destroyers now poised for "Rat Four." Kawaguchi reluctantly agreed to permit this batch to proceed that night as planned, and after bidding farewell to Tanaka returned to the *Sado Maru*.

This inconclusive meeting impelled the admiral to query Rabaul, but no reply was immediately forthcoming. The only dispatch Tanaka received was from Eighth Fleet, which informed him that two transports, a heavy cruiser, and two destroyers were unloading off Lunga. These were to be picked off by Murakami's destroyers after he discharged troops at Taivu.

During late morning of August 30, Murakami returned to the Shortlands to report that although he had landed the troops expeditiously, he had not attacked American shipping because of "moon conditions" and the fact that Henderson planes were airborne.[6] Tanaka, momentarily dumfounded, soon recovered his power of speech. He relieved Murakami on the spot, reported the captain's failure to execute orders to Rabaul, and called a staff conference preliminary to another meeting with General Kawaguchi. The tenor of this gathering was disturbed by scorching messages from the Area commander and Admiral Mikawa respecting Murakami's dereliction.

Commander Reinforcement Force, now in a foul humor, found the general as obdurate as he had been on the preceding day. It was barges or nothing. But the wily admiral had a surprise for Kawaguchi. One destroyer and two destroyer transports were at the moment embarking his troops for "Rat Five"! Over protests from Colonel Akinosuka Oka, his senior regimental commander, and several members of his staff, the general gave permission for this batch to go forward. They landed safely at Taivu just after midnight.

Tanaka's opposition to barging was well founded. The standard 40-foot barges available were cumbersome, slow and, in rough weather, unseaworthy. Fully loaded, their maximum speed was about seven knots. The admiral repeatedly pointed out that the routine of coasting at night and lying up during the day was dangerous and time consuming. Kawaguchi's previous experience with barges, however, had been satisfactory. He preferred them to destroyers. That was that.

At the conference on the following day, Kawaguchi reluctantly consented to proceed by destroyer that night with an increment of 1500 officers and men provided that the remaining 1000 men of his brigade would be shipped by barges as soon as possible. Rabaul directed Tanaka to accede to this, and at noon Kawaguchi embarked headquarters personnel and a reinforced battalion in eight destroyers. He landed at Taivu on the last day of August.

Marine flyers were doing everything possible to stop Tanaka's night runs, but their task was nearly a hopeless one. It was now a period of waning moon, and even traces of ships' wakes could often not be discerned. Mangrum allowed none save the most experienced to fly through the darkness, so heavy it was almost palpable. Only when the Japanese opened fire could SBD pilots discover their targets. Tanaka was quick to issue orders prohibiting his ships from illuminating or engaging with AA.

Meanwhile, Vice Admiral Mikawa, the victor of Savo, had been pondering the lessons of recent operations. He was dissatisfied with army-navy cooperation or, perhaps more exactly, with the lack of it. In a résumé dated August 31, he informed Combined Fleet and his subordinates that the policy of piecemeal reinforcement would lead only to disaster: "Every effort must be made to use large units all at once." These, he continued, must be transported in fast ships. Further, the bad habit of "underestimating the enemy and overestimating our own forces" would imperil the entire "KA" operation:

> Enemy resistance and counter attacks in the Guadalcanal and Solomons area have been extremely stubborn and our operations of the first period were totally unable to cope with them. Unless operations are conducted in accordance with careful and detailed plans based on accurate information the probability of their success is slight.[7]

But for the present, at least, such realism was confined to Rabaul. To be sure, Imperial GHQ was not pleased with the progress being made, but staff officers in Tokyo were not yet so disconcerted by minor American successes that they felt it necessary to heed Mikawa's blunt advice. However, on the same day GHQ did issue instructions assigning first operational priority to the "immediate recapture of Guadalcanal."[8] This directive stipulated that further offensive operations in New Guinea were to be held in abeyance while all available army and navy forces were utilized to regain the lost positions in the Solomons.

Thus, the full weight of Japanese power in the southeastern area swung until it pointed directly at Henderson Field and the shattered coconut groves surrounding it.

The narrow landing strip the Japanese were determined to seize and the marines slightly more determined to hold had taken a pasting during the last ten days of August. But somehow the tired pilots managed to get off it and to stagger back on. And in doing so, they, their crewmen, and their planes shattered another myth. "Cactus fighters," wrote Robert Sherrod, "made a great contribution to the war by exploding the theory that the *Zero* was invincible; the Marines started the explosion on 24 August."[9] On that day, before she was sunk, carrier *Ryujo* launched her entire complement of planes against Guadalcanal. This raid was intercepted by Smith's *Wildcats* and 16 Japanese shot down. Four Marine planes were lost. One pilot parachuted and was picked out of the water off Tulagi. An elementary but efficient air-sea rescue service had previously saved several other pilots.

Two days later, planes from Rabaul reached the field and inflicted considerable damage. Forty drums of valuable aviation fuel went up in smoke as hot fragments riddled parked dive bombers. Smith's boys, temporarily beguiled by *Zeros* aloft, caught the bombers on the way out and flamed thirteen.

The dive-bomber pilots who bent Admiral Tanaka out of shape on August 25 earned their pay again on the twenty-eighth; on the following day, fighters splashed eight Japanese, and on August 30 they brought down fourteen. Fourteen cannon-firing P-400s comprising the U. S. Army Air Force 67th Fighter Squadron, commanded by Captain Dale D. Brannon, had during the previous week flown in from Espiritu Santo: they accounted for four enemy planes that dropped below 12,000 feet, but lost an equal number above. The P-400—an export version of the P-39, and a plane of which General Arnold was inordinately proud—lacked both superchargers and adequate oxygen equipment and was entirely unsuitable for high-altitude combat. After only six days of operations, but three P-400s of the fourteen sent to the island remained in commission, and Vandegrift switched this remnant to close support missions.[10] In this role they proved an invaluable adjunct; in addition to the 37-mm. gun, each could carry a 500-pound bomb.

By August 26, combat and operational losess had reduced

strength at Vunukanau and Lakunai to 19 *Zeros* and 29 *Bettys*, but on the following day, 24 *Zeros* arrived from the Marshall Islands where they had been picked up by escort carriers. The Japanese were now hard pressed. Circumstances were described as "dire," the situation one "difficult to retrieve." Cactus pilots would have derived considerable satisfaction from knowledge of these facts.

Henderson-based aircraft had their own troubles. They were kept operable by maintenance crews who cannibalized a badly shot-up plane with the same loving care the Solomon Islanders had a century previously bestowed on dismembering a plump missionary. Fueling and arming a fighter or dive bomber were complicated operations in which a hand pump, a chamois-skin strainer, muscle and patience were the essential items of equipment. There were no tankers, no bomb dollies or hoists, no machines to belt ammunition for .50-calibre aircraft machine guns, no spare tires, windscreens, wheels or propellers. When it rained, the field became in minutes a rutted slough; when the sun beat on this mush for an hour, its top layer baked into friable, choking dust. Each landing and take-off was an adventure.

Pilots, crewmen and mechanics spent most of every night in foxholes and ate hash, rice and beans for breakfast, and again at dinner. This monotonous diet was actually dangerous for flyers working at high altitudes. Pilots complained constantly of excruciating gas pains, and the problem of providing suitable food for them assumed major importance. Dysentery was rampant and there was no toilet paper. But still the airplanes flew.[11] Of his pilots Vandegrift was immensely proud; in a letter to his wife about this time, he wrote of them simply, "Lord, but these boys are fighters."[12]

On August 30, supply ship *Alhena* slipped in with aviation supplies, equipment and personnel. On the same day, and not inappropriately during a heavy raid, aerial reinforcements arrived. Led by Colonel William J. Wallace, the remaining two squadrons of his Marine Air Group 23 rolled in on Henderson's uneven surface. The fighter squadron (VMF 224) was commanded by Major Robert E. Galer; the dive bombers (VMSB 231) by Major Leo R. Smith. The fighter pilots who followed Galer to dusty landings were aloft and tangling with *Zeros* in less than 24 hours.

Wallace provided a tonic sorely needed. Always one of the outstanding leaders in the Marine Corps, as well as a fine aviator, this humorous, patient and understanding man communicated some of his calmness to air officers and crews living on little more than frazzled nerves and obstinate courage. Foot-slogging marines of every rank were justifiably proud of "their" flyers. When a corporal called: "Captain, didja hear the score?" and the captain replied, "Twelve to one, boy!" or "Eleven to three!" the colloquy did not concern a childish game.

The center which dispensed such basic information was located at the ice plant thoughtfully left in working order by the Japanese. Here hung two large boards, one of which proclaimed in splashing letters:

TOJO ICE FACTORY
UNDER NEW MANAGEMENT
J. Genung, Sgt., USMC, Mgr.

The other board was headed simply: "TODAY'S SCORE." Here the manager of the Tojo Ice Factory conscientiously inscribed with a Japanese paintbrush the record of air activities for the benefit of groundlings who inevitably appeared a few short minutes after rumblings in the heavens abated and hot .50-calibre cases ceased falling into their foxholes. "Ain't gettin' any more cases; let's go up to the ice plant."

But despite difficulties, the air battle was decisively in favor of the marines. The Japanese were surprised; indeed, their feelings were hurt. "The enemy, instead of succumbing to the repeated attacks of our base air units, engaged in determined aerial combat."[13] This was not, then, to be a repetition of China, Malaya or the Philippines.

But how much longer sleep-starved pilots could continue to engage in "determined aerial combat" against the Japanese Navy's "sea eagles" was a problem that worried Admiral McCain, who, the day after Wallace's planes touched down, reported to Cinc-Pac that Guadalcanal pilots were "very tired," and that additional aircraft and crews must be provided immediately. He urged that two full squadrons of *Lightnings* or *Wildcats* be flown to the island at once. "The situation," he stated, "admits of no delay whatever. . . ."

With substantially the reinforcements requested, Guadalcanal can be a sinkhole for enemy air power and can be consolidated, expanded and exploited to the enemy's mortal hurt. The reverse is true if we lose Guadalcanal.

McCain then laid it on the line:

> If the reinforcement requested is not made available Guadalcanal can not be supplied and hence can not be held.[14]

As McCain intimated, events were rapidly and inexorably building to a climax. Although during daylight Marine flyers controlled the air over Henderson and the Navy managed occasionally to send in a ship, the nights belonged to the Japanese, and these nights were long and harrowing. Sleep was banished by float planes based on Faisi in the Shortlands. These, dubbed "Washing Machine Charlie," or "Maytag Charlie," dropped impact-fuzed bombs, after "Louie the Louse" had illuminated with long-burning parachute flares. Almost every night Tanaka's destroyers passing to and fro on "Rat" runs lobbed hundreds of shells in the general direction of Henderson Field. To the victims, this harassment seemed utterly indiscriminate, and for this very reason it fulfilled its primary purpose: to deny the marines any rest, shake them up, wear them down. These night intruders were not sent to attack specific physical targets. Their mission was to destroy morale. They worked at it assiduously.

Clemens's scouts brought daily reports of Japanese newly arrived and active in the vicinity of Kokumbona to the west and Taivu to the east. Turner was worried. On September 1 he radioed Ghormley:

> While always in favor of a move to Tulagi, it may be remembered that I warned that such a move to be permanently successful would entail continuous support by strong naval and air forces. . . . the immediate consolidation of our Cactus position is now possible and advisable, and it is a golden opportunity that ought not to be missed.[15]

The night before this message went on the air, Major General Kawaguchi disembarked with his staff near Taivu Point, in the same general area in which the unfortunate Ichiki had spent his first hours on Guadalcanal. This coincidence did not perturb the general, who established a supply base and immediately directed a small group of engineers to hack a circuitous track through the jungle from Tetere plantation toward the south of the airfield.

Kawaguchi had learned nothing from the failure of Ichiki's hastily organized and ineptly executed attack, and he now proceeded not only to repeat some of the errors which culminated in the defeated colonel's suicide, but to devise a few original variations on the theme.

The general had no information of the terrain over which he proposed to lead his troops. He had neither accurate maps nor satisfactory air photos. He proposed no reconnaissance before committing four battalions to a march through unknown jungle. Anciently, the Chinese military philosopher Sun Tzu wrote: "Those who do not know the conditions of mountains and forests, hazardous defiles, marshes and swamps, cannot conduct the march of an army. Those who do not use native guides are unable to obtain the advantages of the ground."[16] No native guides were available. The natives, all of them, were loyal to the Allied cause. The villages of Taivu, Tasimboko and Tetere had long since been deserted.

And Kawaguchi's intelligence was otherwise faulty. He believed that the defenders, few in number, would yield to the overwhelming "spiritual" authority of Japanese swords and bayonets. Thus he, too, found it easy to read his own meaning into Hyakutake's instructions, although these were unmistakably clear. The Commanding General, Seventeenth Army, had directed Kawaguchi to "view the enemy strength, position and terrain" to see whether it was "possible or not to achieve quick success in the attack against the airfield with [your] present strength."[17] But Kawaguchi was not inclined to spend time "viewing" the enemy strength, position and terrain.

Before leaving the Shortlands, the Japanese general had made his plan. He would capture the airfield on September 13 by a three-pronged attack:

    a) The major blow, a surprise assault by one battalion, One Hundred Twenty-fourth Infantry, and the two remaining battalions of Colonel Ichiki's regiment, would be led by himself and would come in south of the airfield.

    b) One battalion of the One Hundred Twenty-fourth would simultaneously strike due west through the jungle across the Tenaru.

    c) From the Matanikau. Colonel Oka with two reinforced

battalions would drive northeast toward Lunga Point, cross the Lunga River and hit the airfield from the northwest.

d) The main effort would be supported by naval gunfire and air strikes.

This improbable tactical elaboration suggests that General Kawaguchi had spent more time conning textbooks than conducting field exercises. Thus, even before arriving on the island, Kawaguchi was in trouble.

The brigade commander's final argument with Admiral Tanaka also bore bitter fruit. The admiral had vigorously opposed barging the last 1000 men of the Kawaguchi brigade to Guadalcanal but, in the interest of preserving seriously strained army-navy harmony, had been overruled in Rabaul. Accordingly:

> The remaining strength of the Kawaguchi Detachment, numbering 1,000 troops, embarked on 48 large and small landing barges and departed on the night of 2 September from the northern part of Isabel Island. Hiding during the day and advancing by night, the force was scheduled to leave the southern tip of Isabel Island on the night of 4 September, and land on the northwestern tip of Guadalcanal at early dawn on 5 September.[18]

Tanaka consigned the barge party to its fate, and on September 4 made a successful night run:

> The "Rat" landing force succeeded in landing without any enemy interference. After debarking the troops, the destroyer division advanced on the enemy anchorage, and engaged and sank one auxiliary cruiser. It then shelled Guadalcanal airfield, causing fires which lasted an hour, and then returned without any losses.

On the same night the boat amphibious force left the southern coast of Isabel escorted by cruiser *Sendai* and three destroyers:

> The amphibious force separated at a point 21 nautical miles north of the designated landing point in the early morning of 5 September and proceeded independently.[19]

The laboring barges encountered rough seas and were spotted by dawn reconnaissance from Henderson. For the next several hours the tossing boats and their helpless occupants were bombed and strafed without cessation.

Because of inclement weather and disturbances by enemy aircraft on the way, they suffered heavy casualties and the force was torn asunder.[20]

Approximately 300 men landed on Savo and a slightly larger number, including Colonel Oka, near Cape Esperance. Those on Savo made Kamimbo the following night. Four hundred officers and men perished at sea.

9

GENERAL VANDEGRIFT realized that the Ilu battle was only a prelude to more serious attempts to retake the few precious acres his marines had won. There were many evidences of intensified activity outside the position so precariously manned. Native scouts reported Japanese landings to the west, at Tassafaronga and Kamimbo Bay; to the east, near the abandoned village of Tasimboko.

During the first week of September, Vandegrift, a prudent man but not a hesitant one, decided to strike somewhere in sufficient strength to knock the gathering enemy off balance. He had news that the Seventh Marines, reinforced, was en route from Samoa to the South Pacific.[1] But he was aware, too, that Ghormley desired to send this combat team, critically needed on Guadalcanal, to the Santa Cruz Islands. The Seventh Marines was at best no more than a speculative asset. The immediate situation posed its own imperative. Vandegrift could no longer wait to find out what was going on around him. But he dared not undertake any operation that could not be completed between sunrise and sunset.

At this time, the general faced the sort of tactical problem for which textbooks provide no solution. With the recent arrival from Tulagi of the 2nd Battalion, Fifth Marines, both his infantry regiments were at full strength. But the beaches he must defend against anticipated attack from the sea stretched for 8000 yards from the Ilu to a point west of Kukum. Both east and west flanks were bent back into the jungle for a distance of 1500 yards. Six battalions were not adequate to defend this frontage, provide the needed depth, and supply necessary reserves. To gain some operational flexibility, he had, on the last day of the month, ordered Rupertus to ship the Raiders and Parachutists to Guadalcanal.

Edson had not been on the island an hour before he began to urge the need for reconnaissance in force toward either Esperance or Taivu. Indeed, in response to native reports of "Jap an man" on Savo, he had sent a two-company patrol to the island on September 4. On Savo there was no enemy, but beaches littered with oil-soaked debris and newly-dug shallow graves, in which the natives were burying corpses still washing ashore, testified to the fury of the sea battle which had taken its name from this once peaceful island.

The aftermath of the ten futile hours the Raiders had spent climbing up and down the tangled sides of Savo's extinct volcano was tragic. Loaded with sweat-stained men, *Little* and *Gregory* arrived off Kukum in gathering dusk, and after disembarking their exhausted passengers and hoisting boats, found there was not enough time to make Tulagi harbor before full dark. They therefore cruised slowly from west to east, and back to west, in Sealark Channel. And here Tanaka's heavily-gunned, high-speed destroyers, on the first leg of their return trip from another successful run to Taivu, discovered and surprised them.

The one-sided action was brief. The Japanese opened fire at 2:08 A.M. Seven minutes later, thin-hulled *Little* and *Gregory*, their plates ripped apart by accurate gunfire, were reduced to drifting, flaming, exploding hulks which sought their own resting places in Ironbottom Bay. Sailors fought for survival in the black waters that had so quickly engulfed their blood-stained ships.

An hour after darkness on September third, an urgent message had arrived at Air operations. This stated that a DC-3 expected to land momentarily, and requested that the runway be illuminated. Seven jeeps were hastily impressed for the purpose, and stationed at the south end of the strip. The transport roared in, its wheels a few scant feet above the heads of the drivers. This plane brought to Guadalcanal a heavy-shouldered, white-thatched brigadier general of Marine Aviation, Roy S. Geiger. Since winning his wings in 1916, Geiger had flown every type of crate from the *DHs* and *Jennies* of World War I through Fokker and Ford transports to the newest Grumman fighters. With him were the equally experienced chief of staff of his First Marine Aircraft Wing, Colonel Louis E. Woods, and his Intelligence officer, Lieutenant Colonel John C. Munn.

Geiger was curt, cold, and, some said, ruthless. He certainly was determined to squeeze the ultimate ounce of performance from men and machines. And he did. From the pagoda bequeathed by the Japanese, he and the small staff, which the electric Woods drove, took personal control of air operations. The flyers had been performing superbly before Geiger came; this man, with the stern features and the character of a Roman general, imbued them with renewed spirit. He and Woods had spent their aviation careers in open cockpits, not in swivel chairs. Both were undistinguished administrators, and proud of it.

Geiger was cut from the same cloth as Vandegrift; neither was content to permit the enemy unimpeded enjoyment of the initiative. On September 4, and again the next day, his SBDs bombed, strafed and scattered Kawaguchi's troops barging from the southern tip of Isabel; on the two days following, the dive bombers flew up The Slot to strike the Japanese seaplane base at Gizo Bay.

The offensive spirit Geiger and Woods exuded was contagious; within a few days after their arrival, Number One on the Guadalcanal "Hit Parade" was being sung lustily to the tune of "On the Road to Mandalay":

> *In Cactus "Operations"*
> *Where the needle passes free*
> *There's a hot assignment cookin'*
> *For Marine Group Twenty-three.*
> *As the shells burst in the palm trees*
> *You hear "Operations" say*
> *"Fill the belly tanks with juice, boys,*
>
> *Take the Scouts to Gizo Bay.*
> *Take the Scouts to Gizo Bay."*
> *Oh, pack a load to Gizo Bay*
> *Where the Jap fleet spends the day.*
> *You can hear their Bettys chunkin'*
> *From Rabaul to Lunga Quay.*
> *Hit the road to Gizo Bay*
> *Where the float plane Zeros play*
> *And the bombs roar down like thunder*
> *On the natives, 'cross the way.*

Some whose business brought them briefly to Henderson at this time returned to rear headquarters to describe Geiger's air force as on its last legs. Physically speaking, this description was a prodigy of understatement. But even the overwhelming sense of urgency reflected in visitors' reports was not enough to generate the action required: matting, bombs, gasoline and construction equipment arrived at "a pitifully slow rate." Only 1000 feet of runway was matted. After each heavy rain, the remainder became a rutted, potholed swamp which even jeeps found difficult to negotiate. The one saving factor was that the field dried fairly rapidly.

On the morning of September 6, Edson visited Division operations to confer with the G-3. He found both Thomas and his aggressive assistant, Merrill Twining, busy laying plans for just such a raid as he was about to propose. In the evening, Twining drove to the coconut grove back of Kukum to inform Edson that Vandegrift had approved his idea of a foray to the east to break up the enemy concentration reported at Tasimboko.

Even as Twining chatted with Edson, Tanaka's "Rat" destroyers were approaching Cape Esperance, and at midnight landed the headquarters of Colonel Akinosuka Oka's One Hundred Twenty-fourth Infantry, plus its 2nd Battalion, near Kokumbona. At dawn Oka's troops, carrying the regimental flag, began to advance toward the Matanikau to take position to assist Kawaguchi's main effort. About noon on the seventh, a radio informed Oka that the general was encountering unforeseen delays in the jungle.

This message caused a furore in Rabaul and Tokyo. Imperial GHQ had learned that a powerful American convoy had arrived in the Fijis on the 5th, presumably en route from Hawaii to Guadalcanal.[2] Obviously, Kawaguchi must press on speedily, and Hyakutake directed that the attack be launched on the night of the 12th. The general replied that he would do everything in his power to meet the deadline, and dispatched a courier to convey news of this change of plan to Colonel Oka. Mikawa readjusted his schedule of gunfire support. Headquarters, Eleventh Air Fleet, alerted a squadron of *Zeros* to take off for Henderson at short notice on or after September 12, and directed the officer commanding the air transport detachment to ferry essential spares and maintenance personnel to the recaptured field immediately Vandegrift had surrendered.

After dark on September 7, the Raiders embarked for Tasimboko in APDs *Manley* and *McKean* and Diesel-powered "Yippies" 346 and 298.[3] Belching showers of bright red sparks as they chugged eastward through the blackness with engines pounding, the Yippies announced their presence to all but the blind and deaf.

The Japanese at Taivu were not suffering from either of these afflictions, but chance plays strange tricks in war, and on this misty morning the goddess pulled a very special one out of her grab bag. As the Higgins boats headed for the beach, transports *Fuller* and *Bellatrix*, en route to Lunga screened by a cruiser and four destroyers, hove into view from the east. Members of Kawaguchi's excited rear echelon stayed around only long enough to get off a frantic message that a major landing was under way, and abandoning hot breakfasts, rifles, and two antitank guns which could have blown the landing craft out of the water, headed for the boondocks. The Raiders landed unmolested, removed breechblocks from guns, pitched them into the sea, punched inland half a mile, and turned west through a coconut plantation. By the time the unexpected news from his rear echelon—about 300 supply and communication personnel—reached him, Kawaguchi could do no more than order them to "confront the enemy." He could not turn back.

The general had not exaggerated his difficulties. With over 3000 men, he was clawing his way through the humid, putrid jungle. Alternately soaked to the skin by torrential rains and bathed for hours in sweat, his soldiers, in a twisting column over three miles long, slipped and stumbled through ankle-deep mire as they moved foot by foot toward the positions from which they were to launch the planned surprise attack on the airfield.

In Rabaul the news of the American counter-landing was disturbing. Hyakutake pessimistically radioed GHQ that Kawaguchi was "sandwiched." Mikawa planned a night bombardment by a cruiser and eight destroyers. Tokyo alerted two battalions in Batavia to prepare to move at once. Tanaka immediately embarked a battalion of the Aoba Detachment in available destroyers and forwarded it expeditiously to Kamimbo. Commander Seventeenth Army also ordered the Forty-first Infantry to concentrate at Kokoda on the Buna–Moresby trail, in readiness to displace from New Guinea to the Solomons. More than any man, "Red Mike" Edson would have enjoyed every aspect of the major flap his foray had generated.

As the Raiders began moving westward from Taivu the destroyers and Yippies hastened back to Kukum to bring the Parachutists to the scene. By this time, Kawaguchi's rear echelon had pulled itself together sufficiently to man two mountain guns and two howitzers hidden in the coconut grove. *Nambus* began their lethal chatter. Edson was in for a fire fight; the biggest thing he had was a platoon of 60-mm. mortars. He immediately called for close air support, and in 50 minutes Dale Brannon's shark-nosed P-400s were overhead awaiting instructions.

At the same time a Raider company, led by Clemens's scouts, started off on a jungle track to encircle the enemy right flank. By noon this group deployed near Tasimboko, full in the defenders' rear. Surprised, the Japanese fled, leaving 27 dead lying by artillery pieces and draped over six heavy machine guns. Many were shot in the back.

The haul was rich, but there was now no time to load captured weapons, equipment and food, all of which could have been used to advantage. Everything the marines laid their hands on, with the exception of half a dozen *Nambus* with magazines and ammunition, was systematically destroyed. Fifty men were detailed to jab holes with bayonets in several thousand tins of sliced beef and crab meat while others emptied hundreds of bags of rice into the surf.

Dick Tregaskis, the lanky I.N.S. correspondent adopted by the Raiders, poked around and filled a Japanese army blanket with papers, notebooks, maps and charts; marines wrecked a powerful radio set, and burned five thatched huts piled with assorted supplies. Edson viewed the scene with satisfaction. At four o'clock he ordered troops to embark, and a few minutes later all hands were en route to Kukum.

Curiously, during the fast run back to base, the battalion commander discovered that in the confusion attendant upon hurried embarkation, every officer and enlisted man was sagging under a load of tinned crab and sliced beef packed in soy. Twenty-one cases of Japanese beer and seventeen half-gallon flasks of *sake* also found their way on board *Manley*.

"This is no motley of Japs," Edson told Thomas cryptically that night. A few hours later, after he had examined the material delivered to his fetid, blacked-out intelligence shack, "Pappy" Moran confirmed that this was indeed no motley. Clemens's scouts added their careful reports: a large body of Japanese— possibly more than 3000—was on the move generally southwest from Tetere.

The next morning maps and photos were spread at Division operations and latest reports from patrols and scouts studied. Finally, after long discussion, Thomas turned to Edson: "They're coming," he said. Edson, too, suspected they were coming. But from what direction? He drew a forefinger along an air photograph. "This looks like a good approach," he said in his throaty whisper.

The light spot Edson traced represented a broken, rugged, kunai-covered coral hogback which paralleled the Lunga south of the airfield. Jungle lapped at its south, east and west slopes; to the north the ground gave off gently toward battered Henderson. Near this ridge—and over protests from his staff—Vandegrift had decided to establish a new command post. He was sick and tired of jumping in and out of the dugout by the airfield; here he hoped to find some peace.

As the general moved his establishment to an area he thought might be less disturbed by Japanese bombs, Ghormley in Nouméa pondered a most peculiar message from Nimitz. This directed him to turn over to MacArthur one reinforced regiment of "experienced amphibious troops" together with the three transports and the supply ship required for their combat lift! The admiral was perplexed; the Joint Chiefs, who had originated this weird instruction, must have known as well as he that the only such troops in the entire South Pacific were now engaging the enemy in the Solomons. Perhaps the Chiefs desired him to forward the Seventh Marines, then en route to his area, to General MacArthur?

In a quandary, he asked Turner for recommendations. The Amphibious Force Commander restrained himself:

The only experienced amphibious troops in SoPac are those in Guadalcanal and it is impracticable to withdraw them.[4]

The Seventh Marines, Turner continued, had been in garrison on Samoa for several months and were by no means ready to execute an assault landing. Although Ghormley had not solicited advice, Turner gave him some. He obviously stood in need of it:

I respectfully invite attention to the present insecure position of Guadalcanal. . . . Adequate air and naval strength have not been made available. . . . Vandegrift consistently has urged to be reinforced at once by at least one more regiment . . . I concur.[5]

In early September every commander—Kawaguchi, Ghormley, Hyakutake, Turner, Vandegrift—had his own troubles. Geiger and Woods were no exceptions. To the airmen, each day brought its challenge, and not alone from the skies. Operational losses mounted alarmingly; on September 8, eight planes cracked up during take-off. Primitive repair facilities sufficed to return two to a readiness state: the other six were dragged to the boneyard to be cannibalized. Two days later, Geiger could count but 11 *Wildcats* available of the 38 to date flown in. As he glumly surveyed the growing pile of wrecks, one fighter pilot remarked to a visiting member of Harmon's staff: "At this rate we can whip ourselves without any assistance from the Japs."

Critical shortages of starter cartridges, bombs, oxygen, armor-piercing and incendiary bullets, tires, and lubricating oil succeeded one another. And always there was the basic problem: gasoline. The air force existed from one day to the next in a state of crisis. And as each was surmounted, two others developed. Pilots were near exhaustion: the malaria rate was rising gradually, and they were not immune.

As early as the end of August, Under Secretary of the Navy James Forrestal, then visiting the South Pacific, had radioed his friend and colleague, Assistant Secretary of War for Air Robert Lovett, of the desperate need for more fighters able to operate at the altitudes required to intercept. The Army's P-400s simply could not get upstairs. What was needed was the new P-38 *Lightning;* three days after Forrestal's appeal to Lovett, Ghormley appealed in similar vein to MacArthur. The admiral asked for "a small force" of P-38s. MacArthur could not comply; he had only six.

But while McCain, Turner and Vandegrift bombarded Ghormley with urgent pleas for fighters, idle *Wildcats* were available in the South Pacific. These, part of *Saratoga's* air group, had flown to bases in New Caledonia and the Hebrides on the last day of August when the big carrier caught a fish fired by enemy submarine *I-26*. There they had been sitting ever since.

Technically, these carrier aircraft were not under Ghormley's command and he was not free to dispose of them. They belonged to Vice Admiral Fletcher, who continued to operate in Ghormley's area, but still under orders from Nimitz. Fletcher, understandably anxious to maintain the integrity of this carrier air group—even though he had at the moment no operational carrier from which to fly it—had extracted a promise from Ghormley that his fighters would not be committed to Guadalcanal. This, then, was the situation: The Navy had available fighters, manned by experienced pilots, that could reach Guadalcanal in three hours. But they were tied to rear bases. And not only by a command technicality, for Navy doctrine prescribed that carrier aircraft should "normally" operate from carriers.

However, on September 10, Nimitz faced the issue and transferred all carrier aircraft "that could be spared" to Ghormley to use as he saw fit. ComSoPac now acted with a vigor not always characteristic of him, and on the following day ordered Lieutenant Commander LeRoy C. Simpler to fly the 24 *Wildcats* of his "Fighting Five" from Espiritu to Henderson "immediately." Simpler flew immediately.

The squadron did not wait long to acquit itself with distinction. At noon the day after they arrived, Simpler's pilots rose to engage a flight of bombers escorted by twenty *Zeros* which plastered everything within a mile of the pagoda with incendiary bombs, high explosive, and "daisy cutters." With marines, Navy fliers flamed 16 Japanese. One American pilot was killed in an emergency landing.

Twenty-four hours later, two raids came in; air battles were vicious; "Condition Red," first announced in midmorning, was in force during most of the day. Between "Red" alerts other carrier planes arrived; in three days Ghormley threw in a total of 60. Perhaps enough to maintain for a time a condition of stable equilibrium, perhaps not. For in just one day—September 12—Rear Admiral Yamagata brought more than double that number of replacements to Vunukanau and Lakunai.[6]

On September 10, after breakfasting on sodden rice and dehydrated potatoes, Raiders and Parachutists broke camp and started moving to a ridge south of the airfield. "Too much bombing and shelling here close to the beach," Edson remarked. "We're moving to a quiet spot." He smiled. The march to the area the colonel had selected as a "rest camp" was twice interrupted by air raids, but at two o'clock the leading elements of his composite group, 700 in all, began to arrive at the ridge. Edson deployed them as they came up: Raiders around the southern knob, the right flank company thinly spread toward the Lunga; Parachutists—now commanded by Torgerson—on the left.

The gully in which the command post was located was 100 yards south of the newly-established Division headquarters. Here Edson's reserve, a depleted company, scratched out shallow foxholes; here Captain William D. Stevenson's communicators dug in their switchboard.

The next morning, some marines hacked at vines with bayonets. Others strung the few yards of barbed wire available; others dug foxholes. Announcement that the routine raid was on the way disturbed nobody: the Japs always bombed the airfield. But this time the target was not to be the airfield. It was the ridge. On it, 26 *Bettys* unloaded stick after stick of 500-pounders, judiciously mixed with "daisy cutters." Marines who clawed a few inches deeper into their holes or flung themselves behind logs emerged shaking but safe. Those who stood, or ran aimlessly—and a few did—were killed or wounded by flying splinters. And now, in the aftermath, men silently brushing dirt from their dungarees suddenly knew that the Japs would this night, or some night soon to come, swarm screaming out of the jungle just as they had done at the "Tenaru."

"Some goddam rest area," a corporal said. "Some goddam rest area!"

Reconnaissances led before dark by Edson and his executive officer to a distance of half a mile to the south were negative. But Clemens's scouts, who ranged farther and faster, reported a long enemy column moving from the east toward the headwaters of the Lunga. The Jap was there, but precisely where? In what force? All Vandegrift could do was wait, prepare, and hope that his dispositions were correct. They had to be: save the 2nd Battalion, Fifth Marines, now constituted Division reserve, he had no uncommitted troops. Every other fighting man was in the attenuated lines and manning beach defenses.

During the afternoon of September 11, Kelly Turner flew in to Henderson from Espiritu Santo. He had lately spent some time in Nouméa where he had conferred with Admiral Ghormley and his plans officer, DeWitt Peck, a highly educated and dogmatic colonel of Marines. As Turner stepped to solid ground, Vandegrift extended his hand and offered the hospitality of the island. The air-raid siren sounded. "Condition Red" was in effect.

Later, the general escorted his guest to the new command post and promised him a bed. Turner, visibly discomfited, produced from his breast pocket a folded piece of paper, a U. S. Navy message blank, and handed it to Vandegrift without uttering a word. The general opened the paper and began to read. As he continued, for line after line, the color drained from his face and he visibly winced. As silently as he had received the paper, he passed it to Colonel Thomas. Thomas read it. The atmosphere in the hut was now electric—and with good reason.

For this message contained an estimate of the enemy situation drawn up by ComSoPac's staff and approved by him 48 hours earlier. The substance was that overwhelming Japanese naval forces were concentrating at Rabaul and Truk, that air strength at Vunakanau and Lakunai was daily increasing, and that several dozen transports were now lying in Simpson Harbor, taking on stores and troops. A major effort, to be launched in ten days, in two weeks, or certainly before the end of a third week, was anticipated.

This was but the preamble.

There followed a summary of ComSoPac's situation. In this he listed his shortages of cruisers, carriers, destroyer transports, and cargo vessels. The estimate concluded with the stunning statement that ComSoPac could no longer support the marines on Guadalcanal.

Thomas folded the paper and put it in his shirt pocket. (He was to carry this paper in his pocket until the day he left the island, almost exactly three months later.) Turner opened his valise and produced a bottle of Scotch, which he set on the bare table. He then said: "Vandegrift, I am not inclined to take as pessimistic a view of the situation as does Ghormley. He does not believe I can get the Seventh Marines in here, but I believe I have a scheme that will fool the Japs and be successful. Now, I have brought a bottle of whiskey, and we will have a drink and talk this over later." The product of this later discussion was an urgent recommendation to ComSoPac that the Seventh Marines be brought forward at once.[7]

The night the admiral spent on Guadalcanal was not a restful one. For almost two hours, Japanese naval shells combed the nearby ridge. Years later, Vandegrift remarked: "You know, Kelly thought we were 'trigger-happy,' but when those shells began combing us, he changed his mind. The Japanese made a Christian out of him. Before he left the next day, he told me he would bring the Seventh Marines up and land them wherever I wanted him to."[8]

After seeing Turner off, Vandegrift went to confer with Geiger. What was to be done if the state of emergency Ghormley deemed imminent actually developed? Obviously, all planes must be prepared to fly out on short notice. And Geiger? His answer was unequivocal. He would stay.

At the same time, Thomas and Twining were talking, and about the same subject.

"We can't let this be another Bataan, Bill," Thomas said. "We will go to the hills, to the headwaters of the Lunga. We will take our food and our bullets."

Twining agreed and went to his tent. Here, alone, he spent hours drawing up a hand-written draft operation order, which he consigned to his safe. This draft bore neither date nor serial number.[9]

On the morning of Turner's arrival, the Division artillery commander decided that he would take a stroll with his executive officer, Lieutenant Colonel John Bemis. To the ridge Edson was organizing, "Don Pedro" del Valle brought his regimental mapping section. Their labors were not interrupted; the daily raid was intercepted short of Henderson, and artillery draftsmen returned safely with their data to the fire direction center. There Bemis sweated through a long night gridding maps and drawing up fire plans.

Meanwhile, del Valle's 105-mm. howitzers displaced to new positions from which they could render close support to the ridge defenses if necessary. Forward observers joined Edson in an observation post on the southern nose, established communications with the FDC, and directed registration on previously selected check points.

Shortly after noon, "Condition Red" again warned of approaching enemy bombers. This time, marines went to ground fast. Repeatedly, well-placed sticks walked along the ridge. Quarter-ton high-explosive bombs shattered the bordering jungle; 250-pound "daisy cutters" stripped clinging vegetation off trees and mowed down six-foot kunai grass.

No further warning was needed. Men who had slept only fitfully during the preceding 48 hours hurriedly deepened foxholes, cut undergrowth to improve fields of fire on final protective lines, and strung the few available spools of wire stripped from less-threatened positions and brought up by jeep. Extra grenades and belted ammunition were moved into emplacements. Vandegrift shifted his reserve to the south side of the airfield; the commander, Captain Joseph J. Dudkowski (Lt. Col. Rosecrans had suffered a dislocated back during an air raid the day before), his staff, and company officers, reconnoitered routes of approach to be used if the battalion were called forward to the ridge in darkness. Cresswell's battalion of the First Marines moved to backstop Dudkowski. All that could be done had been done.

With darkness came rain, and shortly before ten o'clock a bombarding cruiser and three destroyers began the nightly shoot. But this time the target was not the airfield. Shells sounding like approaching freight trains burst around the ridge; some fell short, others exploded dully in the jungle west of the Lunga. When gunfire ceased, Japanese probing actions began. Rifle and machine-gun fire broke out, now along the right flank, now along the left. Mortars coughed spasmodically; on call, del Valle's artillery broke occasional planned concentrations in the jungle forward of the lines. Only on the right, where the Japanese wriggled through heavy growth, did the enemy displace the defenders. Here they cut off one Raider platoon, which fought its way out and fell back to the west slope of the spine. Seven men were missing.

Just before first light Edson pulled back the left flank. There, the Parachutists, who had been hit half a dozen times, were in disarray. At dawn, which could not come too soon for the marines, the fire fight spluttered out, and as the Japanese faded into the jungle, a local counterattack recovered the right flank position lost during the night. The only item not retrieved was the platoon sergeant's pack, which bulged with newly-arrived and as yet undistributed mail. Nor were the bodies of the seven missing marines ever found.

Before he dipped into a can of hash on the morning of September 13, Edson called a conference of company commanders. He sat on a log, spooned the mixture of cold meat and potatoes slowly and chewed deliberately.

"They were testing," he said. "Just testing. They'll be back. But maybe not as many of them." His mouth smiled but his eyes did not. He chewed a mouthful of hash. "Or maybe more. I want all positions improved, all wire lines paralleled, a hot meal for the men. Today, dig, wire up tight, get some sleep. We'll all need it." The staff officers and company commanders, who had been squatting in a semicircle drinking tepid coffee and smoking, rose. "The Nip will be back," Edson said. "I want to surprise him."

The basis of the surprise was a fall back along the ridge; a contraction and tightening of lines along its sides. This move greatly improved fields of fire for automatic weapons and imposed upon the attacker a trip of about 100 yards from the jungle's edge before he could physically contact the battle position. In traversing this open space he could be brought under killing grazing fire.

Actually, Edson's surmise that the Japanese were "testing" on the previous night was not correct. Kawaguchi had intended his attack to be a decisive one.

> . . . but because of the devilish jungle, the Brigade was scattered all over and completely beyond control. In my whole life I have never felt so helpless. When I looked around I saw only Senior Adjutant Yamamoto, my faithful orderly Noguchi, and four or five others. It was a tragedy. If we had not received the order from Headquarters and had carried out our attack on the night of the thirteenth, such a miserable failure might have been avoided.[10]

Kawaguchi was frustrated and out of touch with the situation, but Japanese commanders in Rabaul were in a much worse position. For, since Edson's raid on Tasimboko, they had been unable to communicate either with the brigade rear echelon or with the general. At Vunukanau and Lakunai, *Zeros* and loaded transports stood with engines idling, their pilots and crews in "ready" huts anxiously waiting word to fly to Guadalcanal and witness surrender ceremonies. True, the last word from Kawaguchi had been received some 36 hours previously. According to that message, he should have occupied the airfield on September 12. The natural assumption was that he had done so. But that no further word had yet arrived was indeed strange!

Commander Eleventh Air Fleet sent four planes to look over the situation:

> It was not definite but it seemed the airfield had been occupied. Thus, steps were being taken to notify all units concerned to this effect. But after the reconnaissance planes had returned, it

was revealed that the airfield had not yet been occupied. It was judged that the Army forces might have postponed their attack. Therefore execution of the proposed plans was postponed by one day.[11]

Still, Headquarters Eleventh Air Fleet did not consider it safe to bomb the airfield or ridge, and decided instead to attack the one juicy target available: the marines who had landed at Taivu six days before, and were presumably still in that vicinity. At noon, 26 *Bettys* escorted by a dozen *Zeros* came in low over Florida and dumped a load on Kawaguchi's hungry and disorganized rear echelon. There was no air opposition, and fighter pilots took the opportunity to strafe Tasimboko viciously. Their targets, frenzied members of Kawaguchi's signal and supply detachments, were slaughtered as they attempted to spread "meat-ball" banners on the sand near the water's edge. These perforated, bloodied flags were later brought in by native scouts.

At nine that night, "Louie the Louse" chugged over Kukum, shut off his wheezing engine, coasted for a minute, then let go a parachute flare which blossomed pale green squarely above the center of the airstrip. On this signal, seven destroyers in Lunga Roads commenced to bombard Henderson. This shoot was sustained for one hour. During the long 60 minutes, Edson's men were fighting—and for much more than their own lives—on the ridge.

In waves, two reinforced Japanese battalions—almost 2000 men —assaulted the slippery slopes. Marine mortars sited in defilade poured out shells as fast as loaders could slide them down the hot tubes. Artillery fires ripped Japanese flesh with steel splinters. On the right, banzais curdled to wordless moanings, but the battle cry was picked up on the left. "Gas attack! Gas attack!" the Japanese shouted as they advanced under greenish flares. "Maline, you die!"

"You'll eat shit first, you bastards!" an automatic rifleman shrieked.

This ferocious attack bent defenses around the ridge as a smith might bend a red-hot shoe. The shoe contracted but did not break, and at eleven came surcease: Kawaguchi withdrew his assault troops to regroup. Gathered in the jungle fringes, the Japanese jabbered. The marines held their peace and prepared.

A few minutes before midnight, Kawaguchi launched another assault supported by cannon and mortar fire. Although Marine counter-mortar fire was not effective, artillery concentrations just forward of the final protective line cut the advancing Japs to ribbons. But still they came. "Bring the fires in," Edson called to del Valle's forward observer. "Closer." And again, "Closer." The F.O. brought them in.

Japanese who dove into marine foxholes to escape enveloping death were pitched out bodily. Dozens of dead and dying marines and Japanese, some with arms and hands torn off, some with shattered legs, some with pierced chests, punctured abdomens, or faces covered with mud and blood, were dragged to a primitive dressing station where two Navy doctors and their men, flashlight beams shielded by ponchos, applied tourniquets, gave transfusions, cleaned and dressed wounds.

By midnight Edson's marines had thrown back two major attacks. At close quarters they had withstood a determined enemy. And the horseshoe still gripped the ridge. Light machine guns and hot automatic rifles had expended ammunition; in forward positions there were no more grenades. Major Kenneth D. Bailey, a one-man supply section, made repeated trips on hands and knees along the fire-swept ridge to deliver grenades and ammunition to marines crouching in foxholes. Edson, standing just behind the front lines, scourged dazed men who stumbled toward him: "Go back where you came from. The only thing they've got that you haven't is guts."

At 2:00 A.M. a mortar barrage plastered both sides of the ridge and cut wires to Division and supporting artillery. Five minutes later flares again illuminated the spine. Along this the Japanese ran, crouching and chanting. "Maline, you die!" "Banzai!" "Maline, you die!" "Banzai!" They were less than 1000 yards from Henderson Field.

The marines had no intention of dying; their wild curses and obscenities rose above the clatter of automatics. One young artillery observer was struck down; a sergeant took his place and sent calls for fire over a supplementary command line just run by the communicators. At half past two the Japanese again fell back. So did Edson, to prepared positions on the ultimate knoll. The ridge was silent. "We can hold," he murmured over the all-purpose line to Thomas. The G-3 had already begun to feed in Division reserve, a company at a time.

The 2nd Battalion, Fifth Marines helped withstand the two halfhearted attacks Kawaguchi sent in before dawn. But these never got off the ground; artillery persistently roving just beyond jungle fringes broke them down. And at six o'clock, Brannon's cannon-firing fighters, flying 20 feet above the marines, began rippping 37-mm. shells through the tangled growth. The Japanese general gave orders to withdraw.

He left behind him a bloodstained ridge littered with corpses. In the grotesque attitudes of those who meet sudden and violent death lay the twisted bodies of more than 500 men who had died gloriously for the Emperor. With heads lolling and mouths agape, the inscrutable dead stared with glazed and sightless eyes at the morning sun.

Snipers were active; teams of marines began to flush them out of trees and underbrush. One sword-swinging Japanese officer rushed wildly through Vandegrift's command post and threw his sword, as one would hurl a spear, at a marine gunnery sergeant. The sword pierced his body. Division Sergeant Major Sheffield Banta, who was at the moment castigating a clerk, heard a scream of "Banzai!" and rushed from his tent, drew his pistol and killed the Japanese with one shot. He then returned to the office and completed unfinished business.[12]

And on the ridge, marines were still being killed. At eight o'clock, a jeep loaded with five wounded crawled slowly toward the airfield. Its occupants, including Edson's operations officer, Major Robert S. Brown, were riddled by three accurate bursts from a hidden *Nambu*.[13]

While Kawaguchi threw attacks against the ridge, another battalion of his brigade hit Lieutenant Colonel William J. McKelvy's battalion of the First Marines in a wired position along the Ilu some 2000 yards due east of Edson. Here, repeated thrusts were thrown back with heavy loss to the enemy. In early morning, five Marine tanks ventured unsupported into mucky terrain. Three bogged down; they were immediately punctured by antitank fire. But the heart was out of these Japanese, too, and they soon withdrew eastward toward Koli Point. During the afternoon, an attack from the west, tardily mounted by Colonel Oka, was repulsed with small loss to either side.

So ended the actions known variously at the time as "Raiders' Ridge" or "Bloody Ridge," or more simply as "The Ridge." No marine needed to ask *what* ridge. Later, this grass-covered hump was appropriately named "Edson's Ridge."[14] Here the Raiders sustained 135 casualties; the Parachutists 128. Of these 263, forty-nine were killed and ten missing.[15]

Kawaguchi's brigade had been grievously hurt. Two hundred and twenty-five officers and 6005 men took part in his attacks; casualties were almost 20 per cent:

Killed and Missing in Action: 708, viz: officers—29; men— 679.
Wounded in action: 505, viz: officers—13; men—492.[16]

Twelve hundred and thirteen officers and men killed, missing and wounded; of this number, Kawaguchi left almost 600 on the ridge. Grim enough, this figure is; it becomes even more so when we know, as we do from Kawaguchi's postwar "Memoir," that of the three battalions allocated to that phase of the fight, one did not engage at all! The two that did were almost annihilated.

What happened, then, to Lieutenant Colonel Kusukichi Watanabe's battalion, the unit supposed "to dash through to the airfield"?

The entire battalion "spent the night without taking any action. This powerful battalion, the one I had counted on most, was completely mismanaged. When I heard of this, I could not help shedding tears of disappointment, anger and regret."

After the general recovered his equanimity, he sent for Watanabe:

"Coward," he shouted as the colonel approached. "Commit hara-kiri!"[17]

Perhaps the Japanese did not realize it on the morning of September 14, but their ordeal was far from finished. Kawaguchi was now faced with a desperate choice. Either he must retreat toward Taivu or break through the jungle and gain the west bank of the Matanikau. He chose the latter course, and in midmorning began to fall back to the south, hacking a path toward the headwaters of the Matanikau. With the column were more than 400 wounded borne on improvised litters, sometimes by four comrades, often by six. He was not harried during withdrawal. There was no marine unit readily available and in condition to pursue.

The Parachute Battalion was wrecked: of 377 officers and men who landed on Gavutu on August 7, a total of 212 had since been killed and wounded—a battle casualty rate of over 55 per cent. The Raiders were scarcely in a better position. Since landing on Tulagi at a strength of slightly over 750, they had absorbed 234 battle casualties, over 30 per cent. Division reserve, which had been committed in driblets, was temporarily disorganized. Thus, Kawaguchi was free to make his way to safety as best he could.

As his long, slow-moving column fought over interminable ridges and into deep valleys where tangles of vegetation trapped humid, heavy air and insects, rice ran short. Safe from relentless strafing and vicious artillery fire, the Japanese now faced a new enemy—hunger—and this was more persistent and more deadly than shells, bullets and bombs. As at a painfully slow pace they negotiated the south slopes of Mount Austen, they ate the last pitiful grains of rice. Three days later, men now ravenous clawed bark from trees, tore at roots of plants, at grass and leaves, gnawed their rifle slings, and drank from puddles. They buried mortars and heavy machine guns before crossing the upper reaches of the Lunga; soon *Nambus*, light mortars, ammunition, helmets, and packs were abandoned.

On the afternoon of the eighth day of this agony, Kawaguchi's advance guard stumbled into Colonel Oka's rear area. Haggard, filthy, barefoot, weak, with clothes in tatters, and minus every weapon but rifles, the disorganized remnants of the 35th Brigade gradually assembled near Point Cruz.

"The Army," one Japanese naval officer later observed, "had been used to fighting the Chinese."[18]

BOOK III

10

IF KAWAGUCHI'S BEATEN and exhausted troops hoped to rest and refresh themselves in peaceful sylvan glades west of the Matanikau they were mistaken, for the Japanese there had no food to give away. Colonel Oka, who had landed with headquarters of his One Hundred Twenty-fourth Infantry plus two weakened battalions, had only sufficient rations to tide his command over until Kawaguchi captured Henderson. After the surrender, the colonel naturally expected his men to subsist on American rice, or whatever marines ate in lieu of it. Provisions had regularly been put ashore at Kamimbo Bay, but the colonel was a long way—almost fifty miles by trail—from the supply center there. Between the rice at Kamimbo and his troops were some 2000 members of the 8th Base Force, who had fled empty-handed from the vicinity of the airfield on August 7. Detachments of various Naval Landing Forces increased by another 700 the hungry Japanese population on the west end of Guadalcanal.

However, things had unaccountably gone wrong; the "marooned" enemy still clung obstinately to the airstrip. With his own command on short rations, Oka could not feed the unwelcome visitors who were descending upon him. Scores of those wounded at the ridge were malarial; hundreds suffered from dysentery; all were enfeebled from their ordeal in the pitiless jungle. Oka, responsible for the defense of the river line, had no choice but to push them all to the west as fast as they stumbled into his area. At Kokumbona, at Tassafaronga, at Cape Esperance, there were doctors, rice and quinine.

One diarist "never dreamed" that coconuts would save his life "in this awful place." His fellow veterans were "nothing but skin and bones"; "pale wild men." He had smoked his last cigarette; there were no matches; he wandered about "with a lit fire cord" begging crumbs of tobacco from more frugal friends. Every morning bombing and strafing planes were overhead;

during most daylight hours he huddled in a sodden foxhole. "Although I have seen our planes they seem to have no effect. The mastery of the sea and air is completely in the enemy's hands. I have become like a primitive man." This disconsolate soldier no doubt derived small pleasure from Tokyo broadcasts which described his adversaries as slowly dying of starvation while in palsied fear they awaited the "righteous bayonets" destined soon to pierce their vitals.

First sketchy reports of the disaster which had befallen Major General Kawaguchi reached Rabaul on September 15, and precipitated a series of conferences attended by officers of Yamamoto's staff and Hyakutake's planners. The result of these deliberations was a request for additional troops, and two days later Imperial GHQ assigned the 38th Division, which had fought at Hong Kong, in Java, on Timor and on Sumatra, to the O/B of the Seventeenth Army.

Even before the 38th Division had been notified to move from the Dutch Indies to a new front, the 1st and 3rd Battalions, Fourth Infantry, plus regimental headquarters and a battalion of 75-mm. pack artillery had arrived at the Shortlands. Tanaka sent the 3rd Battalion forward on September 11; it landed near Cape Esperance at midnight. After an early reveille, these fresh troops, well supplied and equipped and eager to fight, began to march east on the coastal track to reinforce Colonel Oka's battle position. On the fourteenth, the regimental commander, Colonel Nomasu Nakaguma, landed at Kamimbo with the remaining battalion, his headquarters, and more artillery. Major General Yumio Nasu, Commander, 2nd Division Infantry Group, accompanied Nakaguma.

Hyakutake's problem was no easy one to resolve. He had in hand two operations, but lacked both the troops and the means to reinforce and sustain them simultaneously. A choice had to be made, and the general recommended to Imperial GHQ suspension of the attack in New Guinea. This was a bitter decision, particularly as Major General Tomitaro Horii reported that the vanguard of his South Seas Detachment had on the night of September 14 looked down from the slopes of the Owen Stanley Range upon the lights of Port Moresby, less than a tantalizing 30 miles distant.

Horii's men, each now rationed to less than half a pint of rice a day, were exhausted and hungry, but could—or so their commander averred—subsist if necessary on their unique spiritual resources until the goal was reached. Hyakutake refused to entertain this advice and peremptorily directed Horii to fall back at once on Kokoda.[1] Already, as a result of Edson's raid of September 8 on Tasimboko, a part of the Forty-first Infantry had been withdrawn to Buna where it was preparing defensive positions while awaiting transportation to the Solomons.

Thus, events on Guadalcanal during the first two weeks of September had excised the imperial army's immediate overland threat to Moresby. This particular stretch of "the jungle road to Tokyo," later trod by the American General Eichelberger, was, as a result of actions hundreds of miles away, reduced to an area of secondary importance.

For some days before Hyakutake reluctantly directed Horii to halt on the mountain track to Moresby, Admiral Ghormley had been trying to decide what to do with the reinforced Seventh Marines (Colonel James W. Webb), and a detachment of the Fifth Defense Battalion commanded by Lieutenant Colonel William F. Parks. These units, embarked at Samoa some days previously, had been en route to New Zealand when suddenly diverted to Espiritu Santo by CincPac. There they awaited the decision Ghormley was reluctant to make.

On September 12, after his brief visit with Vandegrift, Turner had returned to Espiritu. He found a message from Ghormley awaiting him. This was in reply to his urgent recommendation for reinforcement (in which Vandegrift had concurred) and was not particularly encouraging.[2] Ghormley again temporized; although he approved reinforcement "in principle" he would not authorize it until the situation became "known."[3] The admiral did not intimate when, if ever, he imagined this satisfactory state of affairs would come about. He was content, for the time being, to allow the initiative to rest with the enemy. This procedure is not one ordinarily followed by successful commanders.

In war, situations are the products of mutually exclusive and incompatible wills. Thus, they are practically always fluid. It is this fluidity which generates the miasma called the "fog of war." Frequently, a bold action—a calculated venture—is the catalyst required to dissipate this fog. Ghormley now had at hand the means to take such action. It remained to be seen whether he would make the attempt to send the fresh troops forward.

Turner unfortunately failed to record his immediate reaction to his superior's hesitant message. He did, however, continue to make preparations to sail the transports. He suspected Ghormley must perforce grasp the nettle; on the following day ComSoPac did so, and directed Turner to proceed as recommended.[4] Having finally made the decision to reinforce, Ghormley put everything he had into the effort. And it was well that he did. Radio Tokyo may have helped Ghormley make up his mind; gibing comments on "a reckless invasion" which "left ten thousand men hopelessly marooned" undoubtedly further scarified the already severely lacerated *amour-propre* of the United States Navy; there was enough truth in them to hurt.

The admiral assigned his two available carriers as distant cover for the five transports and two supply ships which Turner sailed with cruiser and destroyer escort from Espiritu Santo at first light on September 14. At about the same time on that morning, Major General Kawaguchi decided to suspend his attacks on the bloody ridge south of Henderson Field.

September 14 was a long day in Kelly Turner's life. While his zigzagging column churned toward the northwest, communication officers sweated. They had reason to do so: they were decoding an unbroken stream of messages warning American ships of Japanese carrier task forces, submarines, and snooping aircraft. But the storm did not break until the following afternoon. When it did, it was short and deadly.

About half past two, two Japanese submarines—*I-19* and *I-15* —planted in waters SoPac sailors already knew as "Torpedo Junction," ran up their periscopes. A carrier task group was what each commander saw. At a quarter before three o'clock, *I-19* torpedoed *Wasp*. In half an hour the carrier was an inferno, and her Captain, Forrest Sherman, gave orders to abandon ship. But the gallant *Wasp*, which Churchill earlier had credited with saving Malta, did not sink. She floated for hours, her red-hot plates a pyre for almost 200 American sailors. Destroyers picked 366 wounded men off rafts and from the water. At 9:00 P.M., Rear Admiral Norman Scott directed destroyer *Landsdowne* to torpedo the incandescent hulk. One operational carrier, *Hornet*, remained in the South Pacific.

Wasp was only the first casualty of that day. Seven minutes after *I-19* holed her, *I-15* let *North Carolina* have one. This torpedo hit deep, penetrated just below the armor belt, and blew

400 square feet of steel out of *Carolina*'s port side. Damage control was instantaneous; the battleship recovered from a slight list almost immediately and continued majestically at 25 knots, a performance which would have been something of a surprise to the captain of *I-15* had he been watching.

But he was not. He had his periscope—and his bow tubes—trained on destroyer *O'Brien*, and two minutes after his single fish penetrated *North Carolina*'s hull, a second tore into *O'Brien*. Score for nine minutes: one carrier, one battleship, one destroyer. The two Japanese submarines, with a very good day's work behind them and 15 destroyers milling about above, departed for less troubled waters, as did the remaining ships of Rear Admiral Leigh Noyes' Task Force.[5]

Kelly Turner also sought more salubrious regions, and just after darkness turned his transports back to the southeast. He continued to withdraw until midafternoon of the following day, when at 3:00 P.M. he suddenly reversed course, bent on 15 knots, and headed for Lunga Point. What Japanese torpedoes might have done to his thin-skinned transports may be imagined. But if there were any submarines along his track, Turner eluded them.

It was then, and still is today, difficult to understand why the Japanese did not make a major submarine effort to stop reinforcement of Guadalcanal. Decisive targets for their undersea boats and their reliable, swift-running torpedoes were not, under the existing circumstances, carriers, battleships or destroyers, but transports and supply vessels. However, submarine doctrine, which prescribed combat ships as primary targets, had apparently congealed. To naval officers in Toyko, and indeed to Yamamoto, destruction of the American fleet had always been, and was to remain, a matter of exclusive priority.

The Japanese were, as we have seen, aware that this particular convoy had arrived in SoPac waters, and had opportunity to concentrate sufficient submarines to destroy it. Yet they failed to do so. The almost total lack of imagination, the hidebound intellectual inflexibility, which characterized alike the High Commands of the Japanese Army and Navy, and which—with notably rare exceptions—filtered down to the senior officers of both services, was to cost Japan dearly to the very end of the Pacific war.

A few minutes before 6:00 A.M. on September 18, Turner brought his convoy triumphantly to the waters off Lunga. In the eyes of the silent, unshaven men who with their commander watched fresh troops disembark, the United States Navy finally stood vindicated.

With the Seventh Marines came tanks, an artillery battalion, engineers; medical and motor transport companies; aviation ground crews, and communication personnel. With over 3000 officers and enlisted men, Colonel Webb brought rations, gasoline, all classes of ammunition, and post-exchange supplies. The latter included button buffers, shoe polish, snuff, starch, blanco for leggings, and 20,000 small round aluminum boxes. In breakfast lines several days later each marine was issued three "Trojans" gratis. If not too tightly knotted, these proved most effective for preserving such perishable items as cigarettes, matches, candy, and letters from sweethearts in the States.

At dusk, the ships pulled out, carrying with them the remnants of the First Parachute Battalion. The men who survived Gavutu and Edson's Ridge had never jumped on a combat mission. Nor would they.

While marines were enjoying a free issue of one chocolate bar per man, Army and Navy Sections of Imperial GHQ issued complementary directives ordering both services to "display their combined combat strength to attack and capture the Guadalcanal airfields" as soon as reinforcements and supplies could be brought forward.[6] GHQ set October 17 as the tentative date for "decisive attack" and ordered Lieutenant General Tadayoshi Sano, commanding the 38th Division, to proceed without delay from the Indies to Rabaul and report in person to Commanding General, Seventeenth Army. Combined Fleet would provide supporting ships and Isoroku Yamamoto would coordinate operations.

At this time, while the Japanese public was misinformed as to the situation in the Solomons, the American public was uninformed. In communiqués, King dished out dibs and dabs designed to obscure the situation. Only those in the top echelons were aware of the gravity of the situation. While marines were hungry in Guadalcanal, and almost every item was in short supply, sixty ships lay in Nouméa waiting to discharge cargos. Most of these were manned by merchant marine crews, who drew exorbitant rates of pay for service in "combat zones." Additionally, their officers and crews demanded "overtime." Forrestal, for one, knew what was going on, and said that if the American people had, there would be revolution at home.[7]

Roosevelt sensed the coming crisis. In a Labor Day address to the nation the President depreciated the strategic importance of the Solomons operation, and referred cautiously to the critical situation on Guadalcanal, "because he knew, as the public did not, of the severe naval losses we had sustained, and he was seeking to prepare the people for possible news that the Japanese had driven the Marines from the positions so precariously held."[8]

Scepticism was rampant in the War Department, where the Army hierarchy recognized that the Navy was "hard pressed on Guadalcanal."[9] On September 16, at a meeting of the Joint Chiefs, Admiral King, after making the—for him—wholly unprecedented admission that the Navy was "in a bad way at this particular moment," had submitted an urgent plea for P-38 (*Lightning*) fighters.[10] General Arnold reluctantly agreed to divert from TORCH, the invasion of North Africa, all that he could spare: fifteen. But there was a slight hitch—these *Lightnings* were not immediately available, nor would they be for some time.

This grudging concession did not satisfy the exasperated admiral, who repaired to his office where, under date of September 17, he prepared a lengthy memorandum to Marshall. In this, King stated that of 62 *Wildcats* delivered to Guadalcanal since 21 August, but 30 remained operational; that the Navy was "unable to meet this rate of attrition and still operate carriers," and that it was therefore "imperative that the future continuous flow of Army fighters be planned, starting at once, irrespective of, and in higher priority than, the commitments to any other theatre." At its destination, this communication was pigeonholed.[11]

A few days later, Arnold arrived in Hawaii. At Pearl, he talked to the Pacific air commander, Lieutenant General Delos Emmons, and visited Admiral Nimitz. Emmons, who had lately returned from a junket through the South Pacific, reported categorically that Guadalcanal could not be held. To buttress this defeatist estimate, he cited an equally gloomy appreciation provided him by MacArthur. Arnold found Nimitz as positive the marines could hold as Emmons was that they could not. But Arnold was not particularly impressed with the views expressed by Admiral Nimitz. Exuding pessimism, the Commanding General, Army Air

Force, departed from Hawaii for the area commanded by Vice Admiral Ghormley.

Happily, on Guadalcanal the atmosphere was less charged with doubt. The day after the Seventh Marines landed, Vandegrift talked to newsmen in his command post.

"Are you going to hold this beachhead, General? Are you going to stay here?" one of them asked.

"Hell, yes," Vandegrift snapped back. "Why not?"[12]

During this interview a small motor launch wheezed alongside the Beachmaster's jetty at Kukum. At the tiller was a heavily-muscled, stocky native in a lava-lava. His frizzled hair rose a full eight inches above his forehead. A tall, lean, lantern-jawed white man wearing a torn khaki shirt tended the cantankerous engine. The launch coughed to a stop, and this ill-assorted pair stepped ashore. After identifying themselves, they borrowed a jeep. The white man was Marion Carl, a fighter pilot of local renown; the black, Corporal Eroni, one of Martin Clemens's scouts.

Carl, shot down above Koli Point on September 14, had bailed out, landed in the water, swum ashore, and encountered Eroni, who had cared for him since. The "one-lunger" in which this modest man—one of the top fighter pilots of World War II—arrived at Kukum was Eroni's patrol boat, assigned to him by Clemens to return such friendly aviators as happened to alight in his vicinity.

Carl and Eroni proceeded at once to wing headquarters, where they encountered General Geiger. The Air commander was happily surprised: Carl had been given up as lost. Among those present at the time was Captain John L. Smith, who, during Carl's five-day absence, had run his score of Japanese shot down to fourteen. After greeting Carl, Geiger said:

"Marion, I have bad news. Smitty has fourteen now; you still have only twelve. What are we going to do about that?"

For a moment Carl hesitated. Then he said:

"Goddammit, General, ground him for five days!"

With his Division assembled for the first time, Vandegrift was able both to revise his plan of defense and to scheme the discomfiture of the Japanese still stubbornly hanging on to the west bank of the Matanikau. The general now had available on

Guadalcanal nine battalions of infantry, a depleted Raider Battalion, four battalions of artillery, two companies of light tanks, and a Special Weapons Battalion commanded by Major Robert B. Luckey, an expert "cannon cocker." In its 75-mm.-gunned half-tracked vehicles, Luckey's hybrid outfit held a "Sunday punch" should the Japanese use tanks.

But of those units landed originally, none now could muster anywhere near table-of-organization strength. For, while battle casualties had not yet reached 1000, twice that number were suffering from malnutrition, the aftereffects of dysentery, virulent fungus infections, and exhaustion. Malaria, shortly to strike down so many, was just beginning to appear; in mid-September only fifty cases were considered sufficiently serious to warrant hospitalization. Mass suppressive treatment with atabrine began on September 10. Rumors at once spread that the yellow pills rendered a man impotent, and marines simply refused to eat them. "Medical personnel . . . were forced to stand at mess lines and not only supervise the taking of this drug" but actually to peer into the mouths "of the recipients" to see that the pills were swallowed. Those who balked at atabrine went hungry.[13]

As the Seventh arrived, its attachments reverted to control of parent units, and infantry battalions were shuffled into new positions. Geiger's aircraft, few as they were, provided reasonable insurance against a major amphibious assault, and skeleton beach defenses were manned during hours of darkness by engineers, pioneers, and amphibian tractor crews. Inland, Vandegrift ordered a cordon defense anchored to the east at the mouth of the "Tenaru" and to the west on the ridge line west of Lunga. The semicircular trace clung generally to high ground. To the south it included Edson's Ridge and from this feature dropped to the impassable "Tenaru."

Defense in depth was out of the question except on ridge positions. In the low-lying sodden ground between kunai-clad spines, jungle vegetation restricted visibility to a few yards. Clearing fields of fire for automatic weapons was enervating work, endless to filthy men who had lived on short rations and little sleep for the preceding six weeks. Nevertheless, dig and chop they must; dig and chop they did.

Dugouts were roofed with coconut logs, sandbagged, and stocked with ammunition, grenades, extra rations and water. Sufficient wire was at last available to surround principal battle positions with two banks of double apron fence. While in the southern sectors very few of these could be sited so as to be mutually supporting, the area forward of the perimeter was constantly patrolled by the defenders as well as by Clemens's scouts. Because they lacked depth these defenses could be fairly easily ruptured, but switch positions, to be occupied on order by troops from adjacent sectors, provided reasonable assurance that penetrations could be sealed off.

But Vandegrift did not contemplate a purely passive attitude. He planned an active defense. With forces now available he could both hold what he had and jab at the Japanese with limited operations designed to keep the enemy off balance and under constant strain. He was in no position to gamble: he anticipated further heavy attacks. Every move must be calculated to harm the Japanese physically and psychologically to the greatest extent possible without risk of serious subtraction from his own force. "The Second Matanikau" was the first of such jab operations.

This move, designed to break up an increasingly threatening concentration between Point Cruz and the Matanikau, started on September 23 when Lieutenant Colonel Lewis B. ("Chesty") Puller, commanding 1st Battalion, Seventh Marines, started overland toward the upper reaches of this ominous and ill-omened stream. After several contacts with Oka's outposts, in which he suffered casualties of seven killed and 25 wounded, Puller approached the Matanikau.

He found fords blocked; all attempts to cross were violently resisted. During the morning of September 26, Puller called for support from aviation and artillery, but the Japanese were well dug in, tenacious and as ready to fight as he. Hoping to force a crossing further downstream, Puller turned north and moved along a narrow jungle trail toward the coast. En route, his column was harassed by heavy mortar fire from the opposite bank; the weary battalion reached the coastal track at sundown. This foray clearly demonstrated that the Japanese were along the river in strength and meant to hold its west bank.

By early afternoon, Division operations had reached the hopeful conclusion that with the application of a little more power, the enemy upriver could be levered out of the positions he had so successfully defended during the morning. The resulting confection, a hastily improvised concept, was generally similar to the design of the August effort in the same area. And as might have been anticipated, the action was to be attended by several of the difficulties which had beset the earlier operation. Both had the same common denominator: They were planned and conducted in total ignorance of the terrain and of the enemy situation.

By this time the Japanese had over 4000 fighting men on the line of the Matanikau and in reserve behind it. Some of them were hungry and others ill. But reinforcements had arrived and fresh troops were on the way. The Japanese were thus not entirely unjustified in believing that the goal they had suffered so much to attain was now in sight. In any event, they were determined to hold the position along the Matanikau. It was under these circumstances that Division directed Merritt Edson, now commanding the Fifth Marines, to establish a command post near the mouth of the Matanikau and coordinate the operation proposed. Essentially:

The First Raiders (Lieutenant Colonel Samuel B. Griffith) would move inland (south) along the east bank of the river to the vicinity of the log crossing known as "The Jap Bridge"; force a passage there or where they could; swing right and attack downstream toward the sea. Air and artillery support were to be available on call.

To assist this sweep, 2nd Battalion, Fifth Marines (Captain Joseph J. Dudkowski), supported by artillery and mortar concentrations and by cannon-firing Air Force fighters, would attack across the sand bar.

Simultaneously, Puller's battalion, boated and under escort of seaplane tender *Ballard*, would proceed to Point Cruz, land to the west of this promontory, swing left and attack to the east down the coastal track.

Trouble began just before noon when the Raiders, strung out along the narrow track hedged by ridges on the left and the river on the right, approached "The Jap Bridge." Here the head of the column was suddenly hit by light mortar and automatic fire from the front. The Japanese, in well-concealed positions, had put a stopper in the jungle bottleneck, which measured about 20 yards from river to ridge. In a short fight, Major Bailey, who had won the Medal of Honor at the Ridge, was killed, and several men wounded.

Leaving a reinforced company to contain the enemy blocking force, Griffith sought room to maneuver, and led the remainder of the battalion up a precipitous jungle-covered spine from which he could move down on the rear of the Japanese. The slow and exhausting development of a battalion in Indian file was not completed until midafternoon, and was discerned by Japanese on an adjacent ridge. Another fire fight ensued in which the battalion commander was wounded. Attempts to push along the low ground or the ridge brought instant reaction from mortars, machine guns and automatics. The Raiders were stalled.

At this moment there occurred a communication muddle of major proportions. A series of garbled messages impelled both Division and Edson to conclude that the Raiders were indeed across the river and ready to jump off toward the sea. Edson therefore ordered the 2nd Battalion, Fifth Marines, to attack across the sand bar and Puller's battalion (less Puller, who remained with Edson to assist him) to land as planned. The attack at the mouth of the river was beaten back, and the few men who gained the west bank recalled.

In the meantime Puller's battalion (commanded in his absence by Major Otho L. Rogers) landed. Rogers moved inland preparatory to swinging left. Unfortunately, the landing was made immediately in front of a Japanese battalion bivouac area. The alerted Japanese pulled out and allowed the marines to penetrate about 400 yards. Then they fell upon them from three sides. Fighting was vicious and in less than five minutes Rogers and half a dozen others were killed. The toll mounted alarmingly as the enemy swung to cut the battalion off from the beach. The situation of these marines was critical; Edson ordered them to pull out and asked for air support.

Before these arrangements were completed, a heavy raid hit Henderson Field, disrupting all Division communications. But fortunately Puller had not dallied. During the raid he hastened to Kukum, commandeered a boat and boarded *Ballard*. With landing craft riding her wake, she moved at once to Point Cruz, established visual communication with the marines surrounded on a kunai-covered knoll several hundred yards inland, and conducted a close-in "boxing" shoot. So aided, the battalion began a fighting withdrawal down the corridor outlined by *Ballard's* exploding shells. With them, marines brought the bodies of 24 dead. Twenty-three officers and men, most of whom had to be carried, were wounded.

Sergeant Robert Raysbrook, who under Japanese fire repeatedly signaled *Ballard*, later received the Medal of Honor, an award also posthumously conferred on Signalman Douglas Munro of the Coast Guard. Munro, who led the landing craft to the beach, was killed by enemy fire while himself firing a boat machine gun to protect embarking marines. At this juncture, strafing planes appeared to cover a second wave of five evacuation boats, and just before dusk Puller's battalion arrived at Kukum.

Meanwhile, Edson ordered the Raiders to withdraw, and by midnight on September 27 all marines were within the perimeter. The "Second Matanikau," the name given this series of blundering actions, exacted a toll of almost two hundred: 67 killed, 125 wounded. Seventy-nine of these were absorbed by Puller's battalion.

Here, it was again proved that coordination of a complicated tactical pattern was next to impossible when it involved movement over constricted trails through unknown jungle. It was again proved that patrol probing actions to determine approximate location and strength of enemy positions were prerequisite to a jungle attack, as they are indeed to any attack. Here Edson, as always supremely confident, had dispersed his force haphazardly to assault an enemy well armed, well concealed, and at each point in superior strength. Second Matanikau hammered home to Vandegrift that a commander who allows himself, or a subordinate, to drift aimlessly into action will pay the price.[14]

At this time, with Guadalcanal in precarious balance, General Arnold arrived in Nouméa. Arnold found the naval officers there "under terrific strain" and "with chips on their shoulders." Admiral Ghormley had been so busy, according to Arnold, that he had not been able to leave his flagship "for about a month." Arnold urged the admiral to stop fighting a paper war and cautioned him that no one could "sit continuously in a small office . . . without suffering mentally, morally and nervously." He advised a change of scene, and although he does not say so, the inference is that he suggested a visit to Guadalcanal.

Arnold left the admiral's headquarters in a curious mood. "The Navy," he later wrote, had "taken one hell of a beating . . . was hanging on by a shoestring." The "logistic set-up . . . to insure success" was lacking. The Navy had paid insufficient attention to development of airfields and to supply of gasoline. Its senior officers in the area "did not understand the technique of ground operations nor the technique of air operations," but were "determined to carry on the campaign in that theater" and equally determined "to do it with as little help from the Army as possible. It was their fight, the Navy's fight: it was their war against the Japanese; and they were going to clean it up if they could."[15]

These statements misrepresent the attitude of the Navy's Pacific command. For weeks before Arnold left Washington, everyone in the South Pacific, including Assistant Secretary of the Navy Forrestal, had begged for fighters. King had pleaded in vain for a few high-performance Air Force fighters, and not until September 16 did Arnold agree to give him any. For weeks thereafter—and Americans are entitled to wonder at whose direction—Arnold's staff insolently neglected to prepare a response to King's memorandum of September 17. And this at a time a dozen more high-altitude fighters on Guadalcanal literally meant the difference between life and death to hundreds of men.

Major General Alexander Patch, commanding the Army's Americal Division in New Caledonia, was able to confirm his distinguished visitor's opinion of the inadequacy of the Navy's supply and replenishment arrangements. Indeed, he informed Arnold, he had withdrawn 20,000 pairs of shoes from his quartermaster's shelves and sent them to Guadalcanal so that marines would no longer be obliged to fight barefoot.

The logistics situation can truthfully be portrayed only as a snafu of monumental proportions. At Nouméa, Ghormley faced an indescribable mess. Practically everything needed to unload the ships riding in the harbor was lacking: piers, mobile cranes, tugs, barges, trucks, workers. The admiral and his staff were at their wit's end to devise means to get these needed materials ashore. Ghormley was, of course, blamed for everything, and he bore it. But the guilty parties were behind snug desks in the Department in Washington.

Arnold's criticism of Admiral Ghormley on this issue was unwarranted, and his attitude little less than deplorable. The decision to enter the Solomons, which Arnold ratified as a member of the Joint Chiefs, had been approved by the President of the United States. It was clearly Arnold's obligation to do all within his power to help the Navy cope with threats which menaced the success of the first offensive effort in the Pacific.

But the general's impressions were not all negative. Before

leaving New Caledonia for MacArthur's headquarters in Brisbane, Arnold visited Tantouta, the air base from which Marine Colonel Perry K. Smith's Douglas transports were operating.

The Marine transport planes, like their other units, were doing an excellent job. A grand job! They made the 800-mile trip into Guadalcanal, carried enough gas for the return trip, and still lugged 3000 pounds of cargo. And they carried out as many of the wounded as their planes would hold.[16]

In Rabaul, Lieutenant General Masao Maruyama conferred with Hyakutake, received his orders, and perfected detailed arrangements for forwarding the remainder of his Second ("Sendai") Division to Guadalcanal.[17] Lifts on October 3, 8 and 11 would be provided by Tanaka's "Tokyo Express," plus seaplane tender *Nisshin* carrying guns, tractors, tanks and trucks. Destination: Tassafaronga. Maruyama proposed to proceed with the first run.

Hyakutake, however, had no idea of entrusting control of the attack set for October 17 to the Commanding General of the Sendai Division. He had no intention of permitting another headstrong subordinate to repeat the costly sacrifices made at the Ilu and the Ridge. Accordingly, he scheduled the displacement of Headquarters, Seventeenth Army to Guadalcanal for the night of October 9. Upon landing he planned to assume personal command. Nor did Hyakutake intend to attack until he disposed of sufficient force. He therefore ordered Lieutenant General Sano to start the 38th Division toward the Shortlands at once.

The principals were thus paired off. Yamamoto, Tanaka and Hyakutake would soon face Ghormley, Turner and Vandegrift in a series of air, land and sea battles that Imperial GHQ estimated might well "decide the fate of the Greater Far East Asia War."

11

ON THE LAST DAY of this September, half a dozen marines in stinking dungarees watched with considerable interest a B-17 taxi laboriously through the mud toward a group of officers gathered under the shredded palm trees along the west side of the runway. The marines hoped it was loaded with nurses, Red Cross girls, or, at the very least, candy bars. A moment after the pilot cut his engines, and even before the choking swirls of dust subsided, a slim, greying officer who wore four stars on the tabs of his shirt collar climbed quickly down the ladder. Vandegrift walked rapidly toward him and saluted. The two shook hands. No smart guard and band, no ruffles and flourishes, no 19-gun salute welcomed Admiral Chester Nimitz, Commander in Chief, Pacific Ocean Areas, on his first visit to Guadalcanal.

Nimitz had flown from his Hawaiian headquarters to learn at first hand what was going on in the South Pacific. Vandegrift had plenty to show him, and even more to tell him. Between air raids, Nimitz was escorted to Edson's Ridge, to Air operations where he talked with Geiger and Woods, and to the Division hospital. Here, a few of those recently wounded at Second Matanikau still awaited transportation in Colonel Perry Smith's supply and evacuation planes to hospitals on the quiet islands to the south. To the haggard sick and wounded men, the admiral spoke words of sympathy and encouragement. Later, in Vandegrift's command post, he was less cheerful. One of Admiral Nimitz's qualities as a great commander—and he had many—was the ability, under constant stress, to be calmly objective. Nimitz was neither an optimist nor a pessimist. He was a realist. He was aware not only that the hold on Guadalcanal was tenuous, but that a major Japanese effort to break it impended.

Before he left for the New Hebrides early the following morning, the admiral awarded decorations to two dozen officers and enlisted men. As he drove to Henderson in misting rain, Nimitz promised Vandegrift "support to the maximum of our resources."[1]

While CincPac conferred with Vandegrift, Admiral Turner was absorbed in laying plans for the occupation of Ndeni in the Santa Cruz Islands, some 300 miles to the rear of the critical battle area. This operation, directed by the Joint Chiefs in their July 2 instructions for WATCHTOWER, had several times been postponed because of continuous pressing demands for fighting men in the front lines. But Ndeni, a strategic red herring if ever there was one, was a project dear to Admiral Ghormley and he was delighted to receive Turner's recommendations.

The Marine commander had always opposed the occupation of Ndeni. Vandegrift was under the guns; he saw no point in diversion of men and material urgently needed on Guadalcanal to this backwash. He therefore viewed these suggestions with profound disapproval, as, indeed, he did certain other projects devised aboard the Amphibious flagship. Vandegrift's constant problem in dealing with his nominal superior in the chain of command was to keep the sailor in his nautical place.

As early as August 29, Turner had, without authority, started to break up the uncommitted remains of the Second Marine Regiment he had carried with him on August 9 when he withdrew from Lunga, in order to form a "Raider Battalion." At the same time, he had informed Admiral Ghormley that as soon as he laid hands on the Seventh and Eighth Marines, he proposed to direct their commanding officers to constitute similar battalions. Vandegrift filed immediate vigorous objection, and Nimitz directed Turner to cease tampering with Marine organization. Every now and then Richmond Kelly Turner behaved like a frustrated general.

On October 3, Nimitz arrived in New Caledonia and immediately closeted himself with Vice Admiral Ghormley, whose pessimistic review of the situation made on him—as later events would prove—a profound impression. When the question of reinforcing Guadalcanal was discussed, Ghormley protested that it was unsafe to strip rear-area islands of their garrisons; he felt the possibility remained that the Japanese "might break through and attack our lines of communication."[2] Fortunately, one of his subordinate commanders had a more acute grasp of the imperative demands of the moment than did Admiral Ghormley.

This was Major General Harmon.[3] Harmon had pondered the situation for some time; Kelly Turner's renewed recommmen-dations respecting Ndeni crystallized his thoughts. Although he had not expressed his opinion formally, Harmon, too, considered the long-delayed occupation of Santa Cruz a complete waste of effort, and the reinforcement of Guadalcanal an urgent necessity. Finally, on October 6, he addressed a lengthy and well-reasoned memorandum to his immediate superior.

In this, a decisive document in the history of the Guadalcanal campaign, Harmon expressed his strong conviction that the enemy was capable of recapturing the island and would do so in the near future unless the position was "materially strengthened." After presenting a full analysis of the existing situation, he recommended that the Ndeni operation be held in abeyance until "a condition of reasonable stability and security" could be achieved in the lower Solomons. He further urged that Guadal-canal be immediately reinforced with one Infantry Regimental Combat Team, that naval surface forces intensify their efforts to disrupt the increasingly dangerous and galling activities of the "Tokyo Express," and that all possible airfield construction per-sonnel and matériel be rushed to Guadalcanal.[4]

The admiral approved. On the following day Colonel Bryant E. Moore's One Hundred Sixty-fourth Infantry Regimental Combat Team of Patch's American Division was alerted for im-mediate embarkation.

Meanwhile, Vandegrift's operations staff was at work on an-other plan to drive the enemy from his positions along the Matanikau. This accomplished, the general proposed to establish an advanced battle position near Kokumbona as well as a strong point to command the river mouth. Here the sandspit, which had already soaked up a considerable amount of marine blood, pro-vided the only east-to-west route for tanks, artillery and wheeled vehicles.

For "Third Matanikau," Division operations slated five of ten available infantry battalions.[5] The plan provided that two would mount fixing attacks along the river while the other three crossed it well inland, turned right, deployed and attacked with air and artillery support along ridge lines toward the sea. Edson was directed to command the operation. The date: October 8. Although Vandegrift was naturally ignorant of the fact, Lieutenant General Masao Maruyama had now arrived on the island with a large part of his Sendai Division and had ordered a limited attack along the river for the same date. His object was to establish a forward battle position on the *east* bank of the Matanikau.

The Japanese commander's purpose was twofold. First, he sought to secure a protected crossing for the tanks to be used in the general assault of October 17. Second, he desired to cover and protect the firing positions selected for the 15-cm. (approximately 6-in.) howitzers Rabaul had promised would soon arrive. With these, Hyakutake would pulverize the airfield prior to the attack he had announced would deliver Henderson into his hands "at one stroke."

Maruyama's presence had boosted Japanese morale, which had reached a low point during the week preceding the general's arrival. Remnants of the Ichiki and Kawaguchi groups, assigned to rear areas to regain health and strength, manned beach defenses from Kokumbona to Cape Esperance. Neither group had fully recovered from the recent ordeal. Many men were still suffering from the effects of exhaustion and exposure. Malaria was common; rations to line-of-communication troops were restricted to a cup of rice per man per day. On October 5, one private who had marched with Kawaguchi and was then recuperating near Tassafaronga, wrote in words which, although they would have wrung tears from a stone, would have wrung none from a marine:

> Rations are gone and our clothing is in rags. I wonder how long this will last and pray it will soon be over. It makes me feel like a little bird in the rain. I am lonesome and think of my native village.

And two days later:

> Since morning we have been in foxholes. We are absolutely helpless.

Front line troops were better supplied. Nor were they as disconsolate as the diarist.

During the first week of October, small combat patrols punched each dismal day at two Japanese companies dug in on a ridge which dominated the upper reaches of this now generally loathed Matanikau River. In all these brief encounters marines were killed and wounded. The casualties had to be accepted: Vandegrift would not again strike blindly at the enemy. By constant aggressive patrolling he sought both to keep the Japanese off balance and accurately to develop the hostile positions.

At the same time, the imperial "sea eagles" increased their pressure on Henderson. During the first three days of October, raids were more than usually violent. In Rabaul, Vice Admiral Yamagata could count almost 200 aircraft, half of them *Zeros*. In contrast, on October 5 (for example) Geiger had but 29 operational *Wildcats*, 16 dive bombers, three torpedo planes, and six Army P-400s. The promised *Lightnings* had not yet arrived; it was rumored in the tents and shacks around Henderson that no such planes actually existed.

October 2 was rough in the skies over Guadalcanal. A top fighter pilot, Robert Galer, who that day ran his score to eleven Japanese planes shot down, was himself shot out of the air. He parachuted and was picked up to fly more combat missions.

And now for seven days from October 4 the Japanese suspended mass air attacks against Henderson. But "Washing Machine Charlie" did his nightly stint. Colonel Pepper's 90-mm. antiaircraft guns vainly sought to exterminate this ubiquitous pest. And although it was a standing joke that his bombs never hit anything, the possibility that one just might was enough to rout marines from soggy blankets into foxholes in which water stood five to six inches deep. Improving foxholes was the universal recreation on Guadalcanal at this time.

Although the operations section was primarily interested in resolving the situation to the west, there were minor problems to the east, where at Gurabusu and Koilotumaria Clemens's scouts had discovered enemy detachments, presumably operating radio stations. These, Vandegrift was for obvious reasons anxious to liquidate. For the purpose, he ordered two companies of Lieutenant Colonel Robert Hill's battalion of the Second Marines, which had seen only minor patrol action since early August, to proceed by boat from Tulagi to that vicinity to land near Gurabusu under cover of darkness, to take the enemy detachments by surprise, and annihilate them. The estimate of enemy strength at each post was of the order of fifty.

On October 7, Clemens left headquarters with a Marine radio

team and three native police. His boat, traveling close to the beach, reached Aola in the afternoon and the party landed without being detected. Clemens set up his radio in the bush, checked with Division, and began his reconnaissance. Hill was expected to land shortly before midnight two days later. On the night of the ninth, Clemens stationed his scouts on the shore, each with a hooded flashlight, and at the appointed hour Hill and a small command group landed. The whereabouts of the remainder of this small attack force was, however, unknown. At dawn, two Yippies appeared, with Higgins boats in tow. One boat had been lost en route, its occupants presumably drowned. Still, Hill had a force sufficient to carry out his mission.

The attack on Gurabusu, launched at dawn on October 11, was a spectacular success. Thirty-two Japanese were killed: but two escaped. There was one marine casualty, Captain Richard T. Stafford, the company commander. The attack on Koilotumaria was, however, a flop. The company delegated to make the attack there could not get into position: when the marines arrived, they discovered that most of the Japanese had sensibly departed. But three enemy were killed. One of the corpses was identified by scouts as that of a Japanese named Ishimoto, the man responsible for the earlier murder of two priests and two nuns of the Ruavatu Roman Catholic Mission. Marines brought back with them the vestments of the priests and the gowns of the nuns, which Ishimoto had neglected to bury in the unmarked graves in which he interred the bodies.

Shortly after dawn on October 7, the five-battalion attack force had marched west from Kukum on the Government Track along the coast to the Matanikau. Soon, two battalions of the Seventh Marines (now commanded by Colonel Amor Leroy Sims) dropped off from the tail of the column and moved southwest across rugged ridges to a point upstream of "The Jap Bridge." They bivouacked for the night a few hundred yards short of the crossing point selected.

At 10:15 A.M., a half mile short of the river, the advance guard (3rd Battalion, Fifth Marines) was stopped by machine-gun fire. But by noon the enemy, estimated as a reinforced company, began to fall back slowly to positions previously prepared. Meanwhile the 2nd Battalion, Fifth Marines, moved up to the left of the engaged battalion and advanced unimpeded to the river line. At the same time, a reinforced battalion group commanded by Colonel William J. Whaling peeled off and marched south toward an assigned bivouac area close to "The Jap Bridge."

Except for the unexpected opposition along the coastal track, deployment progressed on time and without incident. But the Japanese now ensconced about 200 yards east of the sandspit were not in the mood to retreat across it. Edson ordered up a company of Raiders to seal them in, thus freeing the 3rd Battalion, Fifth Marines, for its push across the river on the following morning. But there was no attack on the morning of October 8. The timetable was washed out by a torrential night rain which turned the soft ground bordering the river into an ankle-deep swamp. All Henderson planes were grounded. Vandegrift postponed operations for 24 hours. Edson gave the Japanese tucked in on the east side of the river no rest. All day long he dumped occasional artillery concentrations and methodical mortar fire on them. They lay low and waited. The Raiders, thoughtfully wiring themselves in, attracted no more than sporadic attention from the Japanese.

A few minutes after darkness fell, the Japanese decided they had absorbed all they could take. As one, they rose from their foxholes and rushed yelling at the Raiders. For 45 minutes a fierce fight raged around this pocket. As suddenly as it had begun, the shooting and shouting ceased. Silence fell; the rain stopped. Under ponchos rigged to screen the beams of flashlights held by volunteers, doctors and corpsmen worked until dawn. Of less than a hundred Raiders, 12 were killed and 22 wounded. After sunrise 59 Japanese corpses were picked off the wire. Edson sent the Raiders back to the perimeter. "Third Matanikau" was the last of their five battles in the lower Solomons.

The attack now developed as Vandegrift planned. Whaling's group forded the river, wheeled right, and advanced unresisted down a ridge line toward the sea. Hard on Whaling's heels, Lieutenant Colonel Herman H. Hanneken's battalion of the Seventh Marines passed the same ford, pushed to a ridge about 200 yards west of that assigned Whaling, wheeled right and also drove north. Puller extended the front still more to the west, turned north and attacked in the direction of Point Cruz.

Of the three slow-moving battalion fingers, only Puller's met resistance. Working along the jungle fringes near the bottom of a ravine, his flankers encountered Japanese, apparently in a bivouac area. Puller immediately withdrew this small patrol and called for artillery fire. In minutes, 105-mm. shells began to break with devastating effect over the helpless Japanese, who raced from the concealing jungle toward the ridge opposite. As they emerged from the thick vegetation, marine mortars and machine gunners drove them back into the ravine.

> It was a most effective arrangement for methodical extermination, and Puller and his men kept it up until mortar ammunition ran low.[6]

An unexpected order from Division terminated the slaughter: all units would disengage at once, pass through the Fifth Marines (directed to hold and improve its position at the mouth of the river) and return to Lunga. In this valley of horror, Puller's battalion left the corpses of more than 700 Japanese of the 3rd Battalion, Fourth Infantry. Marine casualties were slightly less than 200. The Matanikau continued to exact its flesh and blood.

The day before the Marine attack jumped off, Maruyama sent Kawaguchi to Rabaul to report on the situation. There he briefed army and navy commanders and staffs on the disaster at Edson's Ridge and its immediate antecedents, on American fighting methods, and terrain of the island "KA." Especially, Kawaguchi emphasized the difficulty of forcing passage through the jungle. Unfortunately for the success of future operations, staff officers who attended the briefing did not attach particular importance to the unpleasant aspects of Kawaguchi's report. The general left that evening for the Shortlands to join Hyakutake, who there awaited destroyer transportation to Guadalcanal.[7]

An hour and a half before midnight on October 9, Lieutenant General Hyakutake, accompanied by his senior staff officer, Colonel Haruo Konuma, and Major General Tadashi Sumuyoshi, commander of 17th Army Artillery, landed on the island from which he intended to eject the U. S. Marines. Several hours later, his command post was established "in the valley of a nameless river about three kilometres west of Kokumbona." His chief of staff, Major General Shuichi Miyazaki, remained in Rabaul to maintain liaison with the navy and coordinate shipment of reinforcements, arms, food, munitions and other supplies.[8]

Bad news did not await the general's arrival at his new post of command. It came to meet him. As he stepped ashore he was addressed by an officer sent by Maruyama to convey the disturbing news that American artillery had "massacred" the Fourth Infantry Regiment, and that Maruyama had been forced to withdraw his front lines to a point about two miles west of the Matanikau.[9] Hyakutake immediately called a conference to convene at daybreak. The situation then detailed to him was not heartening:

> . . . the 2nd Division had retreated and the offensive key points and artillery positions for bombardment of the airfield had been lost. . . . Both Kawaguchi and Ichiki Detachments are practically powerless. . . .[10]

Food and medicines were scarce, roads and trails undeveloped, artillery ammunition in short supply.

The general listened silently to this recital and announced his decision: Offensive operations must proceed as planned. He did, however, get off a priority message ordering Headquarters of the 38th Division, one infantry regiment and an engineer regiment to displace from the Shortlands to Guadalcanal at once.[11] He then informed Imperial GHQ that the situation on Guadalcanal was "far more aggravated than had been estimated."[12]

He urged also that reinforcing activities be intensified. Additional destroyers were put on night runs, and to supplement the "Express," a number of large and small landing craft and barges were collected to operate between the Shortlands and Kamimbo. During daylight hours, the barges lay up in lagoons and creeks on Vella Lavella, Kolombangara, New Georgia, Vangunu and the Russells. The trips were long, tedious and dangerous; "Ant Transport," as the Japanese described these barging operations, was soon abandoned.[13]

Vandegrift's sudden orders to halt the successful operation of October 9 were based on information from Ghormley that a major attack was in the making. Coastwatchers observing Simpson Harbor at Rabaul, as well as those keeping an eye on activities in the Shortlands, reported heavy concentrations of cruisers, destroyers, transports and cargo vessels. The elusive "Tokyo Express" had, too, been more than usually active. Documents removed from the bodies of Japanese killed in patrol actions, and diaries analyzed by Captain Moran, contained intimations that the attempt to occupy the east bank of the Matanikau was only preliminary to an all-out attack which might include direct assault from the sea.

Fortunately, one factor which had complicated evaluation of enemy courses of action before the showdown at the Ridge was no longer present: the Japanese were not in force to the east. Vandegrift felt, therefore, that in the readjustment now essential he could with safety hold the Ilu line in minimum strength. He knew that the One Hundred Sixty-fourth Infantry was on the way, and that barring unfortunate accidents it should be available to him not later than October 13.

This reinforced regiment (less one battalion) loaded expeditiously at Nouméa in transports *McCawley* and *Zeilin* on October 8. Turner sailed the two ships the following morning. Three destroyers and three mine layers provided antisubmarine escort. Ghormley assigned Rear Admiral Norman Scott's Task Force 64—two heavy and two light cruisers and five destroyers—as Covering Force, and sent two Striking Forces, one built around carrier *Hornet*, the other around battleship *Washington*, north.[14] Harmon's letter of October 6 had obviously fired Ghormley's imagination and injected his hesitant spirit with new determination. Guadalcanal was to be reinforced, come what may. Interfering enemy forces would be met and destroyed.

This program suited the aggressive commander of Task Force 64, who viewed the mission as a heaven-sent opportunity to redeem the disgrace of Savo. For three full weeks previous to this assignment, Scott's Task Force had conducted night battle exercises; he had driven himself and his sailors hard. And now he felt that his ships and crews were ready.

In late afternoon of October 11, Scott was cruising south of Guadalcanal when he received the word he anticipated: the Japanese, under Rear Admiral Aritomo Goto, were in The Slot and on the way. Goto's force, as reported by a reconnoitering *Fortress*, consisted of two cruisers and six destroyers. Actually, it was considerably stronger.

Scott now hastened to assume his previously planned night battle formation. In the van, three destroyers of Captain Robert G. Tobin's Desron 12 (*Farenholt, Duncan, Laffey*); following them, *San Francisco* (flag), *Boise, Salt Lake City, Helena;* bringing up the rear, Tobin's remaining two destroyers (*Buchanan, McCalla*). At increased speed the column moved to an intercepting position near Savo. Scott's intention was to "cross the T": to rake each ship of an incoming enemy column from stem to stern. It was now 11:00 P.M. For 35 minutes Scott steamed on course

050° toward Savo. The island now loomed menacingly off his starboard bow and at 11:35 the Admiral directed a 180° column movement to the left to course 230°.[15]

But, for some reason, the leading destroyer did not immediately execute the column movement. Nor did Commander Ralph E. Wilson turn *Buchanan*. He followed the cruisers.[16] Tobin, realizing he had misunderstood the signal, soon turned his column 180° left, rang up flank speed, and attempted to pass the cruisers on their starboard hand—the side from which the enemy would appear, if he were coming. And he was coming.

Helena, the last cruiser in column and the only one equipped with reliable new search radar, had been reporting contacts for some time; she next reported strange ships in sight and at fifteen minutes before midnight requested permission to open fire.

A series of muddled and misunderstood messages now passed between Admiral Scott in flagship *San Francisco* and Captain Hoover in *Helena*. The admiral was reluctant to give permission to Hoover, now practically being rammed by the onrushing Japanese, to commence shooting. Fortunately, however, Captain Hoover put his own interpretation on Scott's replies, and a minute later opened fire on a target less than 5000 yards distant and closing fast. The second salvo from *Helena*'s turret guns smacked Goto's flagship *Aoba;* two minutes later she was engulfed by shells from *Salt Lake City* and *Boise*. On his dismantled bridge, Admiral Goto lay mortally wounded. He passed command to Captain Kikunori Kijima.

Scott, who had by this time determined that Tobin's destroyers were overtaking and passing between his ships and the oncoming Japanese, was in a quandary. Were his ships firing on Tobin's destroyers?[17] He was afraid they were, and over voice radio directed all ships to check fire and show recognition lights. By this time, *Furutaka* was blazing brightly; the scene the flames revealed suggested to Scott that the situation was favorable; he ordered fire to be resumed. But the four-minute hiatus was fatal to his hopes.

The momentarily staggered Japanese recovered fast and proceeded to blast destroyers *Farenholt* and *Duncan*. In exchange, the Americans massed fire on destroyer *Fubuki;* she exploded and disappeared from fire control radar screens. Scott, who apparently deemed the action successfully completed, now inexplicably ordered all ships to cease fire before pursuing. But the

Japanese had no intention of leaving the scene without a few parting shots. *Kinugasa* had not yet been hit; she joined wounded *Aoba* and fatally damaged *Furutaka* in a concentrated and punishing attack on *Boise*. Thus ended, or almost ended, the Battle of Cape Esperance. Its last mortal casualty, destroyer *Duncan*, was abandoned at 2:00 A.M., and took the final plunge off Savo a few hours later.

Scott's valiant effort spared the marines the ordeal of another night bombardment and was good for morale in the States. But his inconclusive victory, expanded in the American press to the proportions of a major triumph, had not prevented the Japanese from landing reinforcements. For while Scott was turning Goto around, Rear Admiral Takaji Joshima was busy unloading aircraft tenders *Nisshin*, *Chitose*, and six destroyers at Tassafaronga. Nevertheless, Japanese morale was shaken:

> Throughout the night battle off Savo Island, Providence abandoned us and our losses mounted. Especially since the enemy used radar which enabled them to fire effectively from the first round without the use of searchlights, the future looked black for our surface forces, whose forte was night warfare.[18]

Admiral Ghormley received first reports of Scott's victory on October 12 and immediately drew up a commendatory message: "Once more the enemy plans have been upset. Congratulations."[19] That this engagement had upset his plans to the slightest extent would have been news to Admiral Yamamoto.

During the night battle northwest of Cape Esperance, and while Rear Admiral Joshima unloaded tanks, artillery, food, and ammunition, Turner was pushing along at best speed. Just after sunrise on Tuesday, October 13, he arrived off Lunga Point. Here *McCawley* and *Zeilin* hove to and commenced discharging almost 3000 officers and men of the One Hundred Sixty-fourth Infantry. Ground personnel of the First Marine Aircraft Wing also disembarked. The "doggies" brought jeeps, trucks, antitank guns, ammunition, tentage, and 70 days' general supplies.

The latter category, as marines soon discovered, included hundreds of cases of assorted candy bars, and by 9:00 A.M. trading was brisk on the beach. All who could find an excuse to sneak down to Lunga hurried through the shadowy coconut groves toward this unexpected bonanza. Most were equipped with Japanese rifles, sabers, pistols, flags, helmets, or officers' map cases. A samurai sword that day went for three dozen large Hershey bars, a "meat-ball" flag—which marines were now adept at manufacturing when supplies of originals ran low—was worth a dozen.

At 11:00 A.M. Japanese bombers temporarily interrupted this flourishing mart, but bartering was resumed on the "All clear." The interlude was short; a noon "Condition Red" announced a large flight of *Zero*-escorted *Bettys*, and two sticks of 500-pounders delivered on the beach closed this unique Exchange. There the One Hundred Sixty-fourth suffered its first casualties. Five hours later, Major General Sumuyoshi's recently emplaced 15-cm. howitzers began to talk and for the first time, but not the last, forced *Wildcats* to displace from Henderson to "Fighter One," a narrow strip about 2000 yards to the east.

The arrival of the One Hundred Sixty-fourth Infantry brought Vandegrift's strength on Guadalcanal to slightly over 23,000, with an additional 4500 on Tulagi. But this regiment brought something more to thousands of filthy and tired marines. The arrival of the soldiers was a signal that somewhere, someone was really interested in trying to hold Guadalcanal, and that at some happy day in the distant and altogether unpredictable future they might get off this cursed island. If they lived.

Yamamoto, who had no intention of allowing the Americans to live much longer, had arranged a lively welcome for the soldiers. If the "sea eagles" could not put Henderson out of business, perhaps sustained bombardment by *Kongo* and *Haruna*, of Vice Admiral Takeo Kurita's Battleship Division Three, could. One cruiser and seven destroyers were assigned to thicken battleship fires. Yamamoto's own force, including carriers and other battleships, would cruise in distant support about 100 miles to the north.

At 11:30 P.M. on October 13, as the two big ships moved with ponderous confidence past Savo and into charted firing positions, "Louie the Louse" dropped the first of a series of brilliant flares over the airfield. Aboard darkened *Kongo* and *Haruna*, gunnery officers began solving the mathematical problems, and at 1:40 A.M. sixteen major-calibre guns opened fire simultaneously on Henderson. In less than 70 minutes, the two battleships fired over 900 rounds of thin-walled high-explosive 36-cm. (14-in.) ammunition into the restricted airfield area.

The . . . scene baffled description as the fires and explosions from the 36-cm. shell hits on the airfield set off enemy planes, fuel dumps, and ammunition storage places. The scene was topped off by flare bombs from our observation planes flying over the field, the whole spectacle making the Ryogoku fireworks display seem like mere child's play. The night's pitch dark was transformed by fire into the brightness of day. Spontaneous cries and shouts of excitement ran throughout our ships.[20]

For 70 minutes, marines and soldiers burrowed as deeply as they could into the mud of foxholes and dugouts while the ground shook and coconut trees smashed down. As flares floated gently toward earth, licking flames devoured tents and ate their way into fuel, ration and ammunition dumps. Kurita's destroyers closed on the north shore and began pouring 5-inch shells into the fires. Few bombardments of World War II equaled this in the amount of large calibre ammunition fired in a few minutes more than an hour on so small a target.

At 2:50 A.M. shelling ceased, and dazed men stumbled trembling from foxholes and shelters. At Henderson, first light revealed a shambles. Jagged pieces of steel matting torn from the runway were found hundreds of yards from the field where they had ripped through tents, blankets and cots. Scores of coconut trees were torn to pieces; a portion of the hospital was completely wrecked. Flaming fuel dumps still cascaded smoke; bombs and ammunition exploded every few minutes. One 36-cm. shell hit a ration dump and blew it apart; eviscerated tins labeled "Spam" were picked up for days. Their contents were plastered over every coconut tree within a radius of half a mile. The rats that infested the coconut groves would have no foraging problems for some time to come.

The Americans could get along without Spam, but not without aircraft. When he turned in on Tuesday, October 13, Geiger had 39 operational SBDs; when he crawled out of his dugout at dawn the next day, he had five. Sixteen of 40 *Wildcats* were twisted hulks. Of 24 remaining, 24 required repairs of some sort—new tires, wheels, tail assemblies, flaps or windscreens. Most of the torpedo planes that had recently arrived were now junk. Vandegrift requested 20 dive bombers "immediately." He would need them. And he needed fighters, replacement pilots, aircrews, and maintenance personnel, too. The shelling, concentrated on the airfield, inflicted over 60 casualties, of whom 41 were killed. Most were aviation personnel, including six pilots.

Wednesday was a relatively quiet day on Guadalcanal. Two of the five SBDs that could still fly took off in midmorning on a search to the northwest. What their pilots saw in The Slot was not reassuring. Six large troop transports, escorted by cruisers and destroyers, were on the way. And so, too, as usual, were *Zeros* and *Bettys*. Mechanics, pilots and crewmen worked to ready as many dive bombers as could immediately be repaired. There were less than a dozen.

In quiet Nouméa, Ghormley estimated the situation as critical, and informed Nimitz that enemy reinforcements must be stopped "if our position in Guadal is to be held."[21] This moment of crisis found the carrier group built around *Hornet* refueling north of New Caledonia. Scott's Task Force 64 was at Espiritu Santo licking its wounds. Neither could possibly reach the scene of action in time to intercept the Japanese task force en route to the island.

During the morning, Geiger sent his handful of SBDs up The Slot. They dive-bombed the zigzagging ships and on return claimed one transport sunk and another damaged. Actually, their bombs, all near misses, inflicted no damage on the Japanese. Nor did they affect Japanese determination to push the convoy through. Vandegrift now got off a brief priority to Admiral Ghormley:

> Urgently necessary that this force receive maximum support of air and surface units.[22]

Before a reply to this message had been received, Henderson took another bombardment, this time from Eighth Fleet cruisers *Chokai* and *Kinugasa*. While high-explosive and incendiary projectiles from their 8-inch guns poured into the airfield, the six transports approached Tassafaronga and began to discharge. By dawn Thursday, over 2000 fresh troops had landed and more than half of ships' cargos—ammunition, rations, antitank guns, howitzers, medical supplies—had been boated to the beach and hidden in the coconut groves.

Henderson aircraft now took a hand in the proceedings and three hours later, after repeated low-level attacks, the convoy commander ordered three damaged transports to beach. Obedient captains rammed their ships hard against the sand, and under an unremitting hail of bullets and bombs continued to discharge. By 10:00 A.M. they reported that 80 per cent of cargo had been landed safely. In the meantime, the three remaining transports wisely withdrew to a waiting position north and west of the Russell Islands.

Where, marines kept asking themselves, was the United States Navy? Was there a United States Navy? If so, what the hell was it doing? Vandegrift, normally an even-tempered man, was thoroughly disgusted, and again attempted to impress Ghormley with the urgency of his situation. Heavy artillery continued to shell his positions; enemy surface craft moved at will in the waters around Guadalcanal and bombarded the perimeter with impunity. There remained but a few gallons of aviation gasoline.[23]

But there was in fact an element of the United States Navy around at the time. This was Motor Torpedo Boat Squadron 3 (MTB3) which arrived at Tulagi on October 12. Lieutenant Alan R. Montgomery's four boats had been brought from the New Hebrides under tow of destroyers *Hovey* and *Southard*. Deepwater sailors, inclined to doubt the efficacy in battle of these temperamental cockleshells, would no doubt as well have deemed it ignominious to be towed to the scene of action. But if Montgomery's crews were suffering from an inferiority complex, it was not apparent: on the night of 13-14 October, he led them in darkness to engage *Kongo* and *Haruna*.

This small but determined "Task Force" slipped in column out of Tulagi harbor before midnight, with engines throttled down, and headed for Savo. The Japanese battleships were not hard to find and the MTBs deployed for torpedo runs. Lookouts had sighted them; the giants took avoiding action and combed torpedo tracks. But the Japanese were sufficiently impressed with the audacity of the attack to recount the episode in their record of the night's work.[24]

All Thursday morning maintenance crews worked feverishly draining gasoline from wrecks (one B-17, stranded at Henderson the day before, yielded over 400 gallons) and repairing *Wildcats*. By noon Geiger could put up over twenty. In relays, some flew high cover while others, their six .50-calibre machine-gun belts loaded with tracer, incendiary and armor-piercing bullets, hit the grounded transports and strafed the beach. Gasoline the Japanese had laboriously brought ashore during darkness went up in smoke;

several low-flying fighters were rocked off course and lifted in the air by pressure waves generated as an ammunition dump exploded under them. A pall of black smoke hung over the beaches from Kokumbona west to Doma Cove.

A group of distinguished visitors happened to be on hand for the show. Among them was Major General Harmon, who had arrived that morning, and watched Vandegrift's Marine, Army, and Navy flyers repay the Japanese in kind for the terrible night they had survived.

And now, in afternoon, with gas again running low, others got into the act. Geiger's aide, Major Jack Cram, put the general's lumbering amphibian "Blue Goose" down on Henderson Field in midafternoon. The "Goose," on emergency from the New Hebrides, was bringing in "supplies"—two torpedoes for the Navy's Squadron Eight. Cram insisted he rated at least one of them; an ensign who had done his day's work said the major could have them both. The fish were mounted so that Cram could release them by pulling improvised toggles, and he took off, escorted by a single fighter, for Kokumbona.

During a long, gliding approach toward target, both Cram and the "Goose" shivered as AA fire from five Japanese destroyers burst above and below. Cram held the course and let go both torpedoes. One ploughed into a beached transport, exploded, and broke her back. The "Goose" wheeled slowly toward Henderson; Cram came in with three *Zeros* on his tail. AA and fighters took them off, but not before "Goose" was thoroughly perforated. When Cram reported success of his mission to Geiger, the general went to look at his command plane. The "Goose" had fifty holes in fuselage, tail assembly and wings. Geiger threatened Cram with a general court-martial for deliberate destruction of government property, returned to his office, and recommended his aide, who had completed one of the most audacious attacks in the history of wartime aviation, for the Navy Cross.

In the Hebrides, "Blondie" Saunders's crews spent the morning of October 15 bombing-up *Fortresses*, and just after Cram returned to base, a flight of B-17s roared over Henderson and headed west at an altitude of under 5000 feet. Minutes later they let go a perfect pattern along the beach, then in majestic climbing turns gained altitude and started their long flight home.

The memorable day was over. Henderson had lost seven planes

in air combat; Geiger's pilots shot five *Zeros* and three *Bettys* out of the air.

At midnight the Japanese retaliated. This time the firing ships —8-inch-gun cruisers *Maya* and *Miyako* and two destroyers— were commanded personally by Admiral Kondo. At ranges of between 8000 and 10,000 yards, Kondo battered the field for over an hour with almost 1500 shells. Again the earth shook, but not with the tremors of "The Night." Nevertheless, again men were killed and wounded; again flamed licked at dumps, and shell fragments tore through parked aircraft. The dawn count was depressing: 15 *Wildcats* completely wrecked. Geiger had only 27 assorted airplanes left; half of them needed repairs.

But help was on the way. Smith sent several transports up from New Caledonia with drummed gas, spare parts and maintenance crews, and at five in the afternoon Lieutenant Colonel Harold Bauer brought in Marine Fighting Squadron 212—19 *Wildcats*. As the last landed, Air operations set "Condition Yellow": enemy aircraft on the way. The squadron commander, who had not yet reported to Geiger, nervously watched ground crews gas a section of his fighters. The planes wobbled to the runway and rolled off. Bauer had been on the ground less than 60 minutes. He next returned to earth almost an hour later. He had shot down four Japanese bombers. His admiring wingman later related the episode tersely: "The Chief stitched four of the bastards from end to end."

12

OCTOBER 15, 1942, was a significant day in the professional career of Lt. Gen. Masao Maruyama, an officer who had a keen appreciation of his own historical importance. The day started well. The general enjoyed a modest breakfast of tea, fish, pickle, and rice. He then picked his teeth, rinsed his mouth, wiped his face with a steaming towel, buttoned his tunic, and sat down at his field desk. An attentive adjutant handed him a document for signature.

This paper prescribed the order of march of Maruyama's command by a concealed route from Kokumbona to assembly areas south of Henderson Field. From these positions, on "X-Day," the Sendai Division would deploy, and then jump off in a dusk surprise attack, annihilate the Americans and take the airfield. "X-Day" was tentatively set as October 22. Movement through the jungle would be conducted over a narrow track which arced to the south of Mount Austen. The general specified that this route, now being prepared by the engineers, be known as "The Maruyama Road."[1]

Lt. Gen. Hyakutake's scheme of attack provided for simultaneous assaults on the perimeter at three widely separated points. The main effort was entrusted to General Maruyama; troop strength allotted for his decisive blow was of the order of seven thousand.[2] This number, Maruyama considered sufficient to overwhelm surprised defenders of a line he correctly presumed to be thinly held, and burst through to the vital areas ringing the airfield. Here were the headquarters, the fuel, food and ammunition dumps; the nerve centers of the American defenses. Here, too, was the artillery. But first the shell of the melon must be ruptured. The soft pulp could be eaten at leisure.

Maruyama's force consisted of two groups, or wings, and a reserve. Kawaguchi commanded the right wing; Maj. Gen. Yumio Nasu, the left. Kawaguchi's wing consisted of three infantry battalions plus antitank guns, trench mortars, mountain artillery and engineers. Nasu's, also with three battalions of infantry, was similarly reinforced. Maruyama held one regiment, Colonel Hitoshi Hiroyasu's Sixteenth Infantry, in reserve, with the mission of exploiting the success of either wing. Service troops included engineer, signal, medical, and water supply units.

To assist Maruyama's decisive drive, Hyakutake activated an infantry-tank-artillery group under Maj. Gen. Sumuyoshi. Sumuyoshi was to conduct a coordinated distracting operation along the Matanikau while his heavy howitzers continued to belabor the airfield and its fringing installations. Sumuyoshi now had the big guns: eight 15-cm. howitzers and other cannon of smaller bore landed from seaplane tenders *Nisshin* and *Chitose* during Scott's tangle with Goto. He also had 16 tanks.[3] As the infantry component, Hyakutake assigned what was left of Colonel Nomasu Nakaguma's Fourth Regiment, one battalion plus several odd attachments. Nakaguma, supported by tanks and artillery fire, was to cross the river at the sand bar. The ubiquitous Colonel Oka, with his One Hundred and Twenty-fourth Infantry (less one battalion, but plus one battalion of the Fourth Infantry) was secretly to ford the river about a mile and a half upstream, make his way to the east, turn north, isolate the American Matanikau battle position, and liquidate its defenders.

From Rabaul, *Bettys* would mount sustained attacks on Henderson; *Zeros* based at Buin were assigned as fighter cover. Under personal command of Yamamoto, battleships and heavy cruisers would conduct sustained bombardment with high-capacity ammunition. A reinforced battalion of the Two Hundred Twenty-eighth Infantry, designated the "Koli Detachment," was alerted to land on order east of the perimeter.[4]

If all went well, then, the Americans were to be hit simultaneously by three separate land attacks, from the air, and from the sea. On paper, the plan looked perfect. But it had been drawn without objective evaluation of terrain, weather, and the enemy, and without consideration of another matter perhaps even more critical. This question, which apparently did not suggest itself to either Hyakutake or Maruyama, was: "Can these movements be coordinated in time and space?" Reliable rapid communication was the prerequisite to such coordination.

At noon on October 16, scouts of Maj. Gen. Nasu's group moved south from the coast on the first leg of the long march.

Maruyama and a small headquarters group marched with Nasu. Kawaguchi's command was next in column. Colonel Hiroyasu's Sixteenth Infantry, plus service troops, brought up the rear. Hiroyasu was directed to march toward the upper Lunga 48 hours after the tail of the main body cleared the coastal track.

Before his column set out, Maruyama conferred with Hyaku-take. The Commanding General, Seventeenth Army, informed his subordinate that the nightly bombardments by warships had proved "a great shock to the enemy," whose strength and morale were "gradually weakening." No marine, soldier or sailor who had endured the recent shelling could have disputed the first part of the Japanese general's statement; some indeed, in the privacy of their foxholes, may have agreed with the second.

In addition to his weapon, ammunition, several hand grenades, individual equipment, and 12 days' rations, each company officer, noncommissioned officer and infantryman in Maruyama's column carried strapped to his pack one or more artillery or mortar shells. The average soldier was toting a load of some sixty pounds. Lt. Gen. Maruyama led a formidable array. But he did not know, as Kawaguchi did, and all too well, what the deceptively peaceful jungle held in store.

As the six assault infantry battalions of Maruyama's force wound and twisted in serpentine column toward the upper Lunga, soldiers and marines prepared for the attacks all felt would soon be launched. But where would the main blow fall? Which would be the sector of decision? Many speculated; none could know. Dive bombers and strafers struck at Japanese boats and barges, suitable areas for troops concentrations between Point Cruz and Esperance, and likely artillery positions.

October 16 was an evil day for the Americans. Seaplane tender *McFarland*, shepherding two barges loaded with drummed aviation gasoline through Sealark Channel to Tulagi harbor, was attacked by dive bombers, her stern blown off, and 11 of her crew killed or wounded. Another bomb hit one of the barges. Twenty thousand gallons of high-test gasoline exploded, throwing flames in every direction. The very waters burned. As the sun set, a flight of dive bombers attacked beach installations at Kukum.

The following morning, 19 *Aichi* 99s covered by eight *Zeros* interrupted breakfast. A Japanese operational dispatch informing

Hyakutake of this raid and containing such interesting details as time of the attack, route of approach, and the number and types of planes participating, had been broken at Nimitz's headquarters the evening before. Geiger launched fighters at daybreak; at seven the neatly aligned formation approached from the north at 10,000 feet. The *Wildcat* pilots pushed over, and downed eight dive bombers and two *Zeros*; six plummeting Japanese fell to accurate antiaircraft fire before they could pull out. One *Aichi* staggered off, smoking. A second raid came in at noon. Vandegrift reported the midday raid tersely:

> 15 twin engine bombers accompanied by many Zeros bombed position 1315. Our planes unable to gain altitude in time to intercept. One bomber probably shot down. Our losses none.[5]

In Nouméa, Admiral Ghormley's communication center worked overtime. Urgent pleas went to MacArthur to intensify efforts against Vunakanau and Lakunai, and to Nimitz for aircraft reinforcements. CincPac appealed in turn to King, but Cominch had nothing more. In the South Pacific, the Navy was no longer scraping the bottom of the barrel. That had been done.

Even with recent reinforcements, Vandegrift's position was brittle. On the ground, his perimeter defense swung generally from the mouth of the Matanikau south and east across the Lunga. Thence, its trace ran east over the ridges toward the Ilu, and north along the river to the sea. The beach chord, from the Ilu to the Matanikau, stretched for almost 12,000 yards; the semicircle to the south covered another 15,000. To man this frontage, he had thirteen infantry battalions. Six (three of Cates's First Marines, three of Edson's Fifth) were tired and more than decimated by malaria. The Seventh Marines were still in good shape. The soldiers were untested. Hunt's battalion of the Second Marines, now in Division reserve, stood at less than 70 per cent of its table-of-organization strength of almost 1,000.

The possibility of a smashing assault from the sea could never be eliminated. The Ilu and Matanikau positions had to be held at all costs. The marines had no guns able to cope with Sumuyoshi's big howitzers. Vandegrift did enjoy the advantage inherent in an "interior lines" position. In daylight, he could shift troops rapidly from one sector to another. He could mass artillery fire to support threatened sectors, and his flyers had proved they could control the local air. Although badly wounded by these aircraft, the Japanese at night continued to push troops, cannon, supplies, and ammunition ashore. The situation, as CincPac viewed it, allowed of no further delay. He so informed King and added: "Allocation of more forces . . . is of the greatest urgency."[6] At the same time Nimitz reassured Ghormley that no effort would be spared to provide him with the tools necessary to hold Guadalcanal.[7]

In Washington, both President Roosevelt and Secretary Knox realized that days of decision in the Solomons were again fast approaching. The President, whose principal concern was the impending Allied invasion of North Africa, spent hours daily in the White House map room, where he received briefings on the situation in the South Pacific. The Commander in Chief of America's military forces was worried about the American position, but did not—at least yet—feel it incumbent to intervene with the Joint Chiefs.

At a solemn press conference on October 17 the Secretary of the Navy parried a number of embarrassing questions.

"Do you think we can hold Guadalcanal?" one reporter asked.

Mr. Knox, unusually grim, cautiously refused to commit himself.

"I certainly hope so, and expect so," he replied. "I will not make any predictions, but every man will give a good account of himself. There is a good stiff fight going on—everybody hopes we can hold on."[8]

The New York Times described Guadalcanal as the focal point in a battle that seemed "likely to develop into one of the decisive struggles of the war in the Pacific."[9] During these trying days, Radio Tokyo had very little to report of the progress of operations in the Solomons.

At 2:00 P.M. on October 18, a four-engined Coronado came in low over Nouméa and circled gracefully above Admiral Ghormley's flagship, U.S.S. Argonne. The pilot lowered flaps, eased throttles back, and brought the heavy flying boat to a gentle landing on the glinting waters of the harbor. Even before she moored, a motor whaleboat drew alongside. Vice Admiral William F. Halsey clambered awkwardly out of the Coronado and lowered himself into the bouncing whaleboat.

Halsey, on a familiarization tour of the South Pacific prepara-

tory to assuming command of a carrier task force, had not expected to visit Nouméa on October 18. Indeed, his schedule called
for him to be in Guadalcanal on that particular day. But en route
he had received a surprise message from Nimitz directing him to
proceed at once to Nouméa.

Even before the admiral made his way to the stern sheets, the
boat officer, a young junior grade lieutenant, handed him a sealed
envelope. Halsey ripped it open. Inside was a second sealed envelope marked "SECRET." The admiral tore this open, extracted
a slip of paper, read it twice, and passed it to Colonel Julian P.
Brown, his Marine advisor and confidant. "Jesus Christ and General Jackson!" Halsey said. "This is the hottest potato they ever
handed me!"

The priority dispatch from CincPac was terse:

YOU WILL TAKE COMMAND OF THE SOUTH PACIFIC
AREA AND SOUTH PACIFIC FORCES IMMEDIATELY.[10]

Strong emotion overwhelmed Halsey; he later recorded his immediate reactions as "astonishment, apprehension, and regret, in
that order."[11] In silence, the admiral and his small party rode to
Argonne.

A few minutes after boarding her, Halsey relieved an old and
dear friend. There was no formal change of command ceremony.
Nor, when the news reached Guadalcanal, were there any signs of
apprehension or regret. An air combat information officer, staggering from repeated attacks of fever, heard the news and wrote:
"I'll never forget it! One minute we were too limp with malaria to
crawl out of our foxholes; the next, we were running around
shouting like kids."[12]

Even as Halsey took the reins in confident hands he radioed
Vandegrift to report aboard *Argonne* as soon as the local situation permitted. Halsey wanted a firsthand report; no one in
Nouméa could give him one. No senior member of Ghormley's
staff had personal knowledge of the situation on Guadalcanal.
Neither he nor his chief of staff, Rear Admiral Daniel J. Callaghan, had during the preceding ten weeks been able to spare a day
from paperwork to fly north and see what was going on.

Halsey's conference opened on *Argonne* after dinner, October
23. Principals, in addition to Halsey and Vandegrift, included
Maj. Gen. Patch, Kelly Turner, Millard Harmon, and Lieutenant
General Thomas Holcomb, the Marine Corps Commandant, who

had recently visited Guadalcanal. Vandegrift outlined his situation; then Harmon spoke.

Archie Vandegrift and "Miff" Harmon told their bitter stories. . . . I asked: "Are we going to evacuate or hold?" Archie answered: "I can hold but I've got to have more active support than I've been getting."[13]

Halsey turned to Kelly Turner. The Amphibious Force commander had problems, too, and they were many and deeply troubling. He lacked cargo bottoms; he was critically short of combatant ships to protect those he did have. Enemy air and submarines were a constant threat. Halsey listened quietly to this pessimistic summary.

When Turner finished, Halsey turned to Archer Vandegrift: "Go on back. I'll promise you everything I've got."

As to Ndeni, ComSoPac was unequivocal: "Cancel it."

King withheld announcement of the change in command for a week. When the news was made public, it produced an orgy of speculation in Tokyo, where one commentator hazarded the opinion that Halsey's appointment presaged "withdrawal of all American naval forces from the South Pacific."[14]

At the time Vandegrift received orders to proceed to Nouméa, Lt. Gen. Maruyama had been four days on the road to which he had modestly given his name. The Commanding General was not entirely pleased with the condition of this thoroughfare. Maj. Gen. Nasu's column progressed slowly, and Kawaguchi's lagged. Men's loads were heavy, the terrain rough, and humid heat vicious, the chilling night rains violent. Mountain and antitank guns and heavy mortars were now far behind; the crews manhandling these awkward loads over slippery ridges and through the muck of countless valleys were exhausted. One by one, artillery pieces were abandoned along the rutted and miry trail, its verges strewn with artillery shells, antitank mines, and other heavy impedimenta. On October 21, Maruyama postponed the attack for 48 hours.

Still the men pressed on doggedly. During this march Japanese soldiers, subsisting on nothing more than a few handfuls of rice softened to edible consistency by rain water, again demonstrated their unequaled qualities of tenacity and endurance. But would these, augmented by the animating spirit of *Bushido*, prove enough to guarantee victory? Hyakutake, at least, thought so, and on

October 22 issued orders to the Koli Detachment to embark at the Shortlands on the following day prepared to land near Koli Point when he released the message which would signify capture of the airfield. This dispatch would consist of one word: "BAN-ZAI."

And although he was not aware of it, Hyakutake had another reason for optimism. The Marine command had not yet the slightest suspicion that a major attack threatened from the south. Previous actions near the mouth of the Matanikau had generated a potentially dangerous fixation that any really serious effort could develop only from that direction. This opinion was apparently confirmed by Sumuyoshi's behavior since October 12, when the Japanese artillery commander's howitzers opened spasmodic bombardment of the airfield.

The first shell to explode on the strip revealed that the enemy had succeeded in putting ashore new weapons of disconcertingly large calibre. Frequently shells fuzed for delayed action burst under the runway to maim members of emergency repair parties. This irregular but accurate harassment forced a shift of air operations to "Fighter One." Marines, never at a loss for the appropriate descriptive, had immediately christened this new menace to their continued good health and peace of mind "Pistol Pete." "Pete" was a menace, and in more ways than one. Not only did he successfully interdict Henderson, but he induced a frustration complex in del Valle's formerly supremely confident artillerymen. They could not locate him. They had no sound and flash ranging section, nor could the Air commander afford to expend gasoline to keep observation planes aloft for hours on end for the sole purpose of trying to pinpoint this newest source of affliction.

While aircraft repeatedly attacked Japanese active west of the Matanikau, pilots and observers consistently reported other areas "Negative." Daily, 3rd Battalion, First Marines, and 3rd Battalion, Seventh Marines, now holding the Matanikau battle position, exchanged shots with Japanese across the river. Sumuyoshi did his best to keep the defenders' attention focused on this sector.

On October 20 he sent out a probe of two infantry-supported tanks, which ostentatiously prepared to cross the sandspit. One was hit and knocked out; the other hastily withdrew. Sumuyoshi replied with the first artillery concentrations the Japanese had produced, and marines now learned what it was to be on the receiving end of heavy artillery fire. Just after sunset the following day, nine enemy tanks milled about in the same area. Again anti-tank fire disposed of one; the others, their engines roaring, disappeared before gunners could lay sights on them.

In early morning on October 23, Maj. Gen. Nasu's two assault battalions moved into final assembly areas to the rear of their lines of departure, and Nasu reported to Maruyama that he could meet the attack schedule. His troops rested. Their harrowing trek over, they were now hidden from aerial observation by the protecting canopy of giant jungle trees. Their morale was high. Officer patrols pushed cautiously through tangled vegetation to focus field glasses on the airfield. The day was brilliantly clear. With mounting excitement, the Japanese observers described to their men routine activities within the unsuspecting perimeter.

In the skies above, there was considerable activity at the usual hour; the Japanese rarely varied from the established pattern of noontime raids. This day, 20 *Zeros* flew escort for 16 *Bettys*. All enemy fighters were shot down, four by a squadron commander, Major Joseph E. Foss, who had recently arrived on the island. One bomber fell in flames and three wobbled westward trailing smoke.

Just after this raid was repulsed, Maruyama received bad news. The right wing—Kawaguchi's—had not yet reached assembly areas and could not possibly jump off at sunset. The Division commander had no alternative but to postpone his attack until 5:00 P.M. the following day. After doing so, he telephoned Kawaguchi from his command post at "Centipede-Shaped Ridge," abruptly relieved him of command, and directed Colonel Toshinaro Shoji to take over the right wing.[15]

And now other difficulties inherent in any complex plan became apparent. Radio communication between Maruyama and Sumuyoshi broke down. Maruyama got through to Hyakutake, however, and Seventeenth Army managed to inform Admiral Yamamoto (whose Combined Fleet was to render direct fire support and cut off the expected American retreat) of the 24-hour delay. Yamamoto, discouraged by these developments, set a rendezvous with fleet tankers and withdrew his striking force to the north to refuel.

A respected U. S. Navy and Marine Corps maxim states a profound military truth: "There is always some poor dope who doesn't get the word." In this case the unfortunate one—and through no fault of his own—was Maj. Gen. Sumuyoshi. The artillery commander, stricken with malaria, now lay in a coma in his dugout shelter. If Maruyama's last message again postponing the main attack ever reached Sumuyoshi's headquarters west of the Matanikau, the general never saw it, and no member of his staff did anything about it.[16] Sumuyoshi's medium tanks therefore jumped off a few minutes after 6:00 P.M. on October 23, exactly as scheduled, and rumbled toward the sandspit. It was their last rumble.

The marines were waiting for just this. Colonel del Valle's expert artillerymen, always ready to respond to calls for fire, brought concentrations down on the sandspit, on the Japanese-held bank of the river, and along the coastal track west of it. Dug-in antitank guns held their fires as gunners counted one, then another, a third, a fourth, a fifth, a sixth, a seventh, an eighth, a ninth tank emerge from the jungle and waddle onto the spit. Behind them, a few infantrymen appeared. Finally, sweating gun captains received the word. Everything that could shoot opened. In less than three minutes the tanks stopped, all but one perforated. As ammunition racked inside their turrets exploded, surviving crew members climbed out and fled, to be shot in the back. The foot soldiers silently withdrew.

One tank made the east bank. A thoughtful marine slipped a hand grenade in its left track as the tank passed conveniently near his foxhole. The explosion tore the treads, and the tank swerved sharply left, making for the sand bar. Three shells from a 75-mm.-gunned half-track ripped into its thin armor plate and exploded dully. No crew members emerged. Japanese infantry never really got started, and for good reason: the artillery slaughtered over 600 as they waited in assembly areas. Concentrations laid on the coastal track blew apart three more operational tanks.[17]

But General Sumuyoshi had succeeded to a degree. He had drawn attention to the Matanikau to the exclusion of other sectors. As yet, Division apprehended no danger to the area where, in a matter of hours, Puller's battalion and the 2nd Battalion, One Hundred Sixty-fourth Infantry, would be put to the test. Indeed, on the previous day, a battalion (Hanneken's) of the Seventh Marines had been pulled out of the southern sector defenses and dispatched to the Matanikau. While on the march, Hanneken was ordered to extend the left flank of the battle position to the southeast. On the day following Sumuyoshi's noisy and costly distractions, this battalion began digging in on a ridge which formed a strong natural defensive position.

In the meantime Division surveyed the ammunition and gasoline situation with justified apprehension. In the preceding 48 hours, del Valle's 75- and 105-mm. howitzers had fired practically all the artillery shells on the island. Barely enough aviation gas remained to fuel fighters for one interception. Urgent messages went to Nouméa begging for shells and gas. That evening Douglas transports landed with sufficient amounts of both to keep artillery in business and planes in the air for about two days.

During the day, Maruyama conferred with his subordinates at the command post south of Centipede-Shaped Heights, and distributed a final order for the attack. This model of brevity was vague:

ORDERS OF THE 2ND DIVISION
(Issued at 1200, 24 October)

The Division has succeeded in reaching the rear flank of the enemy in absolute secrecy.

In accordance with plans of my own, I intend to exterminate the enemy around the airfield in one blow.

Both left and right [wings] will begin the charge at 1700 and penetrate the enemy lines.

I will stay at present location until 1400 [and] will then head for the airfield behind the left [wing] unit.[18]

Now nature intervened. At exactly 3:00 P.M., as Japanese troops started to move toward lines of departure, the heavens opened, and in a few minutes cascading rain turned the jungle floor into a swamp. Communication between units went out. Battalion commanders lost companies, companies lost platoons, platoons lost squads. The attack did not jump off at 5:00 P.M., and confusion reigned for two hours. When the rain stopped, Japanese officers began to pull their scattered units together. And although Shoji's right wing was not yet in position, the impatient Maruyama ordered Nasu to jump off on the left as soon as possible. Shortly after midnight, Colonel Shojiro Ishimiya, at the head of the 1st Battalion of his Twenty-ninth Infantry, fired a flare to signal the attack.[19] Clouds obscured the moon and spattering rain again began to fall. Ishimiya's first wave hit a Marine outpost, engulfed it, and at two places forced a way through the wire in front of one of Puller's companies. The advance was contained and most of the attackers killed.

The rain was now falling steadily. As artillery and mortar fires checked repeated Japanese thrusts, Division began feeding elements of the 3rd Battalion, One Hundred Sixty-fourth Infantry, into Puller's lines. He needed them. The soldiers, led in small groups to their first encounter with the enemy, responded magnificently. By squads and platoons they plugged holes, confined penetrations and, side by side with Puller's marines, threw back every attack save one.

This was almost an individual effort by the commander of the Twenty-ninth Infantry. Ishimiya, accompanied only by nine officers and men, and with the colors of his regiment folded under his tunic, somehow worked his way deep into Puller's position, where for the next 48 hours he and his dwindling group remained.[20] Before dawn a message reached Hyakutake that the airfield was in Japanese hands.

Without waiting to corroborate this, Hyakutake put the report on the air. Could the basis for the false report have been the exploit of the rash Colonel Ishimiya? This has never been ascertained, but in any event the colonel's foray steeled Maruyama's determination. He would regroup and resume the attack. The commander of a proud division could not "turn his back on the fact that the Commander of the 29th Infantry had carried a Rising Sun banner . . . into the enemy lines."[21]

The Twenty-ninth Infantry had taken a terrible beating. Almost 1000 corpses lay on and in front of the American wire and in and around foxholes and emplacements. As Sunday's sun mounted, the bodies began to decompose. It was now apparent that the attack from the south was the main effort, and early Sunday morning fresh units began moving into position to back up Puller's marines and the soldiers commanded by Lieutenant Colonel Robert K. Hall, U.S.A. Several artillery batteries shifted to new locations from which they could reinforce the fire of the single battalion previously in direct support of the southern sector. As the brassy sun beat down, the sickening odor of death enveloped the grassy ridges where marines and soldiers prepared to make another stand.

Vandegrift estimated the total enemy dead as "at least 2000," and added that the corpses stacked in front of his lines presented a "serious disposal problem." He reported his own casualties during the last few days as 86 killed, 119 wounded.[22]

13

AT DAWN on the day to be known as "Dugout Sunday," Sumuyoshi's 6-inch howitzers resumed harassing fires on Henderson. At "Fighter One," where aircraft had earlier sought refuge, "ready" pilots sweated out morning hours waiting for the soggy strip to dry sufficiently to permit slithering take-offs. High-flying fighters from Rabaul, unchallenged, lost no time passing the word to home base that defensive planes were grounded, and minutes later the first batch of *Zeros* rolled down the Buin runway to take advantage of an opportunity long awaited: to blast the Americans with no fear of being shot out of the sky by diving Grummans.

As the blistering sun climbed, Puller's marines and Hall's soldiers silently dug and strung wire. At Centipede-Shaped Heights, Maruyama prepared orders for a new night attack. In Tulagi harbor, World War I flush-deck destroyers *Trever* and *Zane* (Lieutenant Commanders Dwight M. Agnew and Peyton L. Wirtz) quietly finished delivery of torpedoes, high-test gas, oil and ammunition for the four MTBs they had towed in the night before. Yippie *284* and tug *Seminole* left Tulagi for Kukum on a routine run with passengers and freight. This unusual tranquillity was soon to be shattered.

At 9:52 A.M. lookouts in *Trever*'s crow's-nest reported three fast Japanese destroyers rushing past Savo on a course toward Sealark Channel. These ships were carrying Hyakutake's Koli Detachment to its destination east of the perimeter.[1] Vice Admiral Mikawa had planned this move carefully, and given the signal for its execution, "BANZAI," during the preceding night only moments after he received incorrect information from Hyakutake that the airfield was in Japanese hands.

Agnew of *Trever* had no time to discuss possible courses of action with his colleague, Lt. Cdr. Wirtz of *Zane*. There was but one course of action: to get out of Tulagi harbor, and that as speedily as possible. Otherwise, the 5-inch guns carried by the Japanese would mangle the smaller Americans as they lay in harbor.

At 10:04, with *Trever* building up speed to 26 knots, the two "cans" headed for Sealark Channel "cutting all corners as closely as possible." For some strange reason—perhaps because all eyes were turned apprehensively to the skies—the Japanese did not sight them for almost 15 minutes. Then the captain of the leading destroyer picked them out, broke battle signals, rang up flank speed, and swerved to a collision course. The bigger ships closed fast, and at 10:33 their first rounds bracketed the fleeing Americans whose 3-inch popguns could not reach their pursuers. One shell burst on *Trever*'s after gun, demolished it and the "spud locker," killed three sailors and wounded nine. "At this point escape seemed impossible." But Agnew now turned hard left and again hard right and entered Nggela Channel, a pass laced with coral outcroppings. *Trever* and *Zane* were indicating 29 knots; *Trever*'s No. 2 boiler casing burned through. At this moment, three *Wildcats* that had somehow managed to stagger off "Fighter One" tumbled out of the sun and turned the Japanese to the west.[2]

Pursued by rolling fighters, and caught in a storm of armor-piercing and incendiary bullets, the destroyers practically rammed tug *Seminole* and Yippie *284*. These innocents had just arrived off Kukum when they sighted the Japanese. Both turned and lumbered back toward Tulagi. The fast-moving Japanese destroyers let go with everything. Yippie *284* sank in less than two minutes; *Seminole*, loaded with aviation gas, flared immediately from stem to stern. Colonel Pepper's 5-inch guns emplaced near the Point intervened, and holed one of the interlopers. A mixed flight of *Wildcats* and SBDs took to the air to bomb and strafe the Japanese. Dive bombers scored two direct hits, and the enemy departed in the direction of Savo with bloodied decks.

Fire support for this now aborted Koli Detachment landing was to have been provided by light cruiser *Yura* and five destroyers. Before reaching Savo, these six ships sheered northeast to follow the north coast of Florida. They cleared the eastern tip of the island and then swung south at high speed heading for Indispensable Strait. But as they ran along Florida, an unarmed search plane had sighted *Yura* and her brood, made an urgent report, and returned to base. Air operations docketed the group for attention as soon as bombed-up SBDs could lift off.

Geiger's flyers fell on *Yura* at 12:55, when Lieutenant Commander Eldridge, leading the first strike, dove through heavy flak to plant a 500-pounder on the cruiser's forecastle. The bomb chewed through her deck and blew a chunk off her bow. *Yura* turned awkwardly and headed for the open sea north of Santa Isabel. During the afternoon, she was attacked by three flights, the last of which, again led by Eldridge, left her burning and listing. Destroyer *Akizuke* was damaged. At sunset, B-17s from Espiritu and another flight of Henderson SBDs hit her, and her captain requested permission to beach his ship. But *Yura* was sinking, and he abandoned her, a wreck.[3] Destroyer *Yudachi* torpedoed her.

Submarine *Amberjack* had a periscope view of these kaleidoscopic events. Her presence underlined the critical fuel situation: at Espiritu Santo, *Amberjack* had been hastily converted to carry 9000 gallons of aviation gasoline. With tanks full of this precious cargo, and two hundred 100-pound bombs stocked in her forward torpedo compartments, she lay quietly just below the surface of Sealark Channel waiting patiently for things to quiet down. She waited for 24 hours.

While the waters around Guadalcanal were thus disturbed, there was no peace in the air. In early afternoon 16 *Bettys* with 27 *Zeros* arrived. Seventeen *Zeros* were shot down, four by Major Foss, who had bagged a like number the previous day. Two Grumman pilots jumped and were pulled out of the water. Four returning *Wildcats* skidded in on dead-stick landings; six more piled up trying to take off from a still treacherous field. Four *Bettys* fell flaming into Sealark Channel; another crashed less than a mile from Henderson. An hour later, nine escorted *Aichis* wasted their bombs on Geiger's boneyard. After this flurry, "Condition Red"—which had prevailed since early morning—was finally lifted, and those who could do so hastened to view the wrecked *Betty*. By Sunday evening she was a well-plucked bird.

In Rabaul, Vice Admiral Mikawa, understandably disturbed by the events of the day, and "in view of the circumstances," decided to withdraw his forces to safer waters "until the recapture of the Guadalcanal airfield was definitely reported."[4]

The raids and dogfights which punctuated "Dugout Sunday" served Maruyama's purpose well. He was left to his own devices, and spent the day reorganizing his two wings for a "final death-defying night attack." This assault commenced after dark and

resulted only in further slaughter. Maj. Gen. Nasu was killed leading a charge; Colonel Hiroyasu fell, as did four battalion commanders. Half the officers of the Sendai Division were killed or
seriously wounded in this holocaust.

> The commander of the Division had not a single reserve left;
> no food was to be had nor any to be expected. . . . even if all
> died fighting, it would have been impossible to tear the enemy
> positions. No hope was left.[5]

Maruyama directed Shoji to beat his way east to Taivu; the
general led the remainder of his shattered force over the road to
which he had with such optimism given his name on October 15.
He informed Hyakutake of his intention to constitute a strong
base on the upper Lunga, and there prepare for further offensive
operations.

What had Colonel Oka been up to during Maruyama's attack
on October 24, with which his was supposed to be coordinated?
In moving to his jump-off position, Oka encountered terrible
terrain. Although he had opportunity to make a reconnaissance,
he had neglected to do so. His men had to break trail every foot
of the way. In two days, Oka covered less than two miles. He
launched his delayed attack in the early morning of October 26,
by which time Maruyama's goose was thoroughly cooked. Oka,
too, was thrown back with heavy losses. After a short, vicious
fight he was ejected from a foothold gained in Hanneken's position by a hastily collected group of cooks, bandsmen, and run-
ners. The climax was reached and passed in a few wild minutes
that saw 25 marines killed, 14 wounded.[6] The rumor soon spread
that one of the cooks had felled a Japanese officer with a pancake.

The Japanese land offensive of late October failed not just because American artillery was flexible and its fire accurate, or because marines and soldiers fought with skill and determination.
These were the ultimate factors, but the Japanese concept of operations made its contributions. Again a tactical pattern broke
down under the weight of inherent complexity, failure of communications, inadequate supporting fire, and lack of coordination
in time and space.

The debacle earlier suffered by Kawaguchi should have been a
warning to Lt. Gen. Hyakutake to eschew any but a relatively
simple plan, one which would not only exclude movement of

large bodies of troops for any great distance through the jungle, but which also would permit artillery, mortars and flat trajectory antitank guns to support the infantry. The enemy's impetuosity, arrogance, and tactical inflexibility were boons to Vandegrift, who had now profited from them on three occasions.

The positions the Japanese had tried in vain to "tear" were held —and bravely held—by Puller's battalion, and squad and platoon increments of infantrymen. The soldiers, who marched forward through blackness and driving rain, took their places in the lines at a critical moment and, together with marines, saved Henderson Field as it had been saved six weeks earlier at Edson's Ridge.

In this, its first battle, the One Hundred Sixty-fourth Infantry Regiment gained the full respect of marines. Before midnight of October 24, the word "doggie" was a depreciatory term marines used when they referred to members of the United States Army. But after the fight with the Sendai Division, Colonel Bryant Moore's men were respectfully addressed as "Soldier." They had earned the title. A few days after "Dugout Sunday" Clifton Bledsoe Cates, Colonel commanding the First Marines, wrote Moore:

> The officers and men of the First Marines salute you for a most wonderful piece of work. . . . will you please extend our sincere congratulations to all concerned. We are honored to serve with a unit such as yours.[7]

American casualties in the late October ground actions were slight compared to those suffered by the Japanese: fewer than 200 soldiers and marines killed; another 200 wounded.

How many members of the Sendai Division died in the retreat to the upper Lunga will never be known, but they were numbered in the hundreds. For, in the last days of October, Maruyama's routed column suffered as Kawaguchi's had some six weeks earlier, Again, Japanese soldiers ate bark and roots, drank from stagnant puddles, and gnawed their rifle slings. But they could endure—and many would—to fight again.

Although the climax of the October offensive was played out south of Henderson Field on heat-seared ridges and in their bordering jungles, there remained an ultimate act to this particular drama. Its scene was the open sea and sky more than 300 miles east of Guadalcanal. To this area, Yamamoto had dispatched his

"Guadalcanal Support Force"—the Second and Third Fleets. The mission assigned was either to intercept convoys bringing reinforcements or, as Yamamoto thought more probable, to liquidate Americans attempting to flee the "righteous bayonets" of a victorious imperial army. Vice Admiral Nagumo was Officer in Tactical Command (OTC).[8]

THIRD FLEET
(Vice Admiral Chuichi Nagumo)
Fleet Carriers: *Shokaku, Zuikaku*
Light Carrier: *Zuiho*
Battleships: *Hiei, Kirishima*
Heavy Cruisers: *Suzuya, Kumano, Tone, Chikuma*
Light Cruiser: *Nagara*
Destroyers: 12

SECOND FLEET
(Vice Admiral Nobutake Kondo)
Fleet Carrier: *Junyo*
Battleships: *Kongo, Haruna*
Heavy Cruisers: *Atago, Takao, Chokai, Maya, Miyako, Haguro*
Light Cruiser: *Jintsu*
Destroyers: 12

To challenge Yamamoto's powerful fleets, Halsey had Task Force 61 (Rear Admiral Thomas C. Kinkaid), which he expected to arrive in his area from Pearl Harbor on October 24. He directed Kinkaid to rendezvous on that date north of the New Hebrides with Rear Admiral George D. Murray's Task Force 17, and to assume tactical command. At the same time, he ordered Rear Admiral Willis Augustus Lee to operate his Task Force 64 (battleship *Washington*, three cruisers, and six destroyers) separately.

TASK FORCE 61
(Rear Admiral Thomas C. Kinkaid, OTC)
Fleet Carrier: *Enterprise*
Battleship: *South Dakota*
Cruisers: *Portland, San Juan*
Destroyers: 8

TASK FORCE 17
(Rear Admiral George D. Murray)
Fleet Carrier: *Hornet*
Cruisers: *Northampton, Pensacola,*
San Diego, Juneau
Destroyers: 6

Nagumo commanded a force which, if handled properly, could gain the decisive victory Yamamoto had sought in vain since December 7, 1941. The Japanese were stacking four carriers with 212 planes against two with 171; four battleships against one; twelve cruisers against six, and twenty-four destroyers against fourteen. Nagumo had every reason to exude confidence. On October 25 he refueled 450 miles north of the Santa Cruz Islands and headed south. Flight deck crews prepared his combat aircraft to strike any American ships Japanese search planes discovered.

Meanwhile, Kinkaid's much smaller and altogether weaker force steamed north. As had happened before, each admiral was certain that enemy carriers were, or soon would be, within lethal range of his own. The problem each faced was the same: to locate the enemy and strike his flight decks, desirably before he had launched. At eleven minutes after midnight of October 25, a searching *Catalina* of Rear Admiral Aubrey Fitch's land-based air forces provided an answer to the Americans and rang the bell for the first round of the "Battle of the Santa Cruz Islands."[9]

The pilot who spotted the enemy task force illuminated it with flares, reported Japanese strength and approximate location, then dropped a bomb in the general direction of *Zuikaku*. The Japanese reversed course and steered north. The pilot of the PBY shadowed long enough to broadcast this piece of news and disappeared into the night.[10]

A few hours later, Halsey sent his subordinate commanders a three-word message:

"ATTACK REPEAT ATTACK"[11]

This imperative dispatch produced action. Before dawn, American dive bombers and torpedo planes rose from flight decks to find and strike Nagumo's carriers. Their first victim was *Zuiho*: an accurate American pilot scored once on her flight deck. Minutes later she was blazing and her captain reported his ship "impotent to send or receive planes."

Now the big carriers began to hammer each other. At 7:27 A.M. American SBDs delivered a package of 1000-pounders to *Shokaku.* Six pierced her flight deck, exploded in the hangers, wrecked her elevators, tore open fuel lines, ripped cables, and killed and wounded about one hundred of her crew. Twenty dive bombers piled on cruiser *Chikuma;* after five direct hits she slowed, turned north, and limped slowly away, listing. Kinkaid scratched two enemy flattops and a heavy cruiser.[12]

Two and a half hours later Nagumo had the pleasure of scratching one American carrier. This was *Hornet.* Between 10:10 and 10:20 A.M. she caught two 500-pounders on her flight deck. Two near misses started hull plates; an unarmed torpedo plane crashed on her deck and exploded, and two torpedoes pierced her hull. A dive bomber—possibly the first *kamikaze* of record—smashed into her superstructure. In less than ten minutes *Hornet* had been hit by two bombs, two torpedoes and two planes.

She was dead in the water, but officers and men tried valiantly to save their ship. As damage control and fire-fighting teams worked to restore engine power and to confine fires, doctors and corpsmen collected the burned, the wounded and the dying, and began their battle to save limbs and lives. Cruiser *Northampton* closed the carrier, passed hawsers, and took her in tow. During this uproar Japanese submarine *I-21* sank destroyer *Porter.* Fifteen sailors were trapped in her firerooms and went down with their ship.

Nagumo was not yet sure that a second American carrier was in the area. But in a few minutes, intercepts of indiscreet voice transmissions resolved his doubts, and at ten-thirty he launched a search and strike group from *Zuikaku.* These planes located *Enterprise* 40 minutes later, and for the next hour and a half the "Big E" fought off repeated attacks. The first wave, 24 dive bombers, fell on her through broken clouds; she took two hits and an uncomfortably close near miss. Fortunately, these three bombs affected neither power nor steering. Seventeen torpedo planes were next to arrive. Nine attackers closed the carrier, five from the starboard side, four from port. Captain Osborne B. Hardison took high-speed evasive action and his antiaircraft gunners did the rest. The nine Japanese were shot out of the air.

Until this point, Kinkaid had received no mail from carrier *Junyo,* but her air group soon began to deliver it.[13] A few minutes before noon, flights of her dive bombers plunged on battleship *South Dakota* and destroyer *Hughes*. A torpedo plane crashed on destroyer *Smith*. Ten attackers were splashed by ships' AA.

The Americans were about ready to call it quits, but Nagumo was not. He launched another series of strikes. Between 12:20 and 12:45 twenty bombers made gliding attacks on the carrier, and twenty-four planes struck at cruiser *San Juan*. She absorbed one direct hit and was shaken by five near misses. At 4:20 Nagumo's planes hit *Hornet* again. All attacks were pressed home with determination.[14]

As *Northampton* cast off tow lines, Captain Charles P. Mason gave orders to abandon *Hornet*. Members of her crew reluctantly left the shattered carrier. She was dying, but did not want to go. As *Wasp* had done, she hung on. The water was thick with enemy submarines, and Kinkaid wisely decided that *Enterprise*, the only American flight deck remaining in the South Pacific, could not be further jeopardized.

He directed destroyers *Mustin* and *Anderson* to dispose of abandoned *Hornet*. As she had resisted Japanese bombs, this stout ship, the seventh in the Navy to bear her name, now resisted with equal stubbornness the shells and torpedoes which ripped into her torn sides.[15] Finally Kinkaid ordered *Mustin* and *Anderson* to withdraw. Of over 200 casualties, 108 wounded were rescued. *Hornet* was found early the next morning by Japanese destroyers, and suffered burial at their hands.

Enterprise, meanwhile, had recovered her own planes and most of *Hornet*'s. But with her flight deck cluttered, she could not accommodate the last batch of 13 dive bombers. She waved them off and directed them to make for Espiritu Santo. There they landed safely—with enough gas to fly for five more minutes.

Tactically, Santa Cruz was a stand-off. The Combined Fleet returned to Truk; the Americans to their bases in the New Hebrides and Nouméa. But the battle had one important effect on the struggle for possession of Henderson Field: It contributed mightily to the deadly attrition of Japan's naval air arm. Sixty-nine experienced pilots did not return to their flight decks after Santa Cruz. During the ten-day period which culminated in this battle, the Japanese lost 200 aircraft. As they fell into the sea and the jungle, these planes carried with them pilots, bombardiers, gunners, navigators, and radiomen. Since the last week of August, the Japanese Naval Air Force had lost almost 500 aircraft in combat in the South Pacific, and, as a direct result of the inexperience of replacement pilots, had suffered, as well, extremely heavy operational losses.

No inkling of the true situation filtered through to the Japanese public. The navy, close-mouthed as usual, kept the army guessing, too. Broadcasts in Chinese, Japanese, French, and English announced that at Santa Cruz the "invincible Navy" again "achieved brilliant war results," which marked "new achievements in the annals of naval warfare."[16] In a summary on October 28, the naval spokesman announced that since hostilities began, 609 enemy warships and transports had been sunk, 131 damaged, and 9 captured. He was able to give also a figure on Allied planes shot down or otherwise destroyed to date: 3702.

Imperial GHQ was not, however, entirely taken in by its own public information office, and the continuing attrition on land, on sea, and in the air impelled it to make a new appraisal of the situation. The optimism characteristic of previous Tokyo estimates had not entirely evaporated; even after the events of this last week of October, Army and Navy Sections could not bring themselves to face unpalatable facts objectively. That the Emperor's invincible army had absorbed a series of beatings; that his "sea eagles" had been unable to establish air superiority over Guadalcanal, and that his navy could not effectively support the army's operations, were not considered suitable subjects for general staff conversations.

Actually, Imperial GHQ was again misinformed by reports of operational naval commanders. As after Midway they had kept secret the severity of their own losses and inflated those of the Americans, so after Santa Cruz they again misled their superiors in Tokyo. Santa Cruz, they said, had cost the Americans two battleships and three carriers sunk, with other units heavily damaged.[17]

The army, therefore, thought it possible to continue the offensive by a "systematic concentration of fighting forces" whose attacks would be supported by naval guns, air bombardment, and artillery fire. The policy of "making close surprise attacks" was to be discarded in favor of a massive direct effort.[18] Pursuant to this decision, GHQ assigned the 21st Independent Mixed Brigade (less one battalion garrisoning Wake Island) to the O/B of Seventeenth Army and ordered the 51st Division to proceed to Rabaul. Colonel Takushiro Hattori, chief of the operations division at GHQ, was assigned as operational liaison officer on Hyakutake's staff. The new plans provided for concentration of all forces on the upper Lunga and west of the Matanikau. Colonel Shoji, who was near Koli Point with over 2000 men salvaged from Maruyama's right wing, was ordered to start to march around the perimeter on November 3.

But a number of Japanese officers at the front had become increasingly doubtful of the success of any plan which did not provide for neutralization of American air power in the target area. They were convinced that repeated massive bombing attacks with strong fighter cover were the only possible means to break American resistance. These views they now presented to Imperial GHQ. One course of action, urged without success by Admiral Mikawa, was to suspend further attempts to reinforce until a large force of bombers could be assembled at Rabaul and additional *Zeros* advanced to Buin. "To our regret, however, the Supreme Command stuck persistently to reinforcing Guadalcanal. . . ."[19]

The Navy had given everything it could to Halsey, but on Guadalcanal the fighter situation was still precarious. Marshall and Arnold were reluctant to part with more airplanes. Both were fully committed to build-up in the United Kingdom (BOLERO), and to impending TORCH. The decisions to transfer American strength to the British Isles and to invade North Africa had been made by the President and the Prime Minister in accordance with the strategy that dictated liquidation of the European Axis before mounting a major offensive in the Pacific. Marshall and Arnold were caught in a most unpleasant position.[20] On the one hand was the insistent Admiral King; on the other, Roosevelt and Churchill, backed to the hilt by the British Chiefs.[21]

However, through long October weeks, Roosevelt had watched the situation in the Solomons with growing concern, and finally, worried with the reluctance of the Joint Chiefs to allocate resources to secure this important position beyond hazard, addressed a memorandum to them on October 24:

> My anxiety about the Southwest Pacific is to make sure that every possible weapon gets into that area to hold Guadalcanal, and that having held it in this crisis that munitions and planes and crews are on the way to take advantage of our success.[22]

Imperial GHQ realized, as did Washington, that the value of Guadalcanal transcended that of a strategic position, as this term is used in military parlance. In both capitals, the island had become a symbol, and its possession a point of national prestige.

On Tuesday, October 27, 1942, the *New York Times* reported that no one in authority in Washington "would hazard a guess as to the outcome of the current engagement," but that all agreed it would be fought "to a decisive finish" and would probably determine the course "of the war in the south-western Pacific for the next year." Knox refused comment, and King, who detested newspapermen with a fervor equal to that displayed by the American Civil War general, William Tecumseh Sherman, maintained his customary icy silence. In Pearl Harbor, Nimitz confined his remarks to observing that the crisis had not yet been reached.

A less pessimistic attitude was evident on Guadalcanal where plans were being laid in Division operations to drive the Japanese west of the Poha River and establish an advanced battle position at Kokumbona.

14

EVEN BEFORE Roosevelt's instruction of October 24 to the JCS, some steps had been taken to strengthen American positions in the Pacific. On October 19, General Marshall alerted the 25th Division (Major General J. Lawton Collins), on garrison duty in Hawaii, to move as directed to either Halsey's or MacArthur's area. The following day, Halsey had canceled the Ndeni operation and ordered the One Hundred Forty-seventh Infantry (previously detached from the 37th Division and slated as occupying force) to prepare to go forward.

An advance echelon of the Army's 43rd Division, also on the move, was delayed en route. On October 26, the *President Coolidge*, a converted transpacific liner carrying one of its regiments to Espiritu Santo, hit two U. S. mines and sank as she entered the harbor. Few lives were lost, but all the regiment's equipment went down with the ship.

This misfortune was not a fatal one. Other troops were on the way to the island, among them the reinforced Eighth Marines (Colonel Richard H. Jeschke), from Samoa; artillery units; Seabees, and the Second Marine Raider Battalion (Lieutenant Colonel Evans F. Carlson). Replacement planes and pilots, too, were soon to come. At this juncture they were needed more than fresh ground troops: as of October 26, Geiger's strength stood at 29 combat aircraft: 12 *Wildcats*, 11 SBDs, 3 P-400s, 3 P-39s.[1] Most of these required repairs.

As Maruyama's shattered column crawled through the implacable jungle to the south of Mount Austen, and Col. Shoji struggled eastward toward Koli Point, Vandegrift drew plans for still another attack across the Matanikau. Colonel John M. Arthur's reinforced Second Marines (less an infantry battalion) was ferried from Tulagi to take part in this push to the Poha, about one and a half miles west of Kokumbona. The Fifth Marines and the reinforced 3rd Battalion of the Seventh—the "Whaling Group"—were alerted. The attack, scheduled to jump off at daybreak, November 1, was to be supported by artillery concentrations, dive bombers, and ships' gunfire.

And this time there was to be no attempt to force a bloody crossing of the Matanikau at the sand bar. Instead, the Fifth Marines would cross upstream on infantry bridges constructed with planking and empty fuel drums by the engineers. The Whaling Group would ford at the forks, attack to the west, and protect the left flank of the Fifth Marines. Colonel Edson, who had spent a considerable amount of time in this unpleasant neighborhood, would command the operation.

A more imaginative plan would have called for the Second Marines, backed by the available battalion of the One Sixty-fourth, and with Whaling's Group swinging on Arthur's inland flank, to punch along the coastal road, while Edson's battle-tested Fifth moved by sea to hook decisively into Japanese vitals between Kokumbona and Tassafaronga. This scheme, or one similar to it, was indeed contemplated. But various factors weighed against its adoption.

First, it was evident to Vandegrift and the men on whose judgment he heavily relied—Thomas, Twining, Cates, del Valle and Edson—that advantage must be taken as quickly as possible of Maruyama's defeat. A hooking operation demanded detailed prior reconnaissance of the coastal area as far west as Doma Cove. In late September, because of ignorance of the enemy and the terrain, Vandegrift had barely escaped feeding Puller's battalion to the lions in just this type of maneuver. He was not about to repeat his earlier mistake.

Second, this attack introduced Arthur's command to combat, and until a unit—any unit—has gone through the ordeal once, to assess its true effectiveness is difficult. Will the commander be overly cautious, hesitant, vacillating? Or will he be rash, thoughtless, careless of his flanks? These questions, and others similar to them, suggested that the Second Marines go in for the first time under the aegis of the Fifth.

Finally, could a hooking operation be given sustained support by sea and air? Here lay the real crux of the matter. And the decision reached, based on the Navy's record to date and an inventory of aircraft, was that it could not. Circumstances combined to dictate the direct approach.

Accordingly, at midnight on Saturday, October 31, engineers began throwing three foot bridges across the Matanikau. They completed the task at dawn and five minutes later del Valle's artillery broke the first planned concentration in the zone of action of the Fifth Marines. SBDs and P-39s ranged along the coastal track; nineteen B-17s from Espiritu dumped 350 100-pound bombs on Kokumbona, and *San Francisco, Helena* and destroyer *Sterrett,* which during the night had interdicted the track, closed on Point Cruz to deliver close-range destructive fires.

The crossing proceeded as scheduled, and the attack jumped off at seven o'clock. But the Japanese were well dug in. Along the coast, the 1st Battalion, Fifth, met dogged resistance. On its left, the 2nd Battalion (Major Lewis W. Walt) pushed ahead, and further inland the Whaling Group encountered only isolated groups of Japanese. Behind the advancing Fifth Marines, the engineers threw a 10-ton vehicular bridge across the river. Before dark, November 1, Edson halted just short of Point Cruz and organized for the night. His units were well positioned for the compressing attack he planned for the following morning.

At dawn, Edson directed Walt, one of the most aggressive battalion commanders the Guadalcanal campaign produced, to turn his battalion 90 degrees right and attack toward the sea. By midmorning, Walt's assault companies reached the coast west of Point Cruz. The Japanese—estimated as a battalion—were trapped. Edson now called forward Arthur's Second Marines. In column of battalions they bypassed the Fifth Marines and picked up the drive to the west. Edson had committed all he had, but needed more if he were quickly to achieve the results expected. Division released the 1st Battalion, One Hundred Sixty-fourth (Lt. Col. Frank C. Richards, U.S.A.), and Edson constituted it his reserve.

On Tuesday, November 3, the Point Cruz pocket was reduced by the Fifth Marines: over 300 Japanese dead were counted, twelve antitank guns, a howitzer, and 34 machine guns taken. On orders from Division, Edson passed command to Arthur, and the Fifth Marines returned to the perimeter.

The Japanese made frantic efforts to stop the advance to the west. Maruyama was "far in the upper reaches of the Lunga River," and no help could be expected from that quarter. Hyakutake plugged holes with army headquarters personnel, sick, wounded, engineers, service troops; every able-bodied man in the rear area was hurriedly sent forward to fight.[2]

By nightfall on the third day of the attack, the Americans had pushed the enemy to a position about a mile west of Point Cruz and Hyakutake requested immediate reinforcement. At the Shortlands, Major General Takeo Ito, commanding the Infantry Group of the 38th Division, had anticipated this order, and began embarking his headquarters and the Two Hundred Twenty-eighth Infantry (less 3rd Battalion) minutes after it was received. That night, seventeen destroyers brought his troops safely to Kamimbo and Tassafaronga. Ito lost no time; as they landed, the men formed up and started marching to the east.

While the attack continued west of the Matanikau, a new situation was developing at Tetere, twelve miles east of the perimeter, where Colonel Shoji had arrived with approximately 2500 officers and men of his right wing who had survived the night attacks of late October. At Tetere, Shoji found 131 wounded stragglers. He was short of medical personnel and supplies, but was able to give the wounded men rudimentary attention. When the colonel set out on his march to the coast, he had been told to expect reinforcements to land near Koli at about midnight, November 3. On the night of the second, Shoji issued a double ration of rice to his hungry men.[3]

On the same day, Halsey's intelligence section informed Vandegrift that the "Express" would arrive the following night and discharge east of Koli.[4] Division pulled Hanneken's tried but tired battalion out of the lines and ordered it to hit the road east. During late afternoon of November 3, after a 12-hour march, Hanneken forded the Metapona some three miles east of Koli Point, and set up to receive visitors from the sea. Less than a mile to the east, at Gavaga Creek, Shoji prepared to welcome fresh troops, rice and bullets. Neither commander was aware of the other's presence.

Near midnight, marines on beach observation discerned the silhouettes of five ships which they correctly identified as a transport, a cruiser, and three destroyers.[5] The shapes hove to and commenced discharging, but at Gavaga. The night was moonless; Hanneken was unable to intervene. Nor was he able to confirm this anticipated development to Division; his radios, soaked by rain and repeated immersions in the tidal inlets and rivers the battalion had forded, could not raise headquarters. Nevertheless, he determined to attack in the early morning. As his assault companies jumped off, they collided with a group of Japanese on the march toward Koli.

Both sides recovered from their initial surprise, but the Japanese reacted first, and in minutes the marines were catching fire from light howitzers and 90-mm. mortars. As the fight waxed, Hanneken was suddenly hit from the rear. He decided to pull back, and for the next six hours fought a successful withdrawal action. In late afternoon, his battalion gained the west bank of the Nalimbiu River and his radio operators finally reported contact with Division.

Vandegrift acted at once to relieve the situation. Aircraft were dispatched to bomb and strafe the coastal area east of the Nalimbiu, and the cruisers and destroyers which several days earlier shelled Point Cruz now steamed at flank speed toward the east. That the planes did not do too well that day is suggested by the following series of incoming messages logged in the Division operations journal:

1717. Friendly planes strafing and bombing.

1735. Planes are bombing us. Stop them.

1755. Request all planes stop bombing until things can straighten out.

While American planes were killing and wounding American troops, Puller's battalion embarked in landing boats at Kukum and Moore's One Hundred Sixty-fourth Infantry (less Richard's battalion engaged on the west flank) set off from the perimeter to envelop the enemy from the south.

As some marines and soldiers were mopping up west of Point Cruz and others were fighting along the Nalimbiu, one of the silliest actions of the entire Pacific war was being conducted by Kelly Turner at Aola Bay, about thirty miles east of Koli. For two months Turner had been anxious to establish a "fall back" position with an airfield at Aola. Vandegrift, Geiger, Woods, McCain and Fitch had viewed this project with unanimous disfavor, but Turner, as persuasive as he was opinionated, sold the idea first to Ghormley and later to Halsey.

Accordingly, on November 4, when he brought the Eighth Marines to Lunga, Turner dropped Carlson's Second Raiders, the 1st Battalion, One Hundred Forty-seventh Infantry, five hundred Seabees (critically needed for airfield and other construction within the perimeter), Marine AA and coast defense guns, and a battery of the Americal Division's artillery at Aola, with orders to build a strip. The Seabees went to work manfully, but the swampy ground in which Turner had deposited them was totally unsuitable for airfield construction. Such had been the considered verdict rendered previously by a reconnaissance party of Marine engineers who had surveyed the scene.

Not until a month later, and then only after further remonstrances from Vandegrift, Harmon, Geiger and Fitch, did Halsey cancel this abortive operation. Meanwhile, troops which could have been used to great advantage elsewhere wasted weeks waiting to be lifted out of this miserable place. Every time Turner laid aside the sextant for the baton he made an egregious mistake. Aola was no exception.

Vandegrift, disappointed with progress in the west and exasperated with Turner's Aola adventure, determined at least to liquidate the Japanese to the east. On November 4, he temporarily suspended the Cruz operation and ordered Rupertus from Tulagi to assume command at Koli. After listening to reports from Hanneken and digesting information provided by native scouts, the tactical commander concluded there were more Japanese in the vicinity than he had thought, and decided to wait near Koli until Moore arrived before launching his attack.

As the soldiers crossed the river roughly 3000 yards from its mouth and pushed north through jungle, Colonel Shoji received orders to withdraw to the upper reaches of the Lunga.[6] He pulled back toward Tetere and left a rear guard of about 500 to keep the Americans in play at Gavaga Creek while he moved off to the south. His casualties in the Nalimbiu action were slight. In the meantime, Division had (and, as it turned out, belatedly) ordered Carlson to hit the trail from Aola and take the Japanese in the rear.

Saturday, November 7, Moore's two battalions, after encountering but a handful of Japanese, and having fought a noisy but bloodless inconclusive night engagement with each other, reached the sea, and the combined force began a cautious advance toward the Metapona.[7] As night fell they dug in to repel a possible landing, but none materialized. On the following day, the attackers pocketed the Gavaga position, and a series of vicious short-range fights began. At this point, Rupertus fell ill of dengue. Army Brigadier General Edmund B. Sebree, who had accompanied Moore as an observer, assumed command.[8]

Admiral Halsey spent this Sunday on Guadalcanal. He had

wished to visit the island since the day he became ComSoPac, but had been forced several times to postpone the trip. Halsey obviously enjoyed every minute—or almost every minute—of his brief stay. Vandegrift escorted him in a jeep to the "Tenaru," the Ridge, to Henderson and the Matanikau—sites which were of peculiar significance to the general, as indeed they were to every man in his command.

During the night, "Washing Machine Charlie" obliged with a routine call, and destroyers shelled Henderson. As Halsey and Vandegrift hit the general's dug-out, a flare descended; Pepper's searchlights began their interweaving probes; the AA guns cracked, and "Charlie" cut his engine. Interminable seconds later a 250-pound bomb exploded dully.

"Staunch structure you have here, Archie," Halsey said as he belted a sandbag with a hairy fist. Sand began to trickle gently to the ground; another flare blossomed, another bomb exploded. "Charlie" droned off to the west. The "All clear" sounded. As Halsey clambered out of the dugout, the rotten sandbag burst. The Division augurs, of whom there were no less than 15,000, considered this a propitious omen.

The next morning before breakfast, Halsey awarded a dozen decorations and held a brief press conference. One witless correspondent asked the admiral how long he thought the war would last. "How long do you think they can take it?" Halsey snapped.[9]

Another reporter asked the admiral how he proposed to win the campaign in the South Pacific.

"Kill Japs, kill Japs, and keep on killing Japs," Halsey replied.

Before he returned to Nouméa, ComSoPac told Vandegrift that on Guadalcanal he had met "the most superb gang" he "ever knew."

On November 8 a new air commander, Marine Brigadier General Louis Woods, briefed Halsey. Woods had relieved Geiger and inherited the unofficial title of "Com-AirCACTUS" only the day before. During the week prior to his assumption of command, the First Wing had received significant reinforcement. In late October, Marine Air Group II (Lieutenant Colonel William O. Brice) arrived in New Caledonia and the Group commander began pushing planes and pilots forward. On the first day of the month Major Joseph Sailer, Jr., destined to become one of the hottest dive-bomber pilots of World War II, had arrived with his Squadron 132; on November 2, Major Paul Fontana flew in with nine fighter pilots of VMF 112. The long-awaited *Lightnings* had not arrived, but a squadron of Marine torpedo planes commanded by Lieutenant Colonel Paul Moret had.

Two expertly handled photographic aircraft completed mapping the entire western half of Guadalcanal; a week after the pilots finished their work, accurate maps of this portion of the island were at long last available. And during early November, Seabees hacked a new strip—"Fighter Two"—out of the jungle west of Kukum.

With the arrival of two batteries of 155-mm. guns, the artillery could range deep into the Japanese rear. Other guns and howitzers had recently been landed, and del Valle, now a brigadier general, finally had at his disposal a versatile and flexible artillery group.

During this period, the Japanese had been quietly attending to their own knitting. On November 2, 5, 7, 8, 9, and 10 a total of two cruisers and 65 destroyers brought in troops and supplies.[10] On November 7, eleven of Tanaka's destroyers landed over 1300 officers and men of the advance echelon, 38th Division, at Tassafaronga; two night later, the "Express" ran through safely with the Division commander, Lieutenant General Tadayoshi Sano, his staff, headquarters personnel, and over 600 troops.[11] Aircraft from Henderson attacked both groups as they closed the Russells, but neither suffered severe damage.

The big drive was on.

15

WITH THE EIGHTH MARINES ashore, and the Japanese at Gavaga in a bag, Division ordered Arthur to resume the drive to the Poha. Jeschke's newly-arrived regiment (less a battalion) was attached, and marched from the perimeter on Monday, November 9. That day the rain fell relentlessly; Arthur's attack progressed slowly.[2]

On Tuesday, the sun blazed with a ferocity to which officers and men of the Eighth Marines were not yet acclimated, and Jeschke's fresh battalions, which passed through the front lines in early morning, made practically no headway. In airless valleys, overloaded men gasped for breath as they slowly dragged themselves, their machine guns and their mortars up kunai-covered ridges, the scorching sun beating upon steel helmets and gun barrels too hot to touch. The following day the heat was even worse; the regiment advanced but 400 yards.[3]

"Holiday Routine" did not prevail on Guadalcanal on November 11, the anniversary of the armistice which terminated hostilities in World War I. Two raids came in; the Japanese escaped with only slightly heavier losses than they inflicted—eleven *Zeros* to seven *Wildcats*. The "sea eagles" had by this time lost a considerable amount of the enthusiasm they had earlier displayed when briefed for raids on Guadalcanal. The attitude of *Betty* crews, particularly those flying in wing bombers—always the first to be "stitched" by diving *Wildcats*—was now one of stoic acceptance of an end which could be postponed only in increments of twenty-four hours.

The pace of operations west of Cruz worried Vandegrift, as did minatory reports of shipping in The Slot, and when he received an estimate prepared by Halsey's staff, he decided to recall the troops west of the Matanikau, tighten his lines, and prepare for the onslaught which seemed probable. In the afternoon of November 11, he ordered Arthur to withdraw. Marines brought in with them 11 enemy howitzers and antitank guns, 32 machine guns, and 28 mortars. Engaged troops suffered 65 killed, 125 wounded.[4] Japanese casualties during the last phase of this attack were never determined.

To the east, the Japanese at Gavaga made repeated attempts to break out, and some did so. But the bulk of the force was penned—by fire to the south, east and west; by the sea to the north. For them, life was now to be counted in hours and minutes, and on November 12, the last determined defenders were killed or committed suicide. Four hundred and fifty Japanese lay unburied where they had fought. But their sacrifice enabled Shoji, with 2000 men, to get a clear start toward the south and west. Clemens's scouts had reported this movement, and Carlson, hastening westward toward Tetere, was directed to cut into the jungle and catch Shoji. He struck out for the headwaters of the Balesuna River.

American casualties at Gavaga were 40 killed; 120 officers and men, including the indestructible Puller, wounded. Booty included large amounts of rice, two howitzers, mortars, machine guns, automatic weapons, and fifty collapsible landing boats. Sebree was ordered to destroy all captured food and material at once and return to the perimeter.[5]

With 71 killed and missing and 193 wounded in action in the west, and 160 killed and wounded at the Nalimbiu and Gavaga, battle casualties for the first ten days of November totaled well over four hundred. This was a relatively high price to pay, for in the west no lasting gain had been achieved. On the other hand, operations on the east flank had eliminated the possibility of any immediate danger from that direction.

When they later looked back on the first eleven days of November, some of those who lived through them described their island as "quiet." It was, as compared with eventful September and October days and nights, or to those just around the corner.

When Halsey returned to Nouméa on November 9, his chief of staff greeted him with the news that elements of Combined Fleet had sailed from Truk; that other combat ships were assembling in Rabaul; that transports were gathering in Simpson Harbor, and that there was uncommon activity in the Shortlands. Reports from coastwatchers, submarines, and reconnaissance aircraft confirmed decoded Japanese messages. There was no doubt that build-up for a decisive attempt, by which the offensive of late October could be judged minor, was in the cards.[6]

The new Japanese plan was simpler than several earlier ones had been. At midnight on November 12, part of Kondo's Second Fleet, commanded by Vice Admiral Hiroaki Abe, was to close the north shore of Guadalcanal and beat Henderson, the planes parked around it, and its bordering installations to a pulp. Abe's group consisted of battleships *Hiei* and *Kirishima*, cruiser *Nagara*, and fourteen destroyers.[7] The big ships were, as before, to fire high-capacity ammunition, and flashless powder (original with the Japanese) was to be used for the first time.

The remainder of Kondo's Fleet would cruise about 150 miles north of Savo in distant cover.[8] This included carriers *Junyo* and *Hiyo*, with almost one hundred fighters, dive bombers and torpedo planes, battleships *Kongo* and *Haruna*, four cruisers, and nineteen destroyers.[9]

The Commander in Chief Eighth Fleet, Vice Admiral Mikawa, was to provide close support to the landing of Lt. Gen. Sano's 38th Division near Tassafaronga. Mikawa had available six cruisers and an equal number of destroyers.[10] He assigned three cruisers and four destroyers to Rear Admiral Shoji Nishimura and ordered him to conduct shore bombardment when directed.

Rear Admiral Tanaka, who had resumed his post as Commander, Reinforcement Force, was allotted twelve destroyers to convoy eleven transports in which the main body of Sano's veteran division was embarked. A specially organized Combined Naval Landing Force of almost 3000 officers and men was to go ashore simultaneously. Continuous air cover by land- and carrier-based fighters would insure that these sailors, plus Sano's 11,000 troops and their supplies, reached the beach without being unduly bothered by the American planes. This time, no threat was apprehended from Henderson and its two satellite fighter strips; these fields and the planes they harbored would be neutralized by the big guns of Abe's battleships. "Zero hour" for the landing was set for 10:00 P.M., November 13. During debarkation, Mikawa's cruisers and destroyers would complete the destruction of all American air facilities on Guadalcanal. Any American fighters that survived the destructive bombardments would be speedily liquidated by the "sea eagles."

Three hours after midnight on 12 November, Kondo detached Abe's group, which set course for Savo. At six o'clock that evening, Tanaka, in destroyer flagship *Hayashio* ("Fast Running Tide"), led the troop transports and their escorts out of Short-lands harbor. The admiral was not particularly cheerful; he was not sure which way the tide would run, and wondered how many of his ships would survive.[11]

As Admiral Mikawa had urged in his memorandum of late August, a major force, a force capable of destroying the Ameri-cans, was finally on the way "all at once, in big ships." Sufficient aircraft had been allotted to gain and hold air superiority over assault shipping and the beach areas where troops and supplies were to be landed.

Halsey's intelligence division had made an amazingly accurate estimate of enemy strength and capabilities; ComSoPac knew he must put up all he had, from his lone flattop to the cockleshells at Tulagi, to stave off the Japanese. Between the carrier and the MTBs, Halsey was thin, and his forces widely dispersed.

Kinkaid's Task Force 61 (*Enterprise*, two battleships, two cruisers, and eight destroyers) was at Nouméa where electricians, welders and machinists still swarmed over the carrier, repairing damage suffered at Santa Cruz. Despite their best efforts, her forward elevator remained obstinately jammed in "Up" position, which meant that all planes had to be brought topside from the hangar deck, and struck below to it, by the after elevator. Of the two battleships, one (*South Dakota*) was a partial cripple.

Rear Admiral Norman Scott's Task Group 62.4 (cruiser *Atlanta* and four destroyers), which had arrived off Lunga the day before, was still present. Kelly Turner, with the main body of Colonel Daniel W. Hogan's One Hundred Eighty-second Infantry Regimental Combat Team of the Americal Division embarked in four transports, was en route Nouméa to Guadalcanal under escort of *Portland* and four destroyers. During the afternoon he rendezvoused south of San Cristobal with Task Group 67.4, Rear Admiral Daniel J. Callaghan's "Support Group": two heavy cruisers, a light cruiser, and half a dozen destroyers.

When Turner anchored off Kukum on the following morning, soldiers and Marine replacements hastened to disembark, and the first of a stream of warning messages from friendly aircraft and submarines arrived at the command center in "Wacky Mac." By afternoon Turner had a fairly accurate picture of at least a part of the enemy situation. For Abe's group had been sighted in midmorning, slightly over 300 miles northwest of Guadalcanal, and its composition correctly reported.[12] This time Turner did not believe the enemy's design was to establish a seaplane base. He correctly estimated that Abe intended to bombard the airfield. And he ordered Callaghan to prevent him from doing so.

To strengthen Callaghan, Turner attached Scott's group, less a destroyer. He also pulled two destroyers, short of fuel, from Callaghan. This shuffling did give Task Group 67.4 more gun and torpedo potential. But whether the accretions added to the ultimate combat effectiveness of Callaghan's force is doubtful. Here, once more, circumstances forced improvisation and, as had happened before (and would again), ships which had never operated with each other were to go into night battle together.

The crews of all these ships were tired. True, they enjoyed amenities not available to the men whose support was their mission; their sole reason for being where they were. They did not alternately sweat and shiver with malaria, or spend long hours in muddy foxholes. But most of them had been at sea now for many months. Some ships were so shorthanded that officers and men were routinely standing "watch-and-watch"; four hours on, four off. And "General Quarters," in effect at least half of the time from the hour a ship sortied from the New Hebrides until it returned there, allowed crews little leisure to avail themselves of the sleep, the baths, the hot food, that marines and soldiers so envied. The strain was unending, and it told. Turner had aged markedly in three months; some members of his staff, particularly communication personnel, were almost staggering.

Callaghan was no exception. Two weeks previously he had been relieved as Halsey's chief of staff by Captain Miles Browning, and since assuming command of the Task Group "he had had almost no rest. The Admiral was in a state of physical exhaustion."[13]

Aboard ships, the afternoon of November 12 was not exactly relaxing. The last sailors to be served noon chow were bolting it down when "Condition Yellow" was announced and "General Quarters" sounded. Forty minutes later they came in: 25 torpedo bombers with nine *Zeros* covering. Marine and Army pilots jumped the formation, and Turner's ships filled the air with steel. Fighters shot down 16 *Bettys*, AA flamed four. Another bomber crashed into *San Francisco*'s after control, killing thirty men and wounding two dozen more. In the meantime, the *Zeros* made repeated low-altitude strafing runs against Henderson.

That evening Callaghan escorted Turner's unloaded transports safely through Lengo Channel on their way to the New Hebrides. At 10:00 P.M. he wished Turner "bon voyage" over voice radio, and turned his five cruisers and eight destroyers toward the dark waters which lapped quietly at Savo's beaches.

Rear Admiral Dan Callaghan knew that he was going against two enemy battleships with 14-inch guns. He was well aware that he had to surprise the Japanese, and get his torpedoes and first main battery salvos on their targets before Abe's big ships discovered him, and their guns leisurely blew his cruisers out of the water. His one chance, then, was to close swiftly and secretly and start slugging before the enemy even suspected his presence. "We want the big ones," he adjured the gunnery officer of flagship *San Francisco*. But would this couragous admiral's determination suffice?

The cruising disposition Callaghan prescribed for the night battle into which he was leading his ships strongly suggests that he had not carefully analyzed Admiral Scott's experience of the previous month during the midnight engagement with Goto. As Scott had done, Callaghan put his ships in column formation, and divided his destroyers, placing four in the van of his five cruisers, four in the rear. But this was not the most effective formation to cope with the situation he was about to face, for it automatically deprived his destroyers of any fleeting opportunity to make a sudden coordinated torpedo attack at short range.[14]

He failed, as Crutchley had, to issue specific instructions for night battle. Nor did he define the role he expected his destroyers to play. Indeed, Captain Robert G. Tobin, in command of the four bringing up the rear, received no orders whatever from the admiral. Callaghan was thus about to throw his forces against a superior enemy without having taken elementary measures to insure a minimum degree of control. Possibly he felt that instructions were superfluous; that a short-range ship-to-ship battle was inevitable. The Chinese have a phrase for it: "You must go into the tiger's den to get the tiger's pups." Some burst in suddenly; others are more wily. Circumstances had combined to force this admiral to plunge directly "into the tiger's den."

Callaghan now proceeded to compound his difficulties: in positioning his ships in long column he paid no attention to the capabilities of surface search radars. Did he realize that these radars were the principal guarantee that he could achieve the surprise he sought? Apparently not. But a month previously, Captain Hoover of *Helena* had trusted his, to the discomfiture of the Japanese. Of the van destroyers, only *O'Bannon* had the latest search radars. She was fourth in column. Of the five cruisers, *Helena* had the best installation. She was fourth in the cruiser column, which was led by *Atlanta*, a ship with elementary radar. *San Francisco* followed *Atlanta*. She was blind. Choice of *San Francisco* as flagship was not wise. Although she had gunnery radars (for both main battery and AA), she had no SG (surface search) radar.[15]

A few minutes after Callaghan's van destroyers passed Lunga Point, *Helena*'s radar screens showed "blips" identified as enemy. *Helena* dutifully reported them. Six minutes later—at 1:24 A.M. —*Helena* informed all ships that the enemy was on their port bow distant 14,500 yards, steaming at speed 23 knots on course 105°.[16] *Helena*'s plots showed the two forces closing at a rate of almost 1000 yards a minute. No word yet came from the flagship. Indeed no word came from the flagship for many long minutes.

At 1:41 A.M., destroyer *Cushing*, leading the American column, executed an emergency 90° left turn to avoid piling into *Yudachi*, Abe's leading destroyer. Callaghan finally said something. But when he spoke it was not to give the already belated order to open fire.

"What are you doing?" he asked *Cushing*'s skipper over voice radio.[17] Now, with each passing second, the American admiral was allowing the incalculable advantage of the surprise he had achieved to slip away, as sand might have slipped silently through his outstretched fingers. The second sweep on *San Francisco*'s shielded bridge clock pulsed, and again, and again, and again. Finally, 24 minutes after *Helena* positively identified enemy ships closing the range, Callaghan issued an order:

"Stand by to open fire."[18]

It was too late. Japanese lookouts had sighted the Americans.

Atlanta, Rear Admiral Norman Scott's flagship, was the first to catch shells and torpedoes, and even before Callaghan gave the order to commence fire, at least one torpedo had pierced *Atlanta*'s hull. The force of the explosion "lifted her bodily from the water, then set her down shuddering and crippled."[19]

During the next six or seven minutes, two American destroyers, *Cushing* and *Laffey*, attacked *Hiei*. As the Japanese battleship·

swung to avoid their torpedoes, she let them both have the benefit of one salvo of 14-inch thin-walled bombardment ammunition. *Laffey* started for the floor of Ironbottom Bay.

The next two destroyers in column, *Sterrett* and *O'Bannon*, attacked *Hiei* with torpedoes and gunfire. Their fish probably ran deep or, if they struck, failed to explode. The American destroyers, plunging into the middle of Abe's formation, had passed *Hiei* almost close enough to board her. This disrupting attack unnerved the Japanese admiral. He ordered the battleships to withdraw.

Callaghan was confused, but had not lost his nerve and had no intention of pulling out. He sensed, however, that in the melee, American guns were firing on American ships. (They were.) On voice radio, the admiral ordered, "Cease firing own ships."[20] In the sudden silence American gunners waited. So did the Japanese. After a pause of minutes that seemed an age, a 5-inch gun fired. Immediately, Japanese put searchlights on *San Francisco*. Less than two minutes later, accurate salvos demolished her bridge, instantly killing Callaghan, three members of his staff, and mortally wounding Captain Cassin Young, the cruiser's skipper. *San Francisco* was now being conned by Quartermaster Third Class Floyd A. Rogers. All communications were out, and the gunnery officer, Lieutenant Commander Wilbourne,

> proceeded immediately to the bridge, stumbling through wreckage, bodies, blood, and electrical fires from short circuits. Water poured from ruptured fire mains. . . .[21]

Portland and *Helena*, the next two cruisers in column, had joined the bloody fracas, but *Portland* was not long for the battle. Her main battery guns had a target, but a Japanese destroyer captain had her lined up on his torpedo director. He let four torpedoes go at the cruiser. Only one hit, aft, but one was enough. The explosion blew off most of *Portland*'s stern and two of her four propellers. She could no longer steer, and began to circle wildly. *Helena* had better luck. Her captain, Gilbert C. Hoover, conned his ship through the melee in admirable fashion, and *Helena*'s main battery dealt out shells effectively to successive enemy ships. Astern of her, *Juneau*'s guns began flashing. Moments later she was hit by a torpedo that blasted in her Number One fireroom. She began to flood, lost way, and coasted to a stop.

Captain Robert G. Tobin's four destroyers (Desron 12) had

not yet engaged. As we have seen, Callaghan had passed no battle orders to Tobin, and his flagship, *Aaron Ward*, carried obsolete search radars. Tobin was in the dark in more ways than one, but *Aaron Ward* opened fire at 7000 yards on ships she identified as enemy. Astern of her, *Barton* launched four torpedoes against a target on the port beam; she immediately caught two in return. A few seconds later she broke in two and disappeared, taking 90 per cent of her complement with her. *Monssen* lasted only minutes longer. The last of Tobin's destroyers—*Fletcher*—fared better, possibly because she had new radars, possibly because her captain was familiar with them and relied on them. Be that as it may, Commander William M. Cole conned his ship confidently and safely through the shambles.[22]

"Because the visibility was poor, the battle developed into close-range duels and fierce melees, with each ship taking independent action." So reads the summary Japanese report.[23]

Pilots on dawn reconnaissance from Henderson flew toward silent Savo above a calm sea, littered, as these waters were after Mikawa's victory, with orange crates, boards, and life rafts, and dotted with almost 1000 exhausted men, many burned and wounded, who wondered how long the drab grey jackets to which they had confided their lives would continue to hold them up. Below the airmen lay eight ships, five American and three Japanese. A mile northwest of Savo, giant *Hiei* wallowed, attended by a devoted destroyer, *Yukikaze. Yudachi*, veteran of other fights, lay dead in the water. *Akatsuki* had earlier disappeared carrying most of her crew down with her. *Amatsukaze* and *Ikazuchi* had withdrawn, damaged.

In the early morning light, Wilbourne went again to the wrecked bridge of *San Francisco*. One fireroom produced steam; the cruiser moved slowly toward Lunga Point. On the starboard side of the flag bridge he found Admiral Callaghan's body.

A trail of Philip Morris cigarettes led from an open pack in his hand to the emergency cabin. Apparently, when the single shot was fired he had dashed from his cabin. . . .[24]

At that instant had come the holocaust.

This victory was almost Pyrrhic; the American Navy could not afford another such. *Atlanta, Cushing, Laffey, Barton* and *Monssen* had sunk or would soon; *San Francisco, Juneau, Port-*

land, Helena, Sterrett, O'Bannon and *Aaron Ward* were damaged. Only *Fletcher* escaped without a scratch. At least 700 officers and men who had gone into battle with Callaghan and Scott did not live to see the sun rise on November 13.[25] In terms of lives and ships, American losses far exceeded Japanese. Again, the United States Navy had absorbed a terrible beating. But it had won this grim and bloody slugging match, described by Admiral King as "one of the most furious sea battles ever fought."[26] For Abe had not bombarded Henderson. Abe had fled.

As Captain Hoover in *Helena* collected the still seaworthy remnants of Callaghan's Task Group 67.4, *Portland* was nudged, pulled, and pushed to Tulagi harbor, where she was to lay up in deep water against Florida to make repairs. Hoover stood down Lengo Channel with *Juneau, San Francisco, O'Bannon, Sterrett* and *Fletcher*. Behind him dozens of small boats, sent from Lunga and Tulagi, cruised slowly, picking men out of the oily water. As before, practically all the Japanese survivors preferred to die. Most were allowed to do so. After struggling to avoid rescue, some thirty-odd were forcibly pulled into boats for purposes of interrogation.

Meanwhile, Hoover's group continued withdrawal to the east. A few minutes before eleven o'clock, his ships were sighted by Japanese submarine *I-26*. At 10:59 she fired bow tubes; at 11:01 a torpedo struck *Juneau*. The cruiser disintegrated. Within two minutes she had disappeared.

Hoover now faced a frightful decision. Did he dare hazard another ship—possibly even two ships—to pick up survivors, if indeed there could be any? He decided he could not, and sent this message to a *Fortress* overhead:

Juneau torpedoed and disappeared lat. 10°32'5, long. 161°2'E at 1109. Survivors in water. Report ComSoPac.[27]

The message never reached Halsey. Of 100 men who somehow survived the explosion, only 10 lived to tell of it. Approximately 700 were lost.[28]

16

WHILE CALLAGHAN steamed in moonless darkness to his own fatal appointment, Combined Fleet directed Tanaka to turn around and shepherd his transports back to safe haven in the Shortlands. There he arrived at noon, November 13; one hour later he was ordered to proceed again to Guadalcanal. Commander Reinforcement Force "had a premonition that an ill fate was in store."[1] The Americans were determined to justify Tanaka's forebodings.

With forward elevator still jammed tightly in the "Up" position—not even Halsey himself would have dared press the "Down" button—*Enterprise* ploughed north at 26 knots. Repair crews still aboard worked frantically to ready the big carrier for combat flight operations. Willis Augustus Lee's Task Force 64, fast battleships *Washington*, *South Dakota* and four destroyers, was in company.

Meanwhile, flyers from Henderson and B-17s from Espiritu Santo bombed *Hiei* in relays. The first Marine torpedo pilots in the South Pacific (from Lieutenant Colonel Paul Moret's VMSB-131) had plenty of practice this day. But *Hiei*'s AA guns still fired. Five destroyers milling around her made heavy black smoke and threw steel at every approaching attacker. Eight *Zeros* sent to cover salvage operations were promptly shot down. But American pilots were persistent; above all, they wanted to put *Hiei* under. By late afternoon the huge ship had taken all she could and, just before sunset, with battle flags streaming, she began to settle by the stern.

As waters washed over *Hiei*'s maindeck northwest of Savo, word reached Admiral Halsey in Nouméa that Tanaka's force was again on the way, and correctly estimating that heavier ships would cover his entrance into Ironbottom Bay, ComSoPac ordered Kinkaid to send Lee's group ahead to Cape Esperance to intercept. But contrary winds had even further delayed routine air operations still dependent on one elevator. Kinkaid had not been able to make good the distance he had planned, and Lee's ships could not possibly reach the objective by midnight.

Earlier, Kinkaid had launched eight dive bombers with six escorting fighters and directed the flight leader to join Woods's pilots in attacks on *Hiei*, and then proceed to Henderson. And other planes arrived, too, to increase Woods's capabilities for air defense and attack. Dale Brannon, now promoted to major, led in the first long-awaited flight of *Lightnings;* shortly after they landed, eight more of the same type flew in from MacArthur's area. Harmon moved two squadrons of B-26 bombers from New Caledonia to Espiritu. As darkness closed over his runways on November 13, General Woods counted 58 high-altitude fighters, 30 SBDs, 19 torpedo planes, and two P-400s.[2] For the first time in the island's hectic history there were over 100 operational combat aircraft on Guadalcanal. This happy state of affairs was destined to exist for no more than seven hours.

For it was Rear Admiral Shoji Nishimura's mission to do this night what Abe had failed to accomplish the night before: neutralize American air power. A few minutes after midnight his 8-inch gun cruisers *Maya* and *Suzuya* came into waters which, since August eighth, had opened with finality to receive so many brave ships. But Nishimura's cruisers encountered no enemy—at least for the first 50 minutes. During this time, they leisurely pumped almost 1000 bombardment projectiles into Henderson, "Fighter One," and "Fighter Two."

Again, "Louie the Louse" methodically dispensed his apparently inexhaustible supply of flares. Often three or four were drifting gently down; as one candle died, he lit another. Again flames jumped skyward and again ear-splitting cracks of the 90-mm. guns punctuated the more somber theme played by exploding shells from Nishimura's cruisers. During momentary lulls, the steady drone of "Washing Machine Charlie's" toy engine reminded marines, soldiers, and the more than 700 sailors rescued during the day not to relax their hold on the mud where they lay, waiting with wide eyes. Men trembled this night, too. And the night air was not cold.

As suddenly as the firing had started, it stopped, and except for the crackling of flames consuming tents, latrines, and shacks near the strips, all was quiet. Nishimura, attacked by MTBs, withdrew. He had wrecked eighteen planes.[3] Runways suffered no more than superficial damage.

Even before daybreak of November 14, as flames ate into

dumps and hot ammunition exploded, fighter and dive bomber pilots raced toward armed aircraft. The biggest "Express" in history was in The Slot, headed southeast.

As these first reports reached Air operations, Tanaka was 150 miles northwest of Esperance, moving toward Guadalcanal at 11 knots, with a dozen *Zeros* covering him. His eleven transports steamed in four columns; his destroyers, spread in a large vee, gave antisubmarine protection to front and flanks. But the Admiral felt sure his principal danger would not be from submarines. He was right.

Two small strikes hit him about 8:30 A.M.; *Zeros* claimed five attackers.[4] The next flight passed well to the south and west of the transports. Mikawa's rapidly retiring force, now south of New Georgia and heading west, was the target of this "large formation," which Tanaka sighted at about 9:45 A.M. The *Enterprise* strike group, led by Lieutenant Commander James R. ("Bucky") Lee, went directly for the escaping cruisers. There was plenty of time to take care of Tanaka.

Kinugasa had already been holed twice by Henderson-based torpedo planes, and Lee's attack did for her.[5] The pilots now turned to *Chokai*, *Maya*, and *Isuzu*, and damaged all three before bombs were expended. Lee's strike flew off to the southwest, and Mikawa welcomed the interlude to reorganize and struggle on toward the Shortlands.

Except for a few ineffectual *Zeros*, Tanaka was bare. Kondo, hovering only 150 miles away, was obviously in a nervous state; the planes he sent in driblets to cover the transports were shot down, and mixed Navy and Marine strikes from *Enterprise* and Guadalcanal began almost unimpeded assaults on Tanaka's hapless flock. The attacks were deadly. At 11:50, 12:45, 2:00 P.M., at 3:40, and at sunset the Americans struck. From Espiritu, B-17s flew to get in on the slaughter. For slaughter it was. Six transports went to the bottom; a crippled seventh, *Sado Maru*, limped back to the Shortlands under destroyer escort.

> In six attacks this day . . . the enemy had sunk six transports. . . . Crews were near exhaustion. . . . The remaining transports had spent most of the day in evasive action, zigzagging at high speed and were now scattered in all directions.[6]

But Tanaka collected his dispersed charges and steamed doggedly toward Tassafaronga. Three destroyers were now escorting four transports. Welcome night at last embraced this "sorry remnant" of the force that had sortied from Shortlands.[7]

The same darkness that shielded Rear Admiral Tanaka's "sorry remnant" also shielded Kondo, coming down from the north with battleship *Kirishima*, cruisers *Atago, Takao, Sendai* and *Nagara*, and nine destroyers. Kondo, determined to exact revenge for the injuries inflicted on Abe, Mikawa and Tanaka, expected opposition. He was ready to face it. "The point had been reached where the bombardment of Guadalcanal and support of the convoys could be delayed no longer . . . the Kondo Fleet . . . moved resolutely south."[8] With equal resolution, Rear Admiral Lee in *Washington*, with *South Dakota* astern, and four destroyers screening him, pushed north. A monumental collision appeared imminent.

Lee was the first to arrive in Ironbottom Bay. His search radars indicated nothing until 11:15 P.M., when they suddenly showed three "blips" identified as a possible battleship and two cruisers: range 19,000 yards, closing. Lee's gunnery radars fastened on the targets; turrets trained to the indicated azimuth; guns elevated. At the directors, officers pressed firing keys. The big turret guns spoke. The first salvo straddled the enemy; radars showed him turn to retire. After a six-minute shoot, battleships checked fire at 11:21. Their 16-inch guns had dispersed Kondo's cruiser screen.

Lee now swung to course 300° (slightly north of west) to pass south of Savo, which loomed darkly on his starboard hand. As his formation settled on this new course, his van destroyers, 5000 yards ahead, picked up targets. A second enemy formation, destroyers this time, was bearing down on the Americans. Lee's four destroyers opened fire. The Japanese were surprised, but only momentarily disconcerted, and in seconds the water was full of their torpedoes, many of which, as usual, found their marks. In the next minute, guns opened. All four Americans caught Japanese shells; a torpedo hit disintegrated *Walke*'s forecastle as far aft as the bridge; flames wrapped her and she started the trip down. At 11:34 *Preston* sank; Lee ordered *Gwin* and *Benham*, disabled, to haul off. He wanted a clear field for the third round.

Bridge clocks showed exactly midnight as the two American battleships closed Kondo's main body—three cruisers followed by *Kirishima*—at 26 knots. At 8500 yards *Washington* opened main battery fire on the Japanese battleship. Her first salvos hit. A Japanese cruiser, another, and a third, illuminated *South Da-*

kota. Her secondary batteries shot out the questing lights, but not before the battleship's upper works were ripped to pieces by a deluge of shells which carried away search radars and all but one gunnery radar. Radio antennas were shot down. *South Dakota,* deaf, dumb and blind, was no longer an asset but a distinct liability, and at 12:10 A.M. her captain "wisely decided to retire—to the great relief of the Task Force Commander."[9] Kondo withdrew to the north with battered *Kirishima,* leaving Lee, in majestic *Washington,* master of the field.

The American admiral now decided to cruise in search of Tanaka's remaining transports. At that time, these were just passing the Russell Islands, some 60 miles west of Esperance, and the search proved fruitless. Rear Admiral Lee, secure in the knowledge that he had wrecked Kondo's plans for the night and that air would attend to Tanaka in the morning, moved off to the south of Guadalcanal.

Commander Task Force 64, a modest man, gave credit for his decisive victory to everyone but himself. Nor did he neglect to mention the proven fighting qualities of the Japanese:

> We entered this action confident that we could outshoot the enemy. From the instant they retired after our opening salvos, we knew we had the indian sign on the Japs. We, however, realized then, and it should not be forgotten now, that our margin of superiority was due almost entirely to our possession of radar. Certainly we have no edge on the Japs in experience, skill, training or permanence of personnel.[10]

When Tanaka learned of Kondo's rout, Commander Reinforcement Force realized that he was in for plenty of trouble. He could not arrive at Tassafaronga much before daylight on November 15, and radioed Mikawa for permission to run the transports on the beach as soon as he arrived. Mikawa flashed a terse "Negative." But Kondo overruled Mikawa:

> "Run aground and unload troops."

This "resolute approval" of an unprecedented request was "gratefully received" and at dawn the four transports headed for the beach.[11]

Woods's flyers, airborne at first light, had to fly only 15 miles for this day's bloody target practice in which indiscriminate flights of Army, Navy and Marine planes participated. Del Valle hurriedly displaced his eight 155-mm. guns to the Matanikau to shell the beached ships during short intervals between waves of attacking aircraft. Some planes dropped bombs and incendiary "breadbaskets" on the helpless ships, their decks reddening with blood; others came in low to strafe. By nine o'clock the hulls of all four were battered and upper works blazing. But the attacks continued. Despite an unceasing hail of shells and bullets, and the fires which engulfed the ships, 2000 Japanese soldiers gained the beach safely. They managed to land 260 cases of ammunition and 1500 bags of rice.[12] In midmorning, destroyer *Meade* sallied from Tulagi harbor to deliver the *coup de grâce* to the stranded ships. This she proceeded leisurely to do. Then cruising slowly she collected 264 officers and crewmen from *Walke* and *Preston* who had spent almost 12 hours in the water.[13]

First fragmentary reports of this series of vicious night actions, which culminated on November 15 with the destruction of Tanaka's last remaining transports and the scuttling of his ship by the captain of *Kirishima*, were received in Washington with some reserve. But as confirmations arrived, the mood changed to one of confident optimism.

In Tokyo, Imperial GHQ announced another great victory. Under protection of the navy, the imperial army was "streaming" ashore on Guadalcanal; countless American ships had plunged to the bottom, others, "enwrapped in flames," drifted aimlessly in waters dominated by Kondo's "heroic" fleet. Final victory was to be momentarily anticipated.[14] There was, however, one slight problem: The Americans were still *there;* they still, inexplicably, had ships, they still had planes. And, most curious of all, they still seemed willing to fight! But that indomitable spirit which animated Japanese soldiers, sailors, and airmen would of course prevail. The Americans, a people who relied entirely on their engines of war, would soon be ground into the mud of the "insignificant island, inhabited only by natives." Japanese who knew the truth were worried. Admiral Tanaka later wrote: "My concern and trepidation about the entire venture had been proved well founded."[15]

On Monday, November 16, when final reports were in, Secretary Knox, for the first time in months, was almost jovial. His remarks to the press were brief: "We can lick them. I don't qualify that. We'll defeat them."[16] Vandegrift messaged Halsey that the "battered helmets" of the men on Guadalcanal were "lifted in deepest tribute to Rear Admirals Callaghan, Scott, Lee, Kinkaid and their forces."[17] Hanson Baldwin, military critic of the *New York Times*, wrote: "The future is ours to make."[18]

In Nouméa, Halsey read the dispatches and turned grinning to members of his staff: "We've got the bastards licked!"[19]

If one compares only relative losses in combatant ships, as it suited Radio Tokyo to do, the naval battles of mid-November might be counted a Japanese victory. But no battle can be judged by so narrow a measure. For, in addition to two battleships, a cruiser and three destroyers, the Japanese Navy lost the better part of a 3000-man Naval Landing Force and ten scarce transports; the army lost at least half of its 38th Infantry Division with all heavy weapons and equipment.

Even more important, two Japanese admirals, Mikawa and Kondo, definitely lost some of their edge and *élan*. How otherwise can one account for Kondo's failure to commit his fighters on November 13, 14, and 15? How otherwise account for Mikawa's hurried departure from the scene? And other questions remain. Why did not Kondo order a general retirement, beyond the range of Henderson-based aircraft, early on November 14, before the better part of Tanaka's convoy and its precious cargos were destroyed? Why did not Tanaka take the initiative and recommend withdrawal for reorganization? The first air attacks to hit his convoy on November 14 should have told him all he needed to know: that Nishimura's bombardment of the night before had failed to neutralize Henderson Field.

But Japanese commanders again chose, as they had at the "Tenaru," at Edson's Ridge, and in the October attacks, to persist obstinately in a demonstrably losing course of action.

BOOK IV

17

ALL DAY NOVEMBER 16, "Buzzard Patrols" from Henderson picked at the carcasses they had rent the day before. On the beached hulks, flickering flames blistered plates, and holds poured out heavy, oily smoke. Occasional violent explosions along the coastal track west of Tassafaronga marked the destruction of ammunition and drummed fuel landed at such cost in lives and ships. This, Vandegrift decided, was the propitious moment to start west again, to reach the Poha, and to liquidate what remained of Hyakutake's presumably disorganized 17th Army. Division worked up a formidable attack force for the West Sector Commander, Brigadier General Sebree: Hogan's One Hundred Eighty-second Infantry (less a battalion); Moore's One Hundred Sixty-fourth, Jeschke's Eighth Marines, and, in Sector reserve, Cates's First Marines. Del Valle disposed his artillery to fire in direct and general support.

Sebree planned to cross the Matanikau early on November 18, seize a line of departure running south from Point Cruz to Hill 66 (almost 2500 yards inland) on the same day, and jump off the following morning. He then proposed to drive west on a broad front, eject the Japanese from the dominating ridge system, and secure the line of the Poha. During the second week of November, half a dozen reconnaissance patrols (one of them led personally by Sebree) had found the area between the Matanikau and Point Cruz to be free of enemy, and Sebree anticipated little difficulty in occupying his line of departure. But Hyakutake had his own ideas. These did not include withdrawal to the river line which was Vandegrift's objective. Secretary Knox and Admiral Halsey had neglected to inform Commander, 17th Army, that he and his hungry fighting men were licked.

Members of both Army and Navy Staff Sections were even more confident than the general that the situation could be restored to Japan's advantage. Still, the sequence of costly actions culminating in the scuttling of *Kirishima* did force Imperial GHQ to re-evaluate the critical state of affairs in the southern Solomons. The conclusion Tokyo planners reached was that "it was indispensable for the establishment of an advantageous situation in East Asia to crush the U. S. counterattack . . . and to maintain the important areas in the Solomon Islands and New Guinea."[1]

In pursuance of this aim, His Imperial Majesty, on November 16, relieved Vice Admiral Nagumo from command of the Third Fleet and appointed Vice Admiral Jisaburo Ozawa to this important post. Simultaneously, GHQ activated 8th Area Army with headquarters at Rabaul, and named Lieutenant General Hitoshi Imamura as its commander.[2] On the same day, the Army Section created the 18th Army, designated Lieutenant General Hatazo Adachi to assume command, and directed him to report to Imamura. Adachi's mission was to resuscitate the floundering New Guinea operation, but he was not at this time assigned any fresh troops.

Hyakutake, in the new organization also subordinate to Imamura, retained command of 17th Army. His mission was to recapture Guadalcanal. Since late August this effort had engrossed the general's attention, and swallowed at least 75 per cent of the resources available in the Southeast Area. From his jungle command post near Kokumbona, Hyakutake could not possibly control events in New Guinea, where the Japanese position had for some time been slowly but steadily deteriorating under increasing Allied pressure. The activation of an Area headquarters and of an army specifically charged with operations there would, no doubt, enable Commander 17th Army to redeem the situation on the island "KA."[3] But the new arrangement, however desirable from Hyakutake's point of view, did not satisfy the demonstrated need of unified direction of effort at Area level, for Imamura and Yamamoto would function as coordinate commanders.

Before he left Tokyo, General Imamura received instructions similar to those simultaneously sent Admiral Yamamoto.[4] These provided that army and navy would cooperate to speed development of new air bases in the Solomons, and to strengthen existing air installations there. This measure was obviously long overdue. Since early September, a few relatively senior Japanese naval air officers had been trying, with little success, to make it clear to Imperial GHQ that control of the air over Guadalcanal and the waters surrounding it was vital. But despite the debacles of September, October and mid-November, the army refused to see the light. The entire responsibility for air action in the Southeast Area had been borne by the navy. The Japanese Army Air Force was committed on the Asiatic continent, in the Indies, and in Malaya. The army had not contributed one airplane to the Guadalcanal campaign. But now, finally, the general staff capitulated to the navy's insistent pressure. The Army Air Force would cooperate.

As the air build-up proceeded, 17th Army was to secure key positions for future offensive operations, and the navy to use "every means" to check enemy reinforcement and support Hyakutake. After American air strength had been neutralized, the navy was to transport reinforcements. Some time later, at a date not specified by GHQ, the army and navy would mount a combined effort, recapture the Guadalcanal airfields, and annihilate their defenders.

Fresh ground troops for the Area army were immediately slated for early movement to Rabaul. These included, in addition to artillery, tank, transport and engineer units, the 51st and 6th Infantry Divisions and the 21st Mixed Brigade.[5] Substantial additions to his air component were also promised Imamura, but the 6th Air Division (army) remained to be assembled and deployed.[6]

Imamura estimated that all preliminary arrangements could be successfully completed by early January, and set the 15th of that month for resumption of a general offensive designed to drive the Americans from Guadalcanal and to capture Port Moresby. In arriving at this date, Imamura apparently failed to consult the navy. For most of the units ordered to his Eighth Army O/B were far distant from Rabaul; in the empire, in Korea, Manchuria and North China. And what GHQ and Commander, 8th Area Army anticipated (or feared) the Americans might do to improve their own position during these 8 or 9 weeks was nowhere stated, even in general terms.

As Sebree's units queued up within the perimeter to draw emergency rations, extra ammunition, salt tablets, and atabrine, one Marine battalion continued to operate outside its confines. This was Evans Carlson's 2nd Raiders, whose motto *"Gung Ho"* ("Work Together") was soon to become a standard phrase in unofficial Marine Corps vocabulary.[7] Detached from the Aola

Force almost two weeks earlier with orders to march to Koli and take Shoji in the rear, Carlson had later been directed to intercept the withdrawing Japanese column. He had promptly cut inland toward the upper Balesuna River, and on November 10 established a base at the deserted village of Biniu. Here he was hit by two companies of Shoji's rear guard, and for the next 48 hours his 400 Raiders sustained a succession of Japanese attacks. Shortly after the last of these was repelled, Sergeant Major Vouza, leading a select group of native scouts and a carrying party, joined Carlson.

Vouza, now fully recovered from the wounds he had suffered in late August, and proudly wearing the Silver Star medal Vandegrift had personally awarded him for gallantry in action against the common enemy, was ready to go. So were the Raiders, and on November 12 Vouza led a party along narrow native trails through the jungle to Asimana, a village on the upper Metapona River. Here Carlson silently surrounded a company of oblivious Japanese, most of whom were bathing. The massacre lasted only a few minutes. There were no survivors, and the Raiders did not tarry to bury the 120 dead.

Guided by Vouza's scouts, and carrying an iron ration of rice, raisins, tea, and bacon, they set out for the south slopes of Mount Austen in pursuit of Shoji. But the Japanese colonel, too, drove hard, and although the Raiders located and ambushed half a dozen isolated groups of straggling enemy, they could not catch the depleted main body.[8]

Strength reports which reached Headquarters, 17th Army, in mid-November did not make pleasant reading. Of almost 10,000 officers and men of the Sendai Division landed in October and November, Maruyama now counted slightly less than 5500 combat effectives. The 38th Division was in no better shape, for Sano had lost half his troops in the shattering debacle which had overtaken Tanaka's latest "Express." The remains of Colonel Ichiki's Twenty-eighth Regiment (two understrength battalions), and Kawaguchi's 35th Brigade, completed the roster of available infantry. Nevertheless, at this time there were 30,000 Japanese troops of all arms and both services ashore on Guadalcanal.[9]

Hyakutake could not, however, take this impressive figure at face value. It included thousands suffering from malnutrition, as well as the sick and wounded. Medical services in the Japanese

Army were at best primitive as compared with those prevailing in the West, and on Guadalcanal even their low standards were never met. No organized attempt was made to evacuate any but the most gravely wounded to rear areas; the less seriously wounded and the sick fended for themselves, or were attended by their comrades.

> The force at the front line position was divided so that those who could not walk due to illness or injury took charge of the defence of positions; those able to walk by utilizing a stick took charge of transportation and cooking in the rear area, and those who were comparatively healthy disturbed the enemy from the rear.[10]

But Sebree's troops would soon discover that their enemy's will to fight was not impaired. For the rank and file of this army, which refused to acknowledge defeat, were alike dedicated to "easing the solicitude" of their Emperor.

This determination was buttressed by the comparatively low esteem in which the Japanese held American fighting men. American victories, so the Japanese continued to believe, could be ascribed entirely to material preponderance. But this technical advantage was insubstantial; in the scales of battle it must inevitably be outweighed by superior spiritual qualities.

Japanese commanders on the island fully realized—although the Americans as yet did not—that 17th Army no longer possessed an offensive capability. The best they could hope was to hold a position as far to the east as possible. They did not despair of doing so; the terrain favored them. In construction of defensive works, the Japanese were both ingenious and industrious. They seemed to have an instinctive feeling for terrain (which Americans lack almost entirely). This no doubt derived from the fact that the Japanese Army was essentially an army of peasants. And probably because they are an innately artistic people, they were expert *camoufleurs*. The jungle provided unique and unlimited scope for the application of individual and collective skills.

The complex of strongly buttressed and thoroughly concealed reverse slope positions which 17th Army now prepared west of the Matanikau housed heavy and light machine guns, mortars, grenade throwers, and 77-mm. mountain guns. These infantry weapons, plus some artillery for which there was a very limited supply of ammunition, were all 17th Army had to hold off the Americans until the new offensive, set by Imamura for the middle of January, was mounted.

A few minutes after dawn on Wednesday, November 18, Lieutenant Colonel Bernard B. Twombley's battalion of the One Hundred Eighty-second Infantry crossed the Matanikau on an engineer foot bridge, and set off in single file on a cross-country march to Hill 66, the inland extremity of the chosen line of departure. This trail-breaking hike would have tested a superbly conditioned battalion, and Twombley's was far from being one. His troops, who had landed only six days before, "were not yet accustomed to the moist heat. . . . They carried full loads of ammunition, water, and food. Many who had not swallowed salt tablets collapsed. . . ."[11] But by late afternoon the soldiers were on their objective, and as darkness gently fingered the surrounding valleys, they organized Hill 66 for defense. The anticipated night attack did not develop.

On the following morning, the regimental commander pushed his 1st Battalion across the river, and by noon Lieutenant Colonel Francis F. MacGowan's assault companies were digging in on ridges less than 100 yards east of Point Cruz. Between Mac-Gowan's left and Twombley's right there was a gap of almost a mile of tumbled knobs, precipitous spines, and choked ravines.

At first light on Friday, the Japanese, again displaying their almost uncanny ability to sense weak points, hit the left flank of MacGowan's position, and in minutes a fire fight flared along his 700-yard front. As Japanese pressure increased, the battalion gave way. In this potentially critical situation, Sebree came forward. The general found the battalion "somewhat shaken," but his personal intervention, the efforts of his G-3, Lieutenant Colonel Paul A. Gavan, and the exhortations of the battalion commander sufficed to halt the withdrawal. The soldiers rallied, went over to the attack, and pushed beyond their lines of the morning.[12] But Japanese artillery and mortars soon stalled this new effort.[13]

Sebree now committed the One Hundred Sixty-fourth to the gap between MacGowan and Twombley, but the Japanese were determined the Americans would not advance. Sebree, equally determined, called up the Eighth Marines. At the same time, he ordered the soldiers to fall back 300 yards, while artillery fired a

30-minute preparation. Moments after fires lifted, Jeschke's assault battalions passed through the One Hundred Sixty-fourth. But the marines failed to justify the general's sanguine expectations.

The Marines got a surprise. They went forward confidently to show the Army how to do the job and got rocked back on their heels.[14]

The attack was stopped in its tracks; on November 23, Vandegrift directed Sebree to suspend operations and dig in along the line he had reached.

This was the line of departure for his offensive to the Poha.

On Thursday, November 26, Lieutenant General Imamura formally assumed command of the 8th Area Army. In New Guinea and on Guadalcanal, its prospects were grim enough; pending arrival of the promised reinforcements, the Japanese had no choice but to defend with their habitual tenacity. This their new commander adjured them to do:

ADDRESS TO ALL OFFICERS AND MEN

In obedience to the Imperial order, I hereby take the command of the Eighth Area Army.

All officers and men under my command who have been engaged in the operations in the Solomons and eastern New Guinea Area have been fighting hard and painful battles for a long period since the commencement of the operations, under such hardships as heat and hunger, and overcoming jungles and steep mountains, under the persistent attack of enemy planes. Thus, you are frustrating the counter-offensive of the US and Australian forces, and throwing them into panic.

Your loyalty and bravery is enough to make even the gods weep. I should like to express my hearty respect and gratitude to you officers and men for your brave fighting, and, at the same time, my sincere regret to the souls of those who died of wounds and disease.

The outcome of the Greater East Asia War which will decide the fate of our Empire depends solely upon this area army.

I am firmly determined, like all of you officers and men, to defeat the enemy by overcoming all difficulties with ardent and indomitable fighting spirit.

All of you officers and men will realize the responsibility imposed upon this area army and do your utmost for the execution of your respective duties with the spirit of loyalty and patriotism, in order to set His Majesty's heart at ease.

This is my address to you all.[15]

This same Thursday was Thanksgiving Day on Guadalcanal, and Halsey had seen that there was turkey and cranberry sauce for all hands. As members of Vandegrift's Division munched theirs, they gave thanks, and with good reason. For the First Marine Division had received marching orders. It was to leave "The Island" in early December and proceed to Australia for rest and reorganization. As replacement, General Marshall directed the Army's 25th Division, under orders to MacArthur's area, to proceed to Guadalcanal. This arrangement had been satisfactorily concluded only after considerable dickering. MacArthur wanted an amphibious division: he had offered the 25th in exchange for the First. But if ComSouWesPac had known the condition of Vandegrift's troops, it is most unlikely that he would have considered the exchange. For the First Marine Division was no longer combat effective. It was worn out and riddled with malaria.

Medical statistics do not tell the whole story, but the figures speak: in October, almost 2000 malarial admissions; to the last week of November (exclusive) over 2500 more. These reflect only the cases treated at Division hospitals; other hundreds swallowed the quinine capsules available only to active cases at organization sick bays. Many men who in circumstances less demanding would have been on a "no duty" or "light duty" status, worked, patrolled, and fought.[16] One hundred and three degrees Fahrenheit was the critical temperature. Those whose fever hovered below that figure were not considered to be ill.

As one man, the Division shivered, sweat, ate quinine, and waited.

18

Rear admiral raizo tanaka, who did not celebrate the American festival, spent the day aboard his flagship in Shortland harbor composing orders for yet another "Express." Intimations of renewed activity there had earlier reached Vandegrift both from Halsey and the coastwatchers and had brought the general to his decision to suspend Sebree's attack. To assess the effort obviously brewing, Vandegrift ordered Woods to keep The Slot under constant observation. The flyers found no targets.

Halsey, given a fourth star on Thanksgiving Day, had sufficient surface ships under command to cope with any effort the Japanese could mount. The trouble was that his ships were, as usual, dispersed. Possibly Pearl Harbor had taught admirals a lesson they could not forget. But, for whatever reason, this crisis found *Enterprise*, *Washington*, and a light cruiser lying quietly at Nouméa; at Nandi in the Fijis, *Saratoga* idled with battleships *North Carolina*, *Colorado*, and *Maryland*. At Espiritu Santo, or soon to arrive there, were cruisers *Northampton*, *Pensacola*, *New Orleans*, *Minneapolis*, *Honolulu*, and four destroyers.

Halsey had several days previously ordered Kinkaid to fly from Nouméa to Espiritu, take command of this hurriedly assembled cruiser task force, and lay plans to stop the reinforcement attempt which appeared imminent. Kinkaid set to work immediately to draw up an operation plan for the trip to Ironbottom Bay and the night battle he expected to fight. As he put final touches to this on November 28, he was detached by order of Admiral King, and Rear Admiral Carleton H. Wright assumed command.

In the circumstances, Halsey would have been justified in requesting delay of a few days in the execution of Kinkaid's orders, for "there were no pressing duties for him elsewhere."[1] Why Halsey did not do so remains a mystery. Kinkaid, now a veteran of South Pacific action, knew what to expect. Wright, an unproven admiral taking command of ships he had not seen before, must lead them into strange waters, there probably to engage in night battle with an experienced enemy under conditions wholly unfamiliar.

After studying Kinkaid's order, which he adopted—in all save one vital particular—and conferring with his captains, Rear Admiral Wright catapulted cruiser float planes, directed them to proceed to Tulagi, and then stand by, prepared to take off and illuminate as ordered. As the last minutes of Saturday, November 29, ticked off, he ordered Task Force 67 to sea. Halsey had that evening informed him that an enemy group, believed to consist of eight destroyers and six transports, was expected off Esperance about midnight on the last day of the month.

A few hours earlier, Admiral Tanaka had sortied from Short-lands. Was Nimitz's announcement of November 22—that the "critical" phase had passed—possibly premature?

On this occasion, Tanaka's mission was not to put troops ashore, but the more prosaic one of conducting an emergency supply run. The imperial army on Guadalcanal was threatened with disaster:

> . . . by the latter part of the month . . . all staple supplies had been consumed. The men were now down to eating wild plants and animals. Everyone was on the verge of starvation, sick lists increased, and even the healthy were exhausted.[2]

So Tanaka was to write later. The situation, grim enough, was not yet catastrophic. But daring expedients were clearly necessary, and Tanaka had proven himself to be an admiral liberally endowed with both courage and ingenuity.

The method of supply he was chosen to inaugurate was certainly novel. As he later described it:

> Large metal cans or drums were sterilized and then filled with medical supplies or basic foodstuffs such as cereals, leaving air space enough to insure buoyancy. Loaded on destroyers, these drums were linked together with strong rope during the passage to Guadalcanal. On arrival all drums were pushed overboard simultaneously while the destroyer continued on its way. A power boat would pick up the buoyed

end of the rope and bring it to the beach where troops would haul it and the drums ashore. By this means unloading time was cut to a minimum, and destroyers returned to base with practically no delay.[3]

Six of his eight destroyers were deck-loaded with this cargo; to accommodate it, all torpedoes save one per tube were removed. His own flagship, *Naganami*, and that of the division commander, *Takanami*, carried no drums.

During the morning of November 30, Tanaka dawdled at 24 knots to keep out of range of Henderson bombers, but in early afternoon he entered a weather front and upped speed to 30. At the same time, a Japanese reconnaissance plane returning to Buin reported an American formation of combat ships and transports approaching Guadalcanal.

Shortly before 10 P.M. the rain ceased, the skies cleared, and visibility improved from almost zero to four miles. Tanaka's ships passed south of Savo 45 minutes later. Aboard them, crews manned guns and torpedo tubes. The admiral had earlier "exhorted" his captains in these terms:

"There is great possibility of an encounter with the enemy tonight. In such an event, utmost efforts will be made to destroy the enemy without regard for the unloading of supplies."[4]

At the same time, Tanaka had directed his ships not to fire 5-inch guns, but to attack with torpedoes only.

Tanaka was ready for battle. Was Wright?

In darkness, Task Force 67 passed Aola, and two destroyers, *Lamson* and *Lardner*, joined Admiral Wright. He tacked them to the rear of his column. To his van, detailed to make a radar-controlled torpedo attack, Wright had assigned Commander William M. Cole's destroyer division, *Fletcher*, *Perkins*, *Maury*, and *Drayton*. Kinkaid's plan had called for two of these to be positioned well ahead to relay early warning of enemy. Wright neglected to observe this wise precaution. Behind the destroyers, the cruisers were in column: *Minneapolis*, *New Orleans*, *Pensacola*, *Honolulu*, *Northampton*. Tagging along, with no orders of any kind: *Lamson* and *Lardner*.

One hour before midnight Wright entered Ironbottom Bay; six minutes later first "pips" appeared on radar screens, range

23,000 yards. Wright swung slightly left and headed for them. At 11:16, *Fletcher* had Tanaka's column clearly on her screens and the division commander requested permission to fire torpedoes. While Wright delayed, Tanaka's column, on an opposite and almost parallel course, passed his at a distance of 7000 yards. The range, until this moment closing, opened fast, and when Wright gave Cole permission to launch it was too late.

As the Americans' fish leaped from their tubes, and before their guns opened, Tanaka's lookouts reported seven enemy "destroyers." The admiral at once signaled: "Stop unloading. Take battle stations." A moment later, as illuminating shells broke over his ships: "Close and attack!" Tanaka ordered his flag captain to swing *Naganami* about to parallel course, and jump her speed to 40 knots. No hesitation here; no vacillation. Decision. In minutes, the flagship ran abreast of the Americans and when they were broad on the beam, her captain fired torpedoes. Shells burst in the water around *Naganami*, but she was not touched.

The details of this slugging match cannot be reconstructed with accuracy. But Tanaka's marksmen were hitting. As torpedoes ripped into *Minneapolis* and *New Orleans* and blew whole chunks out of their bows, flames leaped through the upper works of *Pensacola*. The Japanese "shouted with joy."[5] But the guns of Wright's ships were finding targets. This was not difficult: three American cruisers and a Japanese destroyer were burning. And so the ship-to-ship battle continued in full fury. *Northampton*, last in column, was the ultimate victim. Two torpedoes hit her and opened a hole in her hull as big as the side of a house. She at once took water and listed dangerously; no damage control measures, however heroic, could save her: she was to sink several hours later. *Honolulu* escaped a like fate only because of canny conning by her officer of the deck, Lieutenant Commander George F. Davis.[6]

And now, at about 11:50 P.M., after an action lasting less than 30 minutes, the Japanese admiral ordered his destroyers to withdraw. Tanaka had made delivery, but not of drummed rice. Behind him, *Takanami* and four American cruisers floundered. *Pensacola*, *Minneapolis* and *New Orleans* were out of action for almost a year. Once again the U. S. Navy had been given a harsh lesson.

How could this debacle, for which there was even less excuse than for Savo, have happened? Here the radar-equipped Americans once again had gained surprise, but once again had shown they did not know what to do with it. Here Wright put four heavy cruisers with a total major calibre armament of 37 8-inch guns, against eight thin-skinned destroyers.[7] He should have blown Tanaka's "Express" out of the water. Here, with all the odds against them, Japanese sailors confirmed their superiority as seamen and as torpedomen.[8] Here as at Savo, courage alone had not sufficed. From this battle, Tanaka emerged to take position with Mikawa as one of very few top naval commanders produced by the Japanese in World War II.

Naturally, a scapegoat was needed on whom to fasten official blame for the catastrophe that had engulfed Task Force 67, and happily a suitable candidate was available. As might have been expected, this was not Rear Admiral Carleton H. Wright, U.S.N., who got himself out of the murderous mess he got his ships into by gracefully accepting "full responsibility for the torpedo damage."[9] The only officer censured was Commander William M. Cole, who in flagship *Fletcher* led the van destroyers.

Tanaka's victory ushered in the last month of 1942 on a distinctly sour note. But there was little pessimism at Halsey's headquarters. And certainly there was none at Vandegrift's. The general spent the first days of December visiting his troops and preparing to turn over his holdings to Major General Patch. His chief of staff, Colonel Thomas, and the sections he supervised, coached the Army officers slated to replace them. The Division surgeon, Captain Warwick T. Brown, and the commanding officer of the hospital, Commander Don Knowlton, conducted a sample survey of Vandegrift's command to determine the overall physical condition. This revealed that more than one-third of the officers and men were unfit for any duty which might involve combat.[10]

On December 7, a year after Pearl Harbor, Vandegrift saluted his Division and all those men who had fought with it in the skies, on the sea and on land:

> In relinquishing command in this area, I hope that in some small measure I can convey to you my feeling of pride in your magnificent accomplishments and my thanks for the un-

bounded loyalty, limitless self-sacrifice, and high courage which have made those accomplishments possible.

To the soldiers and marines who have faced the enemy in the fierceness of night combat; to the pilots, Army, Navy and Marine, whose unbelievable achievements have made the name "Guadalcanal" a synonym for death and disaster in the language of our enemy; to those who have labored and sweated within the lines at all manner of prodigious and vital tasks; to the men of the torpedo boat command slashing at the enemy in night sortie; to our small band of devoted allies who have contributed so vastly in proportion to their numbers; to the surface forces of the Navy associated with us in signal triumphs of their own, I say that at all times you have faced without flinching the worst that the enemy could send against us.

It may well be that this modest operation, begun four months ago today, has, through your efforts, been successful in thwarting the larger aims of our enemy in the Pacific. The fight for the Solomons is not yet won, but "tide what may," I know that you, as brave men and men of good will, will hold your heads high and prevail in the future as you have in the past.

(*signed*) A. A. VANDEGRIFT
Major General, U. S. Marine Corps.[11]

Two days later Vandegrift stood silently for a few minutes at the cemeteries where the bodies of men killed in the first American offensive of World War II lay. Then, at a simple ceremony, he passed command of the CACTUS–RINGBOLT area to Major General Alexander M. Patch. During these hours, Edson's Fifth Marines were marching, and for the last time on Guadalcanal. Their destination this day was Kukum, not the Matanikau.

Embarkation was not as speedy as ships' captains had anticipated. Some men were so weak they could not pull themselves up the swaying cargo nets they had climbed down on that hot morning 125 long days before. As they reached the decks of the transports and rolled their shoulders to slip off combat packs, each sought for a moment to sit quietly in a clean, dry spot and get a good look at the island where he sensed, albeit vaguely, he had helped to make American history.

Cited in the Name of
The President of the United States
THE FIRST MARINE DIVISION, REINFORCED
Under command of
Major General Alexander A. Vandegrift, U.S.M.C.

CITATION

The officers and enlisted men of the First Marine Division, Reinforced, on August 7 to 9, 1942, demonstrated outstanding gallantry and determination in successfully executing forced landing assaults against a number of strongly defended Japanese positions on Tulagi, Gavutu, Tanambogo, Florida and Guadalcanal, British Solomon Islands, completely routing all the enemy forces and seizing a most valuable base and airfield within the enemy zone of operations in the South Pacific Ocean. From the above period until 9 December, 1942, this Reinforced Division not only held their important strategic positions despite determined and repeated Japanese naval, air and land attacks, but by a series of offensive operations against strong enemy resistance drove the Japanese from the proximity of the airfield and inflicted great losses on them by land and air attacks. The courage and determination displayed in these operations were of an inspiring order.

FRANK KNOX
Secretary of the Navy[12]

19

AFTER SURVEYING the forces available to him, General Patch, whose missions were to hold the airfields and to destroy Hyakutake's 17th Army when he could muster sufficient strength to do so, concluded that further attacks must be delayed until the arrival of the 25th Division. He estimated—and correctly—that enemy strength was of the order of 25,000. His own (including attached units) would, when Collins's division arrived, exceed 35,000. The general surmised that the Japanese were having difficulty supporting their position, but he had no way of knowing that only a small fraction of Hyakutake's troops were fit for offensive action. He did know that their defensive capabilities had been sufficient to stop Sebree's November effort, and saw no reason to feed more men into the grinder west of the Matanikau until he could be more than reasonably sure of decisive success.

Tanaka's successful engagement with Wright indicated that the Japanese Navy was still a powerful factor. "Rat" runs to Kamimbo proceeded regularly and without serious attempt by the Americans to impede them. Halsey, suffering from a slight shortage of cruisers, was conserving the battleships for the next major threat. MTBs did what they could to harass and break up the "Express," but nevertheless it ran. And Patch had no way of finding out what the destroyers were bringing. His erroneous assumption that reinforcements were being landed was fully justified by all previous experience.

On paper, Patch had available five infantry regiments; of these, only three were experienced. Moore's One Hundred Sixty-fourth, now reduced to an effective strength of less than 2000 of a T/O establishment of 3325, had sustained almost 500 combat casualties since late October. An equal number, judged too ill to fight, had been evacuated. Malaria raged among those who remained. Arthur's Second Marines had not taken quite the punishment in battle that Moore's soldiers had, but the men had been in the area since August 7. They were tired, and this regiment, too, was riddled with malaria. Nor was Jeschke's Eighth Marines, which had spent months in Samoa before coming forward, in top physical shape. Since its action at the Matanikau, where 103 officers and men were killed and wounded, the regiment had patrolled constantly and aggressively and had suffered 111 additional casualties in the process.[1] Morale was high; all hands were confident the Eighth would give a good account of itself. But every day, nine or ten men reported to sick bays with sensitive swellings in armpits or groin. These swellings were the delayed first signs of "mumu"—filariasis (elephantiasis)—contracted during the Samoan tour.

The bobtailed One Hundred Eighty-second Infantry lacked a full battalion—nearly 1000 officers and men—of its authorized complement, and its battle efficiency had not been truly tested. The remaining regiment of the Americal Division, the One Hundred Thirty-second, had arrived only two days before on the ships that sailed for the south with the first batch of Vandegrift's marines. These soldiers needed time to acclimate and toughen themselves, and to gain a minimum of jungle experience in patrol actions before they could be thrown against the stubborn Japanese. They were neither mentally nor physically ready for sustained combat operations.

The One Hundred Forty-seventh Infantry was fully occupied as a garrison force at Koli, where it provided local defense for Seabees and engineers engaged in construction of a bomber strip on grassy plains near Volinavua, the precise area Vandegrift had several months previously recommended to Turner for new airfield construction.[2] Carlson's 2nd Raiders, after the epic jungle patrol of almost 30 days, during which they killed 450 Japanese, had returned to the perimeter, but were scheduled for early evacuation.

The Cactus Air Force was in comparatively good shape, and its operating facilities were speedily improved after Major Thomas F. Riley's First Marine Aviation Engineers arrived on the scene. "Fighter One," where even the Sixth Seabees could not lick the drainage problem, had been abandoned, and "Fighter Two" commissioned in mid-November. Woods counted almost 200 planes, including 100 fighters. Morale was high, as it invariably had been.

From New Caledonia, Marine Colonel Perry Smith's SCAT (South Pacific Combat Air Transport Command) continued to fly routine supply and evacuation missions to the island.[3] As of December 10, his twin-engined Douglas DC-3 transports had carried out almost 3000 wounded and ill officers and men, three times as many casualties as were evacuated by sea.[4] These reliable and versatile planes, flown by accomplished Marine and Air Force pilots, operated in all weathers and delivered everything from ammunition, drummed gasoline, bombs, candy bars, and barbed wire to bolts of wildly-patterned cotton cloth from which Clemens's scouts, who handled needle and thread as dexterously as they did rifles, made the comfortable and cool lava-lavas they sensibly preferred to dungaree trousers.[5]

Living conditions had not, however, markedly improved since the early days. Menus remained monotonously dreary: canned vienna sausage, dehydrated potatoes, Spam, rice (which as prepared by Marine and Army chefs looked like library paste and tasted worse), string beans, watery carrots, prunes, powdered eggs. Occasionally, Turner's ships put ashore a few days' rations of apples, oranges, cabbages, and frozen sides of Australian beef or mutton (classified immediately as "dead goat" and uniformly detested by all hands). And individual transport captains and crews invariably donated generously of ship's stocks. No one now lacked either tobacco or sweets. Supply officers and clever mess sergeants conducted a brisk trade with sailors in which *Nambus*, "meat-ball" flags, Luger pistols, and samurai swords exchanged for real potatos, real eggs, ham, bacon, and frozen chickens. Some ate better than others, but no one was hungry.

As their predecessors had done, Patch's soldiers and marines lived in pup tents, bitched unceasingly about the food, the mud and the rain, bragged of imaginary sexual exploits, cursed the stupidity of their commanders, reviled the U. S. Navy and MacArthur, scratched mosquito bites, visited latrines frequently, and hit their muddy foxholes every night when "Washing Machine Charlie" paid his compliments.[6] Three or four night fighters would have rid the skies of this pest. These planes had frequently been requested; none was yet available.[7]

Above all, the men wanted to end this seemingly interminable show, and did not relish Patch's decision to await the arrival of fresh troops before mounting a final attack. This, approved by

Halsey, Nimitz, and in Washington, called for the resumption of operations in mid-January. Once again, American and Japanese planning seemed to be in phase.

Although Tanaka, otherwise occupied on the night of November 30, had failed to deliver supplies, his destroyers continued their efforts to float food-loaded drums ashore. They were not too successful, and in early December, Combined Fleet inaugurated a supplementary form of transportation, coded as "Mouse." The "mice" were Fleet submarines; "the system was progressing favorably" until "enemy PT boats began interfering . . . and the method gradually became ineffectual."[8] On December 9, a PT boat from Tulagi "interfered" to the extent of sinking Fleet Submarine *I-9* as she surfaced off Esperance to commence unloading. This was a clear sign that "Mouse" operations had better be suspended.

The Japanese were now almost frantic. Every conceivable expedient was devised to deliver even minimum quantities of food, medicines, and small arms and mortar ammunition. Low-flying *Bettys* attempted to drop bundles of rice and bullets; when an occasional plane managed to elude the fighters its packages fell into the sea or deep in the jungle, and this program was quickly abandoned. Sailing vessels and small motorboats were then collected; these came down the island chain under cover of darkness and lay up during daylight. D. G. Kennedy, a major in the Solomons Islands Defense Forces, whose base was near Segi on New Georgia, kept a sharp watch on this traffic. From his jungle headquarters, Kennedy directed a private amphibious force of natives who, in 12-man war canoes, prowled the bays, lagoons and inlets of his island from sunset to sunrise. Kennedy's intelligence service was not a net, nor even a sieve. It had no holes in it, and very few Japanese barges his scouts discovered managed to escape. "Kennedy's Boys," as they proudly called themselves, took no prisoners unless instructed to do so. They killed quickly and methodically and decapitated enemy corpses with single clean strokes of the captured samurai swords many wore suspended from Japanese officers' belts strapped around their lava-lavas.

The men who manned the coastwatcher organization in the central and lower Solomons put in a very busy six weeks between the first day of November and mid-December. The Japanese had discovered the existence of Commander Feldt's net, and in the northern and central Solomons their patrols made desperate efforts to catch up with the white men who continued to report ship and aircraft movements. On Guadalcanal, Martin Clemens went out for a deserved and needed rest.[9] David Trench relieved him.[10] Dick Horton and Henry Josselyn, who had landed with the 1st Raiders on Tulagi, remained on duty, Horton hidden in the Russells, Josselyn on Vella Lavella. K. D. Hay was left at his post on Gold Field Ridge, high in the mountains overlooking the Lunga plain. His one companion was an aged nun who had survived a massacre a Japanese patrol had perpetrated earlier.[11]

Several days after Patch took command, Harmon flew to Guadalcanal to discuss plans for the January offensive. Harmon was intent that Mount Austen be taken at the earliest possible date. Patch, too, considered capture of this dominant, convoluted hill mass an essential preliminary to successful development of the later operation. The two-phase scheme of maneuver Patch presented to his superior was orthodox. In Phase One, he would take Mount Austen. In Phase Two, he would push west on a broad front, his right anchored to the seacoast. The left flank thus was to be the flank of maneuver.

Some staff officers voiced discreet objection to this concept, which they suggested would be extremely difficult to support, costly, and time-consuming. The terrain west of the Matanikau was corridored from north to south by a series of steep ridges which the attacker would have to assault successively. The Japanese had oriented their defenses against an east-to-west advance, and had organized the reverse slopes of the ridges with networks of strong mutually supporting emplacements. Here the defenders were almost totally immune to artillery fire. Except for a narrow strip along the coast, the terrain was unsuitable for tanks or wheeled traffic. Supply of food, ammunition, and water to the inland flank, and evacuation of casualties from there, would prove problems of considerable proportions.

It appeared to these officers that an amphibious hook—or a series of them—into the Japanese rear would not only obviate the physical difficulties inherent in a cross-corridor attack, but would achieve tactical surprise, cut Japanese supply lines from Kamimbo-Esperance to Kokumbona, and greatly simplify logistic support problems. Others, opting for an even more decisive stroke than such short-range shore-to-shore operations, suggested a major landing on the south coast to be followed immediately by an attack west to Cape Esperance. This, coordinated with a push along the north coast, would put the Japanese "on the horns of a dilemma." Sufficient combat ships and aircraft could, they argued, be found to cover and support such operations.[12]

In elementary terms, the question was whether to push down a succession of stone walls or kick open the garden gate. And, as so often happens in war, the least imaginative counsels prevailed. The reason given for rejecting the indirect approach in favor of the direct was lack of cruisers, destroyers, and landing craft. But almost a full month remained before the tentative D day, and had a concentrated effort been made, these ships and the small craft and crews could have been assembled. This would no doubt have put a temporary crimp in administrative routine in rear areas, but promised the prospect of speedy liquidation of the enemy at relatively low cost. Possibly the specter of defeat in detail ruled these councils, as it had so frequently those of General Patch's predecessor. During Vandegrift's tenure there was more reason to take this factor into account.

On December 10, Brigadier General Sebree, ADC of the Americal Division, ordered the commanding officer of the One Hundred Thirty-second Infantry to send a company "to occupy" Mount Austen. On their long patrol. Carlson's Raiders had passed south of this intricately ramified mass of spines, valleys, and knobs which overlooked the perimeter, and from which the enemy observed activity within it. They had discovered a complicated pattern of Japanese defensive installations in the area, but these, they reported, were not strongly held. Sebree apparently judged that one company would be enough for the job, but told Colonel Leroy E. Nelson that if one proved "not sufficient, you will send a battalion."[13] On December 16, Love Company set out.

On December 17, L Company contacted the enemy; the next day Nelson dispatched the remainder of the 3rd Battalion to the front. The same afternoon, General Sebree made a personal reconnaissance of the area and concluded that Nelson could use another battalion to advantage. He therefore released the 1st Battalion (less a company) to the regimental commander. On the day following, the 3rd Battalion reported that 200–300 Japanese were holding a well-organized position to its front.[14] On three days—December 19, 20, and 21—limited attacks supported by artillery fire and SBD strikes were stopped by Japanese machine gunners. Artillery fire had little effect on the log pillboxes in which the enemy sheltered; observers in the SBDs simply could not locate them. As soldiers on the ground were unable to find the Japanese, it is not surprising that the flyers failed to do so.

On December 21, Nelson asked for his 2nd Battalion. He was having difficulty with supplies of food and water. His troops, not yet acclimated and in deplorable physical condition, were no more able to stand the searing heat than Cates's marines had been on August 7. But the colonel was informed that his 2nd Battalion was not available. It was manning beach defenses. Sebree minced no words: "Make no more requests for 2nd Battalion. Final decision."[15] Nelson could only swallow the rebuff silently. However, he and his battalion commanders had learned one lesson: old information, as Carlson's now was, is rarely to be trusted.

For his attack the following morning, Nelson asked for sustained preparatory fire in the zone of action of the 3rd Battalion. His request was approved, and the colonel promptly ordered the battalion to withdraw 1000 yards.[16] The next morning, Army and Marine artillery shot the heaviest bombardment in the history of Guadalcanal to that date, and planes hit suspected enemy positions. When fire lifted and planes departed, the colonel ordered the battalion to return to its line of departure and jump off. Movement to the position previously held occupied the entire day. A great deal of valuable artillery ammunition and quite a large number of bombs had been expended to no purpose.

On Christmas Day, soldiers on Mount Austen ate cold beans. But their patrols thought they had developed the general limits of the position the Japanese called "Gifu."[17] Nelson directed the 1st Battalion to move into a new assembly area, and to jump off on December 27 to reduce this strong point. The battalion deployed in dense jungle, advanced to its line of departure, and was stopped. At noon on the fourteenth day of this operation, which had degenerated into a bloody fiasco, Patch released the 2nd Battalion to the regimental commander.[18] These fresh troops arrived on the scene on December 31.

At about the same time, Colonel Nelson, ill with malaria, worried over casualties, and under unrelenting pressure, sensibly asked that he be relieved. From December 19 through 30, his 1st and 3rd Battalions had suffered 182 battle casualties. An additional 131 officers and men had been evacuated, many so ill from malaria or dysentery, or both, that they could not stand. Morale was at a low point. The poorly planned and ineptly executed attacks had killed about half a dozen Japanese and made no dent at all in the "Gifu."

Here, the U. S. Army repeated a mistake both marines and Japanese had earlier made: attack without preliminary detailed reconnaissance. This takes time and requires bold, skillful and experienced personnel. Had four or five days been allotted to this project, and the necessary air photos taken and analyzed, the "Gifu" could probably have been economically reduced in a few days. The second error was to send a newly-arrived regiment against a point of such strength. The argument that the strength of the "Gifu" was not appreciated at the time will not wash; patrols should have determined its strength and extent before the attack was mounted. To compound these fundamental errors, Division had assigned a mission to a commander and then withheld from him the means to execute it promptly and properly. Finally, the ridiculous marching and countermarching to which Nelson had subjected his 3rd Battalion might have suggested that appointment of a less timorous regimental commander was in order.

As the thoroughly butchered Mount Austen operation dragged on into January, it became apparent that both Major General Patch and his assistant Division commander had much to unlearn, and perhaps even more to learn.

20   AT ABOUT THE TIME the One Hundred Thirty-second Infantry began operating against the "Gifu," conferences equally indecisive in nature were convened at Imperial GHQ. During late November and early December, members of both Army and Navy Sections had discreetly expressed increasing apprehension that Hyakutake could no longer be supported. This warranted pessimism was viewed by the upper echelons of the hierarchy as defeatist; "no one dared to present or discuss openly such an opinion."[1]

Naval officers, who represented the service responsible for supply and reinforcement of the 17th Army, took a more realistic view of the situation than did their Army Section colleagues. Combat ship losses, particularly of destroyers, were causing the Navy mounting concern. Even more critical was the problem of replacing aircraft, pilots and crews. By mid-December even the most optimistic planners saw little hope that the island "KA" could be effectively reinforced, and GHQ dispatched a liaison group to elicit opinions from Combined Fleet, 8th Area Army, Southeast Area Fleet, and 8th Fleet. "The ultimate conclusion was that there was no chance of success."[2] With this discouraging appraisal the travelers returned to Tokyo, where further study served only to confirm the judgment reached during their trip.

Supply and redeployment of forces widely dispersed in the conquered territories and bogged down in an interminable campaign in China proved continuously increasing worries to GHQ. "More and more ships were needed . . . but the total number of available ships was decreasing daily due to an unexpectedly high ship loss."[3] The American submarine campaign against lines of communication from the empire to the southern "resources area" was beginning to pay handsome dividends. Retrenchment was thus dictated not alone by American and Allied successes on Guadalcanal and in New Guinea.

On December 31, General Gen Sugiyama and Admiral Osami Nagano, in full-dress uniform, answered a summons to the Imperial Palace. Here they obtained approval of the Throne for withdrawal from Guadalcanal. Army and Navy Sections then drew up the usual "Central Agreement," and staff officers began to write orders for the respective commanders concerned. At the time, the High Command recognized that the decision marked "a major turning point of the war in this area."[4]

On January 4, an officer courier, Major General Ayabe, delivered a top secret, numbered copy of the army's order to Lieutenant General Hitoshi Imamura at his headquarters in Rabaul. For several days, Imamura hesitated on the fringe of insubordination. Only when it was impressed upon him that this distasteful directive had received Imperial assent did he reconcile himself to obedience.

The senior naval commander at Rabaul, Vice Admiral Jinichi Kusaka, voiced strong objection to the orders.[5] An evacuation would, he felt, undermine Japan's strategic position in the southeast and demoralize the army and navy. Additionally, the retreat would transfer initiative to the Americans, give them increasing confidence, and enable them "to commence operations against our vulnerable points with audacity."[6] But, as there was "no hope of retrieving the situation," the admiral reluctantly decided to cooperate with the army and "jointly exhaust all possible means in evacuating the Guadalcanal forces in late January to early February."[7]

Although Guadalcanal must be given up, General Ayabe explained that operations in New Guinea would be intensified. Operational bases at Lae, Salamaua, Madang, and Wewak would be strengthened to support a renewed drive on Port Moresby.[8] Airfield construction in the northern Solomons was to be pushed, and New Georgia and Santa Isabel securely held. This summary of future projects did not raise spirits in Rabaul, and only with a reluctance equal to Admiral Kusaka's did Commander 8th Army abandon his "firm determination to annihilate the enemy on Guadalcanal," and turn instead to planning for "a task never before undertaken by a Japanese Army"—a withdrawal by sea.

On Guadalcanal, meanwhile, some changes had been made. Major General J. Lawton Collins had arrived with his 25th Infantry Division, and the Sixth Marines, Reinforced (Colonel Gilder T. Jackson), were setting up camps under the frayed coconut trees. With their arrival, the 2nd Marine Division was complete.

And now a peculiar twist developed. Someone discovered (no doubt quite by accident) that Major General John Marston, U.S.M.C., the Division commander, was senior to General Patch. But Halsey had promised Patch command when he took over from Vandegrift, so Marston was relieved by his ADC, Brigadier General Alphonse de Carre.[9] While this contretemps was being straightened out, General Marshall activated XIV Corps, and Harmon named Patch as Corps commander. Sebree took over the Americal Division.

Patch had now on the island three divisions; a total paper strength of some 40,000. But this figure is deceptive; it included many noneffectives, particularly in the Americal Division. Collins's troops were fresh, as were the Sixth Marines. But no rifle company in any one of the nine infantry regiments was at authorized strength, and many were far below it. These were the officers and men who had, as always, to bear the burden, to do the crawling, dig the foxholes, lie at night in the mud, and break the trails in the morning. And they, who must, sweating and thirsty, locate the Japanese machine guns and then silence them one by one, were again, as always, to be at the end of the supply line.

Several days before the Corps was activated, Woods had relinquished his position as "ComAirCACTUS" to Brigadier General Francis P. Mulcahey, U.S.M.C. Mulcahey inherited a going concern. Henderson, considerably enlarged, was now a completely matted all-weather airfield, from which B-17s operated on bombardment missions to Rabaul. Twin-engined bombers had arrived, too, and for distant reconnaissance there was a squadron of New Zealand-crewed Lockheed *Hudsons*.

Auxiliary naval craft of all types crowded the harbor of Tulagi, where almost two dozen PT boats were on hand to interrupt "Rat," "Mouse" or "Ant" operations. In early January 1943, "The Island" was growing up.[10] There were even movies now and then—but no women. The Navy nurses who flew in on Smith's DC-3s had to run the gantlet if they felt the urge to visit the well-guarded "head" the engineers had built especially for them. The "dope" was that the seats had been sandpapered with loving care.

As the quiet first week of this sixth month of Guadalcanal ended, Colonel Robert B. McClure's 35th Infantry marched from the perimeter to take over investment of the "Gifu" strong point, and to drive the Japanese from a hill—the "Sea Horse"— about 1000 yards west of it. These two were the only organized defensive positions the enemy held east of the Matanikau. The Japanese manning them, elements of the One Hundred Twenty-fourth and Two Hundred Twenty-eighth Infantry Regiments, posed no major threat to the Americans. But from their emplacements in this dominating ground, the Japanese could sally out to raid into the rear, harass supply and evacuation columns, snipe, and in general make lethal nuisances of themselves.

It was manifestly desirable, first to isolate them from their comrades west of the river, and then to liquidate them. This latter, the American general hoped to accomplish by inducing the defenders to surrender. If they would not, extermination by continuous methodical bombardment was to be the answer. To speedy completion of these tasks Colonel McClure's regiment was now assigned. As one of his battalions moved to compress the "Gifu" and the others struggled into position to assault "Sea Horse" from the south, the elements selected to begin the drive west completed preparations to mount their offensive.

The Japanese they were making ready to attack were in a deplorable state. Hyakutake's command was no more than the skeleton of an army. All, including the general and his chief of staff, were hungry. But they had bullets. And determination. They would fight, and fight on, until they no longer had the strength to shove magazines into their *Nambus*, drop shells into mortar tubes, and push bolts home. One must salute the officers and men of this sadly crippled but by no means demoralized army.[11]

Against these men, who expected to die in their emplacements, Major General Patch, on the morning of January 10, 1943, launched his XIV Corps.

The Corps opened its attack on the left (inland) flank at 5:50 A.M. when six artillery battalions fired the first of 6000 rounds on a terrain feature west of the Matanikau dubbed "Galloping

Horse." This intensive bombardment was sustained for 30 minutes. A moment after the last shells burst, each of 12 fighters dumped a quarter-ton bomb on suspected Japanese emplacements. This flight was followed by 12 SBDs which in successive dives dropped thirty-six 325-pound depth charges against enemy positions infantry mortars had marked with white phosphorous shells.

The 1st Battalion, Twenty-seventh Infantry, moved fast off the mark and had no trouble seizing its first objective on "Galloping Horse." On its left, the 3rd Battalion encountered sporadic resistance, but it, too, was on the assigned objective by late afternoon. Next morning, after preliminary bombardment, both battalions again jumped off. But the 3rd ran into trouble. The soldiers had received no fresh supplies of water, and none reached them until midday. In the meantime, several score parched, dehydrated and exhausted men crumpled under a brassy sun. The battalion could make little progress, and in midafternoon its commander, Lieutenant Colonel George E. Bush, decided to pull his advance elements back to tenable positions. This day, altogether frustrating for Bush's battalion, was climaxed when Japanese 90-mm. mortars ranged-in on several groups of retiring soldiers.

On the following morning, the 2nd Battalion relieved the 3rd, and immediately attacked along a spiny kunai-covered ridge toward a well-concealed and strongly held Japanese position on its southern tip, designated "Hill 53." The battalion could not know, at the moment its companies jumped off, that its lonely battle on this desolate ridge would bring merited distinction to itself, the regiment, and the 25th Division.

Throughout its course, the Guadalcanal campaign had resolved itself into a series of platoon, company and battalion actions. Except by calling for artillery fire, arranging for air strikes, or committing his reserve, a regimental commander—or even a battalion commander—could exercise very little control over the battle joined. Thus, young company officers and noncommissioned officers, endowed with the ability to work out imaginative tactical combinations and to lead in their execution, had ample opportunity to display these talents, which are not as commonly possessed as is frequently supposed. However, the fight for the southern spine of "Galloping Horse" was, on January 13, to develop into precisely this sort of combat, fought and ultimately decided at such close range that hand grenades were exchanged at less than 20 yards.

The first problem that faced Lieutenant Colonel Herbert V. Mitchell, his executive officer, Captain Charles W. Davis, and his staff was to locate the center of resistance from which light and heavy machine guns fired against any individual who exposed himself. During the hot day, and without water, two companies, one on each side of the ridge, attempted repeatedly to approach its southern nose. Each time they were stopped, and by afternoon the men, their clothes black with sweat and dirt, their throats dry as sandpaper, were on the verge of collapse. But a three-man officer patrol led by Captain Davis had discovered the mutually-supporting Japanese emplacements on Mitchell's objective, Hill 53, and Davis was sure he could take the largest of them with no more than a small patrol.

Before noon on January 13, he and his five-man patrol did so, first crawling to within ten yards, then showering the Japanese with grenades and finally rushing the position and killing most of the enemy in it. A few dazed men stumbled out and fled toward the jungle. This "bold rush" was witnessed by hundreds of soldiers on adjacent ridges, and inspired them to assault and overrun remaining Japanese positions on "Galloping Horse."[12] The left flank of XIV Corps was now firmly anchored about 4500 yards from the sea, and Collins had the maneuver room he needed.

The Japanese were not slow to realize that a decisive effort was in the making, but other than exhort his troops to hold, there was very little Hyakutake could do. He had no reserve either to counterattack or to localize American penetrations. On January 10, the first day of the attack, the 17th Army had burned its secret files and was now preparing to displace headquarters to Tassafaronga.[13]

The last lot of supplies to reach the stubborn men garrisoning the "Gifu" strong point was delivered on January 13, when a small carrying party worked its way through American lines. At the same time, 17th Army ordered the position abandoned. Possibly the isolated Japanese deliberately ignored this order, or possibly the senior officer present thought the attempt could not succeed. For whatever reason, they remained, and continued for some days to repel every attack thrown against them by the 2nd Battalion, 35th Infantry.[14]

On January 14, Rear Admiral Koniji Koyanagi, who had relieved Tanaka as Commander, Reinforcement Force on December 29, sent an important "Express" down The Slot.[15] The night was dark, visibility poor, and the destroyers closed Esperance slowly. After discharging passengers and cargo with customary celerity, they began a high-speed withdrawal. They were not alone in these waters lashed by intermittent rain squalls. Seven PTs were waiting for them. The fireworks lasted but a few minutes, during which Japanese skippers had a series of bad scares. But they got away safely. Two PTs were damaged in the melee, but this did not deter their crews, who gained an accolade from the Japanese: "The enemy has used PT boats aggressively . . . on their account, our naval ships have had many a bitter pill to swallow—there are many examples of their having rendered the transport of supplies exceptionally difficult."[16]

A morning strike group from Henderson located the Japanese off the coast of New Georgia, but failed, as the PTs had, to derail this run of the "Express." Nevertheless, January 15, 1943, was to be a memorable one in the annals of Marine Aviation, for on that day Foss shot down three Japanese planes and became the top ace in the history of American aviation, with 21 enemy aircraft destroyed in combat.[17]

On this day, too, a first echelon of the Second Marines finally said farewell to the island. Withdrawal of this regiment from further combat assignments reduced the Second Marine Division to two combat teams, of which one, the Eighth, needed rest. General Patch pulled it back to the perimeter, and activated a Composite Army Marine Division (CAM) consisting of Headquarters, Second Marine Division, the Sixth Marines, the One Hundred Eighty-second Infantry, and the One Hundred Forty-seventh Infantry. This improvised division was to attack along the seacoast in the second drive of this new year, scheduled to jump off on January 22, 1943.

The unpleasant task of delivering Imamura's order to evacuate the island "KA" and explaining plans to Hyakutake had been assigned to Lieutenant Colonel Kumao Imoto.[18] He and a party of officers and enlisted men from the operations division of Eighth Area Army debarked at Cape Esperance a few minutes before midnight on January 14, and after a short rest set out for the command post of 17th Army. Each officer and man carried a pack weighing almost 100 pounds which contained "consolation gifts"—small flasks of whiskey, sweet cakes, dried fish, and cigarettes.

Just after dawn, American planes appeared to bomb and strafe the coastal track. The colonel and his companions sheltered themselves behind fallen trees. As they resumed their march toward the Bonegi River they observed the bodies of "many soldiers who had died from hunger and disease, and noted that hospital facilities were deplorable." The depressing and frequently interrupted journey along the coast required 18 hours.

When the weary party reached the mouth of the Bonegi River, the short tropical twilight was dying into night. Overhead, planes roared toward Henderson. A guide appeared to lead the visitors from the mouth of the river upstream to the headquarters area. Here they were challenged, responded, identified themselves, and asked for the chief of staff. As they groped their way toward General Miyazaki's tent, he called out, addressing Imoto by name. Imoto entered the tent, dimly lit by a guttering candle.

Colonel Haruo Konuma, the senior staff officer of the 17th Army, was lying on a bed made of twigs. Miyazaki snuffed the candle, and in the blacked-out tent, Imoto began to explain his mission. As he talked into the heavy silence, he sensed that both officers were stunned. Both apparently expected that he had brought orders for a new offensive. When Imoto finished, Miyazaki said abruptly, "The army cannot withdraw under present circumstances regardless of the order." Imoto listened as the chief of staff and his deputy explained in detail the situation of the army.

"If," said Miyazaki, "we take the offensive after we have been strengthened and sufficiently supplied, that would alter the situation. But if the army cannot be strengthened and sufficiently supplied, then we have no other choice but to cut our way into the enemy lines and bring into our own one last bit of glory." Such had been the decision Hyakutake and his senior commanders had reached. To withdraw, the chief of staff concluded, would be "more difficult than to pass over the raging seas." The discussion lasted until the sun rose. With daylight came planes, cruising in the skies "like hawks searching for game," and from the east "continued, choked sounds of violent firing." A few minutes later, Imoto was taken to see the commanding general.

I found him sitting on a blanket in a cave which had been dug underneath the roots of a big tree. I handed him the withdrawal order and plans relating thereto, as well as a personal letter from General Imamura. He listened to my explanations with closed eyes. When I had finished, he said very slowly, "The question is very grave. I want to consider the matter quietly and alone for a little while. Please leave me alone until I call for you."

At noon, Imoto was summoned to Hyakutake's cave. The general spoke slowly:

"It is a very difficult task for the army to withdraw under existing circumstances. However, the orders of the Area Army, based on orders of the Emperor, must be carried out at any cost. Therefore, I will respectfully comply with the conditions of the order."

It was now his task to explain the order to the senior and junior staff officers. He faced a hostile audience. When he finished, one of them said, "There is really nothing else to do but cut our way into the enemy lines and die with honor." This, Imoto remarked, was not the object of the proposed exercise. After a general discussion which lasted some time, all present pledged "to exert their greatest efforts to effect the coordination necessary."

That afternoon, Colonel Konuma proceeded to the front to explain the orders to Major Generals Maruyama and Sano. He returned the following evening, January 18, with the news that the two division commanders "had decided to abide by the decision of the Commanding General, 17th Army."[19]

On the same day, XIV Corps stood on commanding ground 1000 yards west of the Matanikau. Here de Carre's marines and Collins's soldiers were busy consolidating positions on the broken ridges which extended from the seacoast 4500 yards inland to the southernmost extremity of "Galloping Horse." Some of these Americans, and many Japanese, were to die violently during the final two weeks of this last battle on "The Island of Death."

Here the offensive which earlier had engulfed Malaya, Guam, the Philippines, Hong Kong, the Indies, and the Bismarcks reached its terminal point. Here for the first time in World War

II a Japanese army checked, held, and thwarted of its purpose, was preparing to abandon the field. But not without striking back as it did so.

Nor in dishonor did its commander now prepare to save what could be saved of his 17th Army, and to pass with it "over the raging seas."

21

THAT THE ARMY was falling back preparatory to withdrawal from the island was a secret withheld from all but senior commanders and their principal staff officers. The rank and file were told that troops were being redisposed for a future offensive.[1] Arrival of a fresh battalion from Rabaul on January 15 followed immediately by deployment of its companies to critical front-line positions apparently confirmed this. In the meantime small detachments, composed of men in relatively better physical condition than most of those in the front lines, filtered forward to relieve soldiers now so weak they could scarcely drag themselves around. All such movements were made at night.

Detailed instructions were issued for last-minute burial or destruction of artillery pieces, trucks and tractors. All ammunition other than that needed for personal weapons, light and heavy machine guns, mortars, antitank guns and howitzers were to be sunk in the sea or buried in the jungle. Emergency rations, landed by destroyer, were stocked at Kokumbona, Tassafaronga, Esperance and Kamimbo. Patients were collected in the vicinity of the Cape. Those for whom there was little or no hope were to be left. Cruel, this, perhaps. But it was now of paramount importance to salvage what could be saved of the 17th Army.

As the Japanese slowly fell back, XIV Corps advanced to the west. Every day massive artillery concentrations broke over Japanese positions; every day fighters and SBDs strafed and bombed the inland ridges and coastal track; every day Americans and Japanese died. On the left (south) flank two infantry regiments pushed rapidly along ridges, and on January 22 the 1st Battalion, 27th Infantry, looked down on Kokumbona. In this phase of the Corps offensive, Collins's division suffered exactly 300 casualties.[2] Meanwhile, CAM Division, attacking with its right resting on the coastal track, ran into a series of positions the Japanese held to the last. Here it was that a fiercely mustachioed company commander, Captain Henry P. Crowe, sparked a Marine attack the Japanese had broken down: "Get up, you sons of bitches, you'll never get Purple Hearts lyin' in those goddam foxholes."[3]

And now, in the last days of January 1943, as the "sea eagles" mounted a new aerial offensive against Guadalcanal fields, coastwatchers again reported combat ships gathering in Simpson Harbor and the Shortlands, and Combined Fleet again sortied from Truk. These signs were interpreted by Admiral Halsey and General Patch as clear indications of another major effort to reinforce. Patch suspended the offensive, and called the 25th Division back to defend the airfields against an assault from the sea.

This action has been the subject of much criticism, not all of it unbiased. Psychologically, the Japanese had the Americans just where they wanted them. Perhaps the fault here was that the two responsible senior commanders again attempted to divine enemy intentions rather than to analyze capabilities. What the Americans feared was that, with the bulk of infantry strength sucked out to the west, the enemy would strike the one vital spot. Perhaps a more audacious command would have played the situation both ways. But here Halsey and Patch deemed prudence advisable.

At 9:30 P.M. on the night of February 1, 1943, the first of 2316 emaciated officers and men, all who were left of almost 8000 Major General Tadayoshi Sano had brought to the island, waded silently toward the ramps of barges beached near Cape Esperance. In less than two hours the dim shapes of Rear Admiral Tomiji Koyanagi's "Express" destroyers slipped away from this "Cape Hope," now such a familiar landfall to the captains who had served under Admiral Tanaka.[4]

Three nights later, the main body of Maruyama's Sendai Division embarked without interference. At the same time, General Hyakutake and senior members of his staff wearily climbed the gangway which scraped and clanked rythmically against the stained hull of destroyer *Hamakaze*. The general greeted her captain briefly and went immediately to his cabin. He did not look back. On February 7, Colonel Matsuda's rear guard, slightly more than 3000, left from Kamimbo.

In these three nights, the navy lifted from the island almost 11,000 officers and men. Behind, the army left nearly 21,000 corpses.[5] Many lay unburied where artillery shells or strafing aircraft had cut them down. Others, now no longer sick, tired, and hungry, huddled in the protecting root structures of the giant trees. There they clasped with bony hands, over which the parchment skin was drawn taut, the rusting barrels of rifles they would never again aim or fire. The western end of the island was become a silent amphitheater of decaying death, where the only living things were jungle birds and intent battalions of ants. Of the dead, 8500 had been killed in action. Over 12,300 had died of wounds, disease or starvation. Of the evacuees, six hundred died before they could receive proper medical care; 3000 more recuperated slowly in rear-area hospitals.

That this minor Dunkirk, characterized by the chief of staff of the 17th Army as a "rare miracle," was successfully completed without loss of a man is a remarkable tribute to meticulous Japanese planning and to their characteristically superb seamanship. The one thing the Japanese feared above all, in late January, was that the Americans would press them hard and turn a staged withdrawal into a bloody rout. But the opportunity to destroy Hyakutake's army was missed, and 10,000 Japanese Army and Landing Force veterans lived to fight another day.

In the cold perspective of history, the relative importance of a military campaign is not judged by statistics. That a greater or lesser number of men were killed or maimed, or so many ships sunk, aircraft shot out of the skies or prisoners taken are criteria, of course; but it is the ultimate effect which the battle, or connected series of battles, exerts on the conduct and result of the war that should be considered.

Guadalcanal lasted for almost exactly six months. During this time, six naval battles were fought and sixty-five combat ships sunk.[6] Japanese aircraft losses were staggering; though the figures have never been precisely computed, between August 7, 1942, and February 7, 1943, the naval air arm lost upwards of 800 planes and 2362 pilots and crewmen.[7] The Japanese Army, in the words of Major General Kawaguchi, was not the only service "buried in the graveyard of Guadalcanal."

This protracted and bitter battle undermined the bulwarks of provincial arrogance which protected the Japanese High

Command from the contemplation of unpleasant reality. For the first time, some senior officers in Tokyo and in combat commands attempted seriously to evaluate future prospects. Now some, at least, knew that the beguiling dreams of a timeless empire embracing the strange, ever-warm, lush islands of the southern seas would never come true. After Guadalcanal, they could hope only that ultimate defeat would not be totally disastrous. For on that "insignificant island, inhabited only by natives," those who were not willfully blind had learned that they could not win:

> "There is no question that Japan's doom was sealed
> with the closing of the struggle for Guadalcanal."
> —Raizo Tanaka

And Americans, too, had learned: That the jungle could be friend or enemy. That the island war would demand all that soldiers, sailors, marines and airmen could give. That the road to the empire would be long and bloody. But Guadalcanal resolved all their doubts. There they conclusively demonstrated that they could win.

One need but to look at a map of the vast South and Central Pacific to realize what the seizure and successful defense of Guadalcanal meant in strategic terms to the Allied cause. Not only did this remove the menace to the long lines of communication to Australia and New Zealand, but Allied forces based on the island now stood on the flank of the Palau–Truk–Marshalls line, the outer cordon of empire defense, behind which the Marianas sheltered. From Guadalcanal, the First Marine Division would one day sail to seize the Palau Islands; the Third, first to eject the enemy from Bougainville, and later to recapture Guam. From Guadalcanal fields, planes flew in direct support of the 1943 operations against New Georgia and Bougainville. And from these fields were mounted the sustained air assaults which reduced Rabaul to isolated impotence.

Some day, the natives say, the Americans are coming back. With them, this time, they will not bring guns, but shiploads of strong black twist tobacco, and bolts of cotton cloth for lava-lavas.

On 7 August 1962, Sergeant Major Vouza sent the following message to the First Marine Division Association:

"Tell them I love them all. Me old man now, and me no look good no more. But me never forget."

NOTES

CHAPTER I

1. Tokyo date. Unless specifically stated otherwise, all times are local.
2. Record, International Military Tribunal for the Far East. Exhibit 802.
3. Pearl Harbor Striking Force—Vice Admiral Chuichi Nagumo.

> ATTACK FORCE—Vice Admiral Nagumo
> Carriers: *Akagi* (flag), *Kaga, Soryu, Hiryu, Zuikaku, Shokaku*
>
> SUPPORT FORCE—Vice Admiral Gunichi Mikawa
> Battleships: *Hiei, Kirishima*
> Heavy Cruisers: *Tone, Chikuma*
>
> SCOUTING FORCE—Rear Admiral Sentaro Omori
> Light Cruiser: *Abukuma*
> Destroyers: *Tanikaze, Hamakaze, Urakaze, Asakaze, Kasumi, Arare, Kagero, Shiranuki, Akigumo*
>
> SUPPLY FORCE

Ito, Masanori; Pineau, Roger; Kuroda, Andrew W. *The End of the Imperial Japanese Navy* (New York: W. W. Norton & Co., Inc., 1962), pp. 31, 32.

4. When King commanded Aircraft, Battle Force in the late 1930s, a story was current that shortly after the admiral had gone to Heaven a naval aviator knocked at the Gates. He was greeted by Saint Peter with the news that the once easy-going place had been turned inside out, reorganized and put on a "combat readiness" footing. "I'm not surprised," the aviator said, "Ernie King always thought he was God Almighty." "That's not our trouble," Saint Peter replied. "It's far worse than that. God Almighty thinks He's Ernie King!"

5. King, Fleet Admiral Ernest J., and Whitehill, Commander Walter M. *Fleet Admiral Ernest J. King, A Naval Record* (New York: W. W. Norton & Co., Inc., 1942), p. 325.

6. Commander in Chief, United States Fleet, hereafter Cominch. The office had been abolished on 1 Feb. 1941 when the Atlantic, Pacific, and Asiatic Fleets were created as independent fleets. The previous title was CincUS. For reasons obvious after Pearl Harbor, King thought this (pronounced "Sinkus") singularly inappropriate.

7. "ABC" was short title for American-British Staff Conversations of January 1941, code name: "Arcadia."

8. Bryant, Arthur, *The Turn of the Tide* (Garden City, N. Y.: Doubleday and Co. Inc., 1957), p. 446 n.

9. King and Whitehill, *op. cit.*, p. 382.

10. *Ibid.*, p. 383.

11. *Ibid.*, p. 385.

12. Bryant, *op. cit.*, p. 288. But Alan Brooke (as he was then) is not an entirely reliable source respecting either the motives or behavior of Admiral King. To state the case mildly, the CIGS was not exactly one of the American admiral's most enthusiastic admirers.

13. Ghormley, Vice Admiral Robert L. Unpublished ms. (Office of Naval Records and Library, Arlington, Va.), p. 1.

14. This model was the justly celebrated Grumman F-4-F3, soon to be replaced by the F-4-F4, an improved version.

15. Roosevelt once described King in these words. A rumor was current in Washington that the President purchased a small blowtorch and presented it to the admiral on his sixty-fourth birthday.

CHAPTER 2

1. *Nampo Sakusen Riku Kaigun Chuo Kyotai*—"Central Agreement Covering Army-Navy Cooperation in the Southern Areas." Concluded 10 November 1941. Such concordats are hereafter referred to as "Central Agreements."

The Japanese had no body such as the U. S. Joint Chiefs of Staff responsible for strategic direction of the war. There were two "Sections," or "Divisions," in Imperial General Headquarters. These were the Army Section (*Dai Honei Rikugunpu*) and the Navy Section (*Dai Honei Kaigunpu*), over which presided, respectively, Chiefs of the Army General Staff (*Rikugun Sanbo Honpu*) and Navy General Staff (*Kaigun Gunreipu*). The strategic concept, objective, and scope of each operation, the outline plan, and the allocation of forces, were decided by consultation between the Sections, with preliminary work invariably being done at fairly low staff levels. When the two Chiefs reached agreement, a "Central Agreement" was prepared, on the basis of which the Chiefs issued complementary directives to the service commanders responsible. They in turn consulted at implementing level.

I am indebted to Lieutenant General Shuichi Miyazaki for this description of the functioning of Imperial GHQ.

2. The South Seas Detachment, later to play such an important role in New Guinea, consisted of an infantry group headquarters, one regiment, a battalion of mountain artillery, a company of engineers, cavalry and transport. Total strength was slightly under 5000 officers and men.

3. At this time, the American designations *Zero, Emily, Betty*, etc., used to identify Japanese aircraft types had not been developed. Later, all fighters were given masculine designations (*Zero* being changed to *Zeke*); all other types, feminine names.

4. The Mitsubishi model *Zero*, a maneuverable navy fighter, climbed fast and turned tightly. Its armament was good: two 20-mm. cannon and two machine guns. But the cockpit was not armored and the gas tanks were not self-sealing. The *Zero* could not "take lead," and incendiary bullets flamed it readily.

The twin-engined Mitsubishi *Betty* navy bomber was an easily flammable, dual-purpose attack plane which could be armed with either torpedoes or bombs.

The *Kawanishi*, a slow, heavy boat, was designed for distant overwater reconnaissance.

5. Imperial GHQ, Navy Directive No. 47 of 29 Jan. 1942, addressed to Admiral Yamamoto.

6. Japanese heavy cruisers of the *Miyako* class displaced 10,000 tons, without fuel, ammunition and food, and were 640 feet over-all. Speed was upwards of 32 knots. The ships carried ten 8-inch guns mounted in five turrets, and eight torpedo tubes. As in the *Zero* fighter, the design sacrificed armor for speed and maneuverability. Hull lines were unmistakable and clean, but top hamper was (by American and British standards) excessive and cluttered. No Japanese combat ship was at this time equipped with either search or fire control radar. *Haguro* was a sister ship of *Miyako*. *Jane's Fighting Ships* (London: Sampson Low, Marston & Co., Ltd., 1940. Ed. Francis E. McMurtrie, A.I.N.A.), p. 310.

7. *Daikairei Dai Jukyo-go* (Imperial GHQ Navy Order No. 19, 1942).

8. Fuchida, Mitsuo, and Okuniya, Masatake. *Midway—The Battle That Doomed Japan*. Edited by Clarke Kawakami and Roger Pineau (U. S. Naval Institute, Annapolis, Md. Third Printing, November 1955).

9. Clemens, Martin. Unpublished ms. p. 50.

10. *Ibid.*, p. 53.

11. According to Captain Toshikazu Ohmae, 8th Fleet operations officer, there were at this time 2,571 officers and men of the 11th and 13th Base Construction Units on the island. Toshikazu Ohmae, *The Battle of Savo Island*. Edited by Roger Pineau, with amplifying note by Vice Admiral Gunichi Mikawa (United States Naval Institute Proceedings, Annapolis, Md. December 1957).

CHAPTER 3

1. Vandegrift was not officially informed until 23 April, 1942, by CMC serial 003D11342 of that date. It is interesting to note that as "no regular officer courier" was available, this document was transmitted by registered mail.

2. Cominch serial 00322 of 29 April, 1942: "Basic Plan for the Establishment of the South Pacific Amphibious Force." Office of Naval Records and Library (hereafter ONRL), Arlington, Va.

3. Originally BANDBOX. LONEWOLF is revealing.

4. S.S. *Electra* sailed from Norfolk 10 May, 1942; *Wakefield*, ten days later.

5. S.S. *del Brazil* sailed from New Orleans 12 May.

6. The marines who traveled on the chartered M.V. *John Ericsson* from San Francisco had a bad time. They were fed rancid butter, rotten eggs, spoiled meat, no fresh foods. Hundreds suffered from dysentery and all from undernourishment. The owners of the ship, and its master, should have been sent to the penitentiary.

7. Ghormley, *op. cit.*, p. 9.

8. Correspondence, General Merrill B. Twining, U.S.M.C. (ret.). Twin-

ing was at this time a Lt. Col., Assistant G-3, First Marine Division. Hereafter this source is cited as "Twining correspondence." I have used the designation "G" for Staff Sections. At this period, the Marine Corps used "D" to indicate Staff Sections of a Marine Division.

9. Cominch 022100, July 1942, ONRL.

10. CincPac Ltr. Instructions WATCHTOWER to ComSoPac of July 9, 1942, ONRL.

11. Ghormley, *op. cit.* His italics. He found particular fault with the Bureau of Aeronautics, the Chief of which was Rear Admiral John H. Towers, U.S.N.

12. Ghormley, *op. cit.*, p. 52.

13. The map was later located and delivered to G-2, 1st Division, in December, after the Division had arrived in Australia from Guadalcanal.

14. ComSoPac Opn. Plan 1—42., 16 July, 1942, WATCHTOWER. ONRL. In *Coral Sea, Midway and Submarine Actions* (Volume IV of his *History of United States Naval Operations in World War II*), Rear Admiral Samuel Eliot Morison discusses planning for the operation and writes (p. 268) that after Turner assumed command of the Amphibious Force in Wellington on July 18, he and his small staff promptly "began intensive planning for the landings, working day and night. This admiral, like President Roosevelt, had an equal capacity for broad views and for minute details, and, although his was the first amphibious operation of the war, he carefully planned it down to the employment of every landing craft and the exact times and amounts of naval gunfire support." The suggested inference is that until this time there had been no such planning. The fact is that *complete plans* for unloading of personnel, equipment and supplies, employment of boats, naval gunfire and air support, organization of beaches, etc., were drawn up before Turner's arrival by cognizant divisions of Vandegrift's staff. Admiral Turner was at this time practically completely ignorant of the amphibious planning process. He and his staff did no doubt work "day and night" during that hectic interval in Wellington, but credit for preparation of the many detailed and complicated plans necessary must be given impartially to all those who deserve it.

15. In fact, the directives relating to airfield construction were inserted at the instance of Vandegrift's Operations Section.

16. *United States Naval Administration in World War II.* Commander in Chief, Pacific Fleet, Amphibious Force, Vol. I. (unpublished), ONRL.

17. Correspondence. General Alexander A. Vandegrift, U.S.M.C. (ret.).

CHAPTER 4

1. Shakespeare's *King Henry V*, Act III, Prologue, lines 13–16

> *O! do but think*
> *You stand upon the rivage and behold*
> *A city on the inconstant billows dancing;*
> *For so appears this fleet majestical. . . .*

I am indebted to my friend Martin Clemens for calling my attention to the apposite phrases which I have used for the title of this chapter and in the text.

2. *War Diary, Japanese Eighth Fleet,* 7 August, 1942. ONRL. Document No. 161259. p. 6.

3. CRUISER DIVISION 6:

Aoba (flag)	*Furutaka*
Kinugasa	*Kako*

Each of these cruisers carried six 8-inch guns in turrets, formidable broadside batteries, and twelve 24-inch torpedo tubes. American designers had some years earlier removed torpedo tubes from cruisers. They did not anticipate cruiser actions at close range. Japanese thinking was less orthodox.

4. *Meiyo Maru* was sunk the following day by American submarine *S-38,* lying off Cape Saint George, New Britain.

5. All Allied operators guarded coastwatchers' "Bells" frequency at all times. All American operators additionally guarded "Fox" frequency. "Fox" broadcasts, which emanated from Pearl Harbor, were addressed to all naval units in the Pacific Ocean Areas. "Fox" broadcasts were scheduled, and were not ordinarily used to broadcast emergency warnings.

6. When he heard the news the Emperor, with more prescience than his advisors, was disturbed and wished to go at once to Tokyo.

7. Hattori, Takushiro. *The Complete History of the Greater East Asian War.* Office of the Chief of Military History (OCMH). Dept. of the Army 8-5.1, AF. VII, p. 6.

8. U. S. Navy designation for destroyers converted to troop transports. These World War I four-stackers had been modified to carry 175 officers and men. Accommodations left much to be desired.

9. Marine Corps Historical Branch has no summary casualty figures for this or any other engagement of the Guadalcanal campaign. The only data available to the researcher are scattered through reports and in a machine records tabulation. In this tabulation, I discovered several obvious errors. The figures given here are the most accurate I could produce from existing records. *First MarDiv Final Report* gives 90, of whom 36 were KIA or DOW on the island.

10. See note 9, *supra.* Figures for Gavutu show 28 KIA, one DOW, 49 WIA, 6 missing (presumed dead).

11. Report of W. Wyeth Williams, Protestant Chaplain, 3rd Battalion, Second Marine Regiment. Miscellaneous Reports. Historical Branch, U.S.M.C. Document A11-2.

12. *First MarDiv Final Report.*

13. *Ibid.* U. S. Marine Corps machine records. Casualty figures for Tanambogo must be presumed to be incorrect. They show 39 KIA, 3 WIA and 1 DOW, a total of 43, plus 6 killed by aerial bombs on Gavutu before Tanambogo was attacked. Something is obviously wrong here. Hunt's report of the action on Tanambogo did not detail casualties. The figure of 56 given in *Final Report* is therefore used advisedly.

14. Personal letter. Vandegrift to Lt. Gen. Holcomb, August 11, 1942.

15. *Ibid.*

CHAPTER 5

1. Admiral Nimitz in a later review of all reports of the Battle of Savo decided not to censure any individual commander, but did describe Fletcher's withdrawal as "most unfortunate." Potter, E. B., and Nimitz, Fleet Admiral Chester W., U.S.N. (Editors), *The Great Sea War: The Story of Naval Action in World War II* (Prentice-Hall, Inc. Englewood Cliffs, N.J. 1960), p. 254, note.

2. *Naval Administration.* Turner's communication center logged this message at "1807"—that is, 6:07 P.M. local time. It must have been broken and in Turner's hands between 6:30 and 7:00 P.M.

3. But later, others could and did. Morison, Rear Admiral Samuel Eliot. *History of United States Naval Operations in World War II: The Struggle for Guadalcanal* (Boston: Little Brown and Company, 1950). Vol. V, p. 28 and note. Here Morison presents an analysis based on detailed studies made by Lieutenant Roger Pineau, U.S.N.R., and by the U. S. Naval War College, which categorically refutes Fletcher's statement that his ships were short of fuel.

4. As drafted by Captain Ohmae and approved by Mikawa. Ohmae, *op. cit.*, p. 1271.

5. *Ibid.*, p. 1272.

6. Two reports of Japanese surface forces south of the Bismarcks were made on August 7. The first, a sighting in early afternoon by a B-17 of MacArthur's command, was vague, but relevant to the context which was developing. This plane sighted Goto's Cruiser Division 6 before Goto rendezvoused with Mikawa. At dusk U. S. submarine *S-38* made a more accurate report.

7. This message was apparently received, or decoded and distributed at Admiral McCain's headquarters, too late for the search to be executed as requested.

8. Of these destroyers, only *Ralph Talbot* played a significant role in the battle. Those with the southern group were *Bagley* and *Patterson*. *Blue* was outposting. With the northern group were *Wilson* and *Helm*. *Ralph Talbot* was outposting.

9. Author's translation.

10. Ohmae, *op. cit.*, p. 1273.

11. Quoted by Morison, *op. cit.*, Vol. V, p. 45.

12. Roscoe, Theodore. *United States Destroyer Operations in World War II*. United States Naval Institute (Annapolis, Md., 1953) "Damaging of U.S.S. Ralph Talbot," p. 172.

13. The assumption was correct. She was attacked by Japanese torpedo planes on the afternoon of August 9. Her lost complement is included in the casualty figures given, which are from Morison, *op. cit.*, Vol. V, p. 63, note 52.

14. *Japanese Eighth Fleet War Diary*, p. 7.

15. All quotations in this and the two preceding paragraphs are from monitored Japanese broadcasts. National Archives, Washington, D. C.

16. *Naval Administration.*

17. *Time*, 24 August, 1942, p. 25.

18. "In retrospect this division of the substantial forces available to cover the approach routes certainly seems to have been mistaken; but as the Admiral *lacked accurate information of the enemy's strength and intentions, it must have seemed at the time the natural thing to do.*" (italics mine) Roskill, Captain S. W., D.S.C., R.N. *The War at Sea, 1939–1945.* Vol. II, *The Period of Balance* (London: Her Majesty's Stationery Office, 1956), p. 224.

19. Newcomb, Richard F. *Savo, The Incredible Naval Debacle off Guadalcanal* (New York: Holt, Rinehart and Winston, 1961), p. 235. Newcomb made a thorough investigation of this battle, a fact which his conclusions reflect.

20. Ghormley, *op. cit.,* p. 25.

21. *Ibid.,* pp. 87–88.

CHAPTER 6

1. The river bounding the perimeter on the east was the Ilu; not, as shown on Marine maps, the Tenaru. Vandegrift had five infantry battalions to defend a front of over 10,000 yards.

2. Pepper's four 5-in. naval guns did not arrive until early September.

3. Letter, Vandegrift to Holcomb, August 22.

4. Letter, ComGenSoPac to Chief of Staff, U. S. Army, August 11, 1942. OPD 381, PTO 1. World War II Archives, Alexandria, Va.

5. Incident witnessed by the author. The battery was one of those under command of Major Manley L. Curry, whose 3rd Battalion, Tenth Marines, landed on Tulagi. An account of the episode from the more personal point of view of one of those in the boat is contained in *Guadalcanal Diary,* Richard Tregaskis (Garden City, N. Y.: Blue Ribbon Books, 1943), pp. 75–78.

Exactly a week later a measure of revenge was exacted. On the morning of August 19 two destroyers, *Hagikaze* and *Yamakaze,* closed Tulagi and began with deliberation to shell the impertinent American battery that had fired on the submarine. While so engaged, they were attacked by a three-plane flight of B-17s. One bomb of a well-delivered stick hit *Hagikaze* between her after turret and stern. Shore watchers cheered madly as they saw flame and smoke erupt. The destroyer at once lost speed and began turning in wildly erratic circles. Her steering repaired, she was escorted from the scene by *Yamakaze.*

CHAPTER 7

1. From the well-known couplet which appears in the Emperor Meiji's Rescript to soldiers and sailors:
> *"Death is lighter than a feather;*
> *Duty, heavy as a mountain."*

2. *Josei Ni Ozuru Tobu Nyu Giniya—Soromon Gunto Homen Sakusan Ni Gansuru Riki-Kaigun Chuo Kyotei,* August 10, 1942.

3. Citations from Japanese documents in this chapter are drawn largely from *Seventeenth Army Operations,* Vol. I. OCMH File 8-51, AC 34.

4. As related by Colonel Nishiura in a personal conversation.

5. There has been much discussion relating to the strength and composition of the first echelon, Ichiki Detachment. Japanese records show these as below:

Detachment Commander—Colonel Ichiki

Detachment Headquarters	163
Battalion Headquarters	23
1st to 4th Companies (105)	420
M.G. Co.: 12 heavy MG	110
One platoon Bn. Gun Unit: 2 guns	50
Engineer Company	150
TOTAL	916

6. Tanaka, Vice Admiral Raizo, with the assistance of Pineau, Roger. *Japan's Losing Struggle for Guadalcanal* (Annapolis, Md., United States Naval Institute Proceedings, July (I) and August (II) 1956). I., p. 690.

7. Curiously, the exact time of the first attack has never been established. The Division *Final Report* says 0310. Pollock put it even earlier than 0240, a time given to me by a participant.

8. Clemens, *op. cit.*, pp. 152–153.

9. Vandegrift to Holcomb, letter of August 22, 1942.

10. Phrases ascribed to General Matsui, commander of the Japanese troops which sacked Nanking.

11. Including seven suffered by Captain Brush's patrol, and three by 3rd Battalion.

12. *Seventeenth Army Operations*, p. 32.

13. Vandegrift to Holcomb.

14. Tanaka, *op. cit.*, I, p. 691.

CHAPTER 8

1. Correspondence. Major General Richard C. Mangrum, U.S.M.C.

2. Hough, Lieutenant Colonel Frank D.; Ludwig, Major Merle E.; Shaw, Henry I. Jr. *History of U. S. Marine Corps Operations in World War II, Pearl Harbor to Guadalcanal*. Historical Branch, G-3 Division, Headquarters, U. S. Marine Corps. U. S. Government Printing Office, Washington 25, D. C., p. 276.

3. Neither the destroyers attending *Wasp* nor the carrier herself needed fuel. See Morison's analysis, *op. cit.*, Vol. V, p. 83, note 7.

4. Tanaka, *op. cit.*, I, p. 694. Vice Admiral Nishizo Tsukahara, whose headquarters were at Rabaul, commanded both Southeast Area Force and 11th Air Fleet. Vice Admiral Mikawa, commanding 8th Fleet, was Tanaka's immediate superior.

5. *Ibid.*, p. 695.

6. The moon was waning and Henderson's planes were airborne.

7. *War Records, Japanese Navy*. Desron 2. ONRL. Doc. #161711, p. 9.

8. *Daikaishi Dai Hyakunijushichi-go*. Imperial GHQ Navy Directive No. 127, p. 9.

9. Sherrod, Robert. *History of Marine Corps Aviation in World War II* (Washington: Combat Forces Press, 1942), p. 81.

10. ComAirSoPac's evaluation of this Army fighter: "No good at altitude and disheartening to the brave men who fly them." (Sherrod, *op. cit.*, p. 82.) Despite constant validated reports of the inability of this fighter to meet high-altitude combat requirements in the Solomons, Arnold's battery of Washington quill-drivers kept insisting that it would. See Craven, Lesley Frank, and Cate, James Lea, *The Army Air Forces in World War II*, Vol. IV, *The Pacific: Guadalcanal to Saipan* (The University of Chicago Press, 1950), pp. 40-42. Sherrod, *op. cit.*, (p. 82) cites the words of the 67th Fighter Squadron's historian:

"We can't maneuver and dogfight with the Zero—what good are we? Our enlisted men are risking their lives every day trying to get the planes patched up—for what? We're just eating up food—and there's not enough to go around anyway, and using up valuable gasoline—and the gas supply is getting lower every day. Hell, we can't fight. When the Japs come we're told to 'go on reconnaissance.' What good are we?"

11. Under Secretary of the Navy Forrestal is reported to have said: "Grumman saved Guadalcanal." The Grumman *Wildcat* was a fine airplane, but marines did not exactly appreciate this remark.

12. *Life*, Nov. 16, 1942.

13. *Southeast Area Naval Operations*, Vol. I. OCMH 8-5.1, AC 98, p. 18.

14. ComAirSoPac to CincPac, 31 August 1942. ONRL.

15. CTF 62 to ComSoPac, 1 Sept. 1942. ONRL.

16. Author's translation.

17. *Seventeenth Army Operations*, p. 41.

18. *Southeast Area Naval Operations*, p. 20.

19. *Ibid.*

20. Correspondence, Lieutenant General Kumao Imoto.

CHAPTER 9

1. When the Seventh Marines embarked in Samoa, their commanding officer was told that his regiment was to be sent to New Zealand for further training and ultimate transfer to MacArthur's theater.

2. Actually from Samoa. This convoy was lifting the Seventh Marines and the 5th Defense Battalion.

3. Navy designation "YP," hence to the marines "Yippies."

4. Turner to Ghormley 092300, Sept. 1942. ONRL.

5. *Ibid.*

6. The 26th Air Flotilla at a strength of 140 aircraft, over half of them *Zeros*.

7. ComAmphforSoPac 120530, Sept. 1942. ONRL.

8. Vandegrift, Thomas and Twining correspondence. Twining was not present at the conference described, but read the memorandum a few hours later.

9. Thomas and Twining correspondence.

10. *Jitsuroku Taiheiyo Senso* (Personal Records of the Pacific War). Kawaguchi memoir: "Struggles of the Kawaguchi Detached Force." I am deeply indebted to Mr. Yukihisa Suzuki, author of *Autobiography of a Kamikaze Pilot* and presently Director, Asia Library, University of Michi-

gan, for his translation of this personal account of Edson's Ridge as seen by the Japanese commander.

11. *Outline of Southeast Area Naval Air Operations*, Part II. OCMH 8-5.1, AC 121, p. 22. Details of Japanese strikes during the period are largely from the same record.

12. Twining correspondence. Colonel Twining witnessed Banta's act.

13. The author identified Major Brown's body a few minutes later.

14. In *First MarDiv Final Report*.

15. The ten missing (seven Raiders, three Parachutists) were later presumed dead.

16. *Seventeenth Army Operations*; Kawaguchi, *op. cit.* Kawaguchi's brigade consisted of the units listed below, at the effective strength shown as of departure from Shortlands:

	Officers	Men
Hq. Co., 35th Inf. Brig.	12	40
One Hundred Twenty-fourth Inf.	120	3550
2nd and 3rd Bns., Fourth Inf.	44	1272
	176	4862

Additionally:
One antitank platoon (4 guns) (two left at Tasimboko)
One Btry. Mountain Arty. (4 guns) (two with Kawaguchi)
One Btry. Howitzers (4 guns) (two with Kawaguchi)
Signal Detachment
Medical Detachment
Engineer Detachment

In all, about 210 officers and something over 6000 men. Of the original strength, some 400 had been lost in barges at sea. The 2nd and 3rd Battalions, Fourth Infantry, still known as the "Ichiki Detachment," were incorporated in the 35th Brigade.

17. Kawaguchi, *op. cit.* Actually, Kawaguchi relented. The colonel had a very good excuse. His feet were in such terrible condition from the jungle march that he could barely hobble. But why he did not turn over command to his executive officer is a mystery.

18. *U. S. Strategic Bombing Survey* (USSBS) Interrogation.

Of the Ridge, Rear Admiral Morison later wrote: "The Battle of the Ridge was one of the crucial actions of the Pacific War. It was won by Edson's inspired leadership and the skill and courage of individual Marines. If this battle had been lost, Henderson Field would have been lost. . . ." (Morison, *op. cit.*, Vol. V, p. 130.)

CHAPTER 10

1. Hattori, *op. cit.*, II, p. 22. The failure of Kawaguchi's attack "proved fatal to the overland advance of the South Seas Detachment to Port Moresby."

2. In reply to Turner's 120530 to ComSoPac, previously cited.

3. ComSoPac 122346, Sept. 1942. ONRL.

4. ComSoPac 130540, Sept. 1942. ONRL.

5. ComSoPac blamed Admiral Noyes for loss of *Wasp*. It is true that the

two carrier Task Groups were not steaming at high speed, and that they were not "zigzagging." But a carrier cannot very well "zigzag" when she heads into the wind to launch aircraft. This was the maneuver in which *Wasp* was engaged when struck. Both Nimitz and King reviewed the circumstances and fully exonerated Admiral Noyes.

6. Imperial GHQ Navy Directive No. 135. World War II Combat Archives, Alexandria, Va.

7. Had the Merchant Marine been Federalized at outbreak of war and put under jurisdiction of the Navy, this scandalous situation would not have developed.

8. Sherwood, Robert E. *Roosevelt and Hopkins* (New York: Harper and Bros., 1948), p. 632.

9. Arnold, General of the Air Force H. H. *Global Mission* (New York: Harper and Bros., 1949), p. 337.

10. *Ibid.*

11. General Arnold's staff got around to preparing a reply almost three weeks later, but General Marshall deemed the letter submitted to him for signature on October 5 "a little too brisk" and refused to sign it. During the next two weeks the Air staff somehow found time to draw up a more temperate response to King's memorandum of September 17. This they accomplished by October 18. The letter went for signature to General Marshall with the following interesting notation: "The situation in the South Pacific has gone through such a change since the date this communication [King's] was written that an answer to the same at the present time is thought to be unnecessary." Equally unnecessary is further comment on this incident. (OPD 452.1 Pacific Theater of Operations. Sec. 1, World War II Combat Archives, Alexandria, Va.)

12. This exchange was first printed in the *New York Times* on November 3, 1942.

13. First MarDiv "Medical Experiences and Problems in the Guadalcanal Operation." MarCorps Historical Branch, Doc. A7-19.

14. Vandegrift, quoting *Field Service Regulations*, admitted that at Second Matanikau he "drifted" aimlessly into action. *First MarDiv Final Report*, V, p. 9.

15. Arnold, *op. cit.*, p. 348.

16. *Ibid.*, p. 343.

17. Maruyama received Seventeenth Army Opn. Order No. 9-291500 when issued. His division was so called because it had been raised in and near the city of Sendai, Miyagi Prefecture, Honshu.

CHAPTER 11

1. Correspondence, Fleet Admiral Chester W. Nimitz, U. S. Navy.

2. Ghormley, *op. cit.*, pp. 128–129.

3. Harmon was ComGen United States Army Forces in South Pacific Area (USAFISPA), and commanded U. S. Army Air in the South Pacific. He was ex officio a member of Ghormley's staff.

4. This important letter is reproduced as "Appendix A" in Miller, John

Jr., *Guadalcanal: The First Offensive*. Historical Division, Department of the Army (Washington, D. C., 1949), pp. 357–59.

5. Three Marine infantry regiments, the First, Fifth and Seventh, were now present. Battalions of the first two were at about 60 per cent of authorized strength; the Seventh at about 80 per cent. The extra battalion was Hunt's (of the Second Marines, recently brought from Tulagi). The First Raiders, now reduced by casualties and malaria to half strength, were still present, awaiting evacuation, in Division reserve.

Japanese strength at this time was of the order of 15–16,000 officers and men, of whom roughly two-thirds were infantry. This estimate is possibly conservative. *17th Army Opns.*, Vol. II, p. 51, gives October average as 18,000.

6. *History of Marine Corps Operations in World War II*, p. 321.

7. Miyazaki correspondence.

8. *Ibid.*

9. This information was conveyed to Hyakutake personally by Staff Officer Hirama of Sendai Division.

10. *Seventeenth Army Operations*, p. 75.

11. The 228th Infantry of the 38th Division and the 19th Independent Engineer Regiment were ordered forward at this time.

12. Hattori, *op. cit.*

13. Although some air cover could now be afforded; on October 9 the fighter strip at Buin in South Bougainville was activated.

14. Scott's Task Force 64 consisted of heavy cruisers (CA) *San Francisco* (flag) and *Salt Lake City*, light cruisers (CL) *Helena* and *Boise*, and destroyers *Duncan, Farenholt, Buchanan, Laffey* and *McCalla*.

15. A misunderstanding of this signal was to cost the Americans dearly. What Scott apparently intended was for the leading ship in *each division* to turn left simultaneously to course 230° with ships of each division turning in the same water as had the lead ship (Divisions 230 Corpen). This would automatically have reversed the roles of the destroyers. That is, the two ships previously astern of the cruisers would have been in the van, while the three previously in the van would be astern of the cruisers.

16. Wilson must have interpreted the order received over voice radio (TBS) as "230° Corpen," which would have meant that the *column* was to turn left to course 230°, with each ship turning in the same water as had the *lead* ship. Accordingly, he continued to follow in trace of *Helena*, and turned where she had turned. I am indebted to Rear Admiral William W. Wilbourne, U.S.N. (ret.), then a lieutenant commander and gunnery officer of *San Francisco*, for the details of the "tragic mix-up" which followed close upon Scott's change of course signal.

17. There is reason to believe that one or more of them were. *Duncan* received hits on her port side.

18. *Southeast Area Naval Operations*, Vol. I, p. 35.

19. This message appears in ComSoPac War Diary in proper sequence, but lacks date-time group.

20. Tanaka, *op. cit.*, II, p. 815.

21. ComSoPac 141410, Oct. 1942, to CincPac. ONRL. The tenor of this

message affected Admiral Nimitz profoundly, and convinced him "that a tougher leader was needed." (Nimitz correspondence.)

22. ComGen First MarDiv 141942, Oct. 1942, to ComSoPac. ONRL.

23. ComAirSoPac 150921, Oct. 1942 to ComSoPac. ONRL.

24. *Southeast Area Naval Operations*, Vol. I, p. 36.

CHAPTER 12

1. *Seventeenth Army Operations*, pp. 85-86.

2. *History of Marine Corps Operations in World War II* gives 5600, but this is an error. *17th Army Opns.*, VI, p. 51 gives 20,000 troops on the island as of Oct. 25. Maruyama's force consisted of nine infantry battalions at an average strength of about 600. Additionally, both light and heavy mortar units, mountain guns and quick-firing gun batteries, engineers, signal, medical and other service troops marched with him.

At this time the entire Sendai Division (less one artillery battalion and part of the reconnaissance battalion) was on Guadalcanal. According to Colonel Kazuo Taguchi, then operations officer of the Division, its ashore strength on October 19 was 9372 officers and men. Colonel Taguchi states also that as of that date, 176 artillery pieces of all calibre had been landed. Some of these (for instance, the twelve landed by Kawaguchi at Taivu) were, of course, no longer available. (Taguchi correspondence.)

3. Maj. Gen. Tadashi Sumuyoshi does not recall exactly how many tanks he had, but thinks "about sixteen." (Sumuyoshi correspondence.)

4. This reinforced battalion was to land near Koli Point and seize an area suitable for construction of an airfield.

5. ComGen 1st MarDiv 170410, Oct. 1942, to ComSoPac. ONRL.

6. CincPac 180315, Oct. 1942, to Cominch. ONRL.

7. CincPac 180319, Oct. 1942, to ComSoPac. ONRL.

8. Secretary of the Navy Frank Knox. Press interview, Oct. 17, 1942. *New York Times*, Oct. 18, 1942.

9. *New York Times*, Oct. 18, 1942.

10. Halsey, Fleet Admiral William F., and Bryan, J., III, *Admiral Halsey's Story* (New York: Whittlesey House, McGraw-Hill, 1947), p. 109. Quoted by permission of the copyright holders.

11. *Ibid.*

12. *Ibid.*, p. 116.

13. *Ibid.*, p. 117.

14. Monitored Tokyo broadcasts. National Archives, Washington, D. C.

15. "Just before the night attack was launched, Maj. Gen. Kawaguchi was relieved of his post as Commanding Officer of the Right Wing by a telephone order from Commanding General, 2nd Division. . . . It is said that the reason for the dismissal of Maj. Gen. Kawaguchi was due to the fact that he insisted on the need to change the direction of the attack further to the right (east) than that given in Division instructions. Maj. Gen. Kawaguchi was a very able and brave officer, but he had the habit of at times stubbornly insisting on his own views. Later the Major General was ordered to return home and was placed on the Reserve List." (Miyazaki correspondence.) Kawaguchi died in 1960.

16. Sumuyoshi correspondence.
17. *Seventeenth Army Operations.*
18. *Ibid.*
19. *Ibid.*
20. *Ibid.*
21. *Ibid.*
22. *First MarDiv Final Report.*

CHAPTER 13

1. DDs *Akatsuki, Ikazuchi* and *Shiratsuyu.*
2. Detailed account of action of U.S.S. *Trever* and *Zane* in *Combat Narratives, Miscellaneous Actions in the South Pacific, 8 August 1942–22 January 1943.* ONRL, Document No. 2583.
3. Sherrod, *op. cit.,* p. 104, and *S.E. Area Naval Opns., op. cit.,* p. 41.
4. *Southeast Area Naval Operations,* p. 41.
5. *Seventeenth Army Operations,* p. 98.
6. Colonel Oka has been grievously maligned in American histories. His own seniors considered him an able and brave officer.
7. *Unit History, 164th Infantry, Americal Division, 300 Inf.* (164) 0.2 (2342), National Archives, Alexandria, Va.
8. Morison, *op. cit.,* p. 206, puts Kondo in command, but USSBS No. 75, "Interrogations," from which the Japanese O/B is drawn, names Nagumo.
9. Rear Admiral Aubrey Fitch had relieved McCain, who was ill, as ComAirSoPac on September 20, 1942.
10. I have been unable to determine whether it was this PBY pilot or one of his colleagues who sent the classic message: "Sighted enemy carrier task force Lat. 'a' Long. 'b' course 'c' speed 'd' x-ray. Please notify next of kin."
11. Halsey's message to all SoPac Task Forces, Oct. 25, 1942.
12. Hits scored on Japanese ships as given in USSBS No. 75.
13. *Junyo* was attached to Kondo's "Advance Force," but her air group was under Nagumo's command for the battle. This air group consisted of 24 fighters, 21 bombers, and 10 torpedo planes.
Aircraft available at Santa Cruz:

	U.S.	Japanese
Fighters	70	87
Dive Bombers	72	68
Torpedo planes	29	57
	171	212

14. Details of Japanese air attacks from *Narrative of Japanese Anti-Shipping Attacks, 1941–43,* A.I.D. No. 3—Part II, August 1943. Air Information Division, Office of the Chief of Naval Operations.
15. The sad story of the American Mark 14 torpedo with its Mark 6 exploder ("the arch-villain in the melodrama of malfunction") has been told in detail by Theodore Roscoe in the semiofficial *United States Submarine Operations in World War II* (United States Naval Institute, Annapolis, Md., 1949). Briefly, this 21-inch torpedo, with a warhead carrying

507 pounds of TNT (the 24-inch Japanese torpedo carried almost 1000 pounds) was almost totally unreliable. The depth-setting mechanism was inaccurate, and the torpedo ran anywhere from 10 to 15 feet too deep. For instance, at a 15-foot depth setting, these torpedoes passed under targets drawing 25 feet. The influence exploder, designed to operate by induction as the torpedo passed through the magnetic field generated by a ship, failed to function more often than not. The impact exploder worked only when the torpedo head struck its target at an acute angle. Further, due to another built-in peculiarity, there were many "prematures," *i.e.,* explosion before the torpedo hit the target.

Not until eight months after Pearl Harbor, and then only as a result of forceful intervention of Admiral King, could operational submarine officers force the Bureau of Ordnance to admit the Mark 14 was running deep. Finally, a full year later, submarines managed to convince the Bureau that drastic steps must be taken to provide a reliable torpedo.

That despite a faulty weapon American submarines compiled the good record they did in the first year and a half of World War II is irrefutable testimony to the skill and persistence of officers and men of the Submarine Force. That the mistakes in design were finally admitted and rectified is a tribute to the dogged determination of Rear Admirals Robert H. English (ComSubsPac) and Charles A. Lockwood, Jr. (then ComSubsSouWesPac). These, "after hundreds of hours had been expended in fruitless approaches and many thousands of dollars worth of ammunition had gone down the drain" (Roscoe, p. 146), finally got a torpedo that would do what torpedoes were supposed to do: sink enemy ships. Had such torpedoes been available in the fall of 1942, many "Express" runs to Guadalcanal would have been permanently derailed.

16. Monitored Japanese Broadcasts, *op. cit.*

17. *Seventeenth Army Operations,* p. 100, states these figures on American losses were given in American broadcasts. This is incorrect, and if it were correct would be an amazing justification for the imperial army's continued optimism. Actually, what must have happened was this: shortly after dawn on October 26, a search plane from cruiser *Tone* reported sighting an American force of three carriers, two battleships, five cruisers, and twelve destroyers. This news was of course relayed to Yamamoto. Nagumo's "face" demanded that after the battle he report all enemy capital ships sunk. Hence the fiction which misled army planners.

18. *Ibid.*

19. Tanaka, *op. cit.,* p. 818.

20. Even today, marines can get quite worked up over what some describe as "betrayal" of Guadalcanal. The prime culprits, as those who hold this view aver (usually profanely), were MacArthur, Arnold, and Marshall. But Halsey had full authority to strip rear areas of fighters, which he did not do. One basic question, usually overlooked, was the existing capacity of Guadalcanal airfields to support additional aircraft. This might have been solved by a series of airlifts of matériel and personnel from New Caledonia, but, again, there was the problem of how to support the shuttling transport aircraft based there. Fuel supplies on that island were limited and operating conditions relatively primitive.

21. The British Chiefs at this time were no more than vaguely interested in the Pacific. They considered Hitler the enemy who must be first eliminated.

22. Sherwood, *op. cit.*, pp. 622–23.

CHAPTER 14

1. Sherrod, *op. cit.*, p. 110.

2. Miyazaki correspondence.

3. Correspondence. Major General Toshinaro Shoji.

4. Japanese operational messages were frequently intercepted and broken at Pearl and in Washington.

5. According to *Seventeenth Army Operations*, pp. 101-02, these Japanese ships brought to Gavaga Creek one infantry company, two field guns, and a signal detachment, plus ammunition, general supplies, and rations for 2000 men for 10 days. These supplies were to sustain Shoji's column during a march to the upper Lunga, where he was to begin as soon as they arrived. Major General Takeo Ito, 38th Division Infantry Group Commander, later stated that no troops were landed at this time. (Miller, *op. cit.*, p. 196, 196 n.). Hough, Ludwig and Shaw, *op. cit.*, say (p. 347, 347 n.) 1500 troops were landed, but also cite Miller's note. I rely here primarily on information kindly supplied by former Major General Toshinaro Shoji.

6. Shoji correspondence.

7. Miller, *op. cit.*, p. 198, 198 n.

8. Sebree, ADC of the Americal Division, accompanied Moore, as he later said, "to observe and learn." Sebree had but recently arrived on Guadalcanal to prepare the way for the remainder of the Americal Division.

9. Halsey, press interview on Guadalcanal, Nov. 9, 1942.

10. *Southeast Area Naval Operations*, p. 45.

11. Tanaka, *op. cit.*, II, p. 820.

CHAPTER 15

1. A phrase used in a *New York Times* editorial at an earlier date, but equally appropriate here.

2. *Report of First* [sic] *Matanikau Engagement.* 164th Infantry. File: 300-Inf(164)—0.3. 23808. (National Archives, Alexandria, Va.) Actually, this was the fifth action at the Matanikau. Curiously, *First MarDiv Final Report* says (p. 31) that action was resumed on 10 November, yet according to ComSoPac War Diary (ComGen 1st MarDiv to ComSoPac 082245 and 092235) the attack jumped off on November 9.

3. The circumstances under which this regiment was committed to combat for the first time reflect the operational improvisation characteristic of the campaign as a whole. Jeschke received no warning orders; he was not afforded opportunity for personal reconnaissance; he was not given detailed air photos which were then available. The regimental commander's complaints were justified. Still, the Division staff was seriously undermanned and the situation demanded speedy action.

Jeschke's regiment was not properly indoctrinated for jungle conditions or jungle combat because "no information had been received regarding lessons learned by other Marine units in the Guadalcanal operation during the three months prior to the landing of the Eighth Marines." (*8th Marines, Report of Operations, Guadalcanal.* Historical Branch, G-3, Hq., U.S.M.C. Document A24—1.)

Headquarters, Marine Corps was singularly derelict during the first six months of World War II in providing rear-area units with timely "Action Reports" and summaries of lessons learned.

4. *First MarDiv Final Report*, Phase V, p. 30.

5. *Ibid.*

6. Halsey, *op. cit.*, p. 124.

7. *Southeast Area Naval Operations*, p. 46.

8. Nagumo's Third Fleet with battle carriers returned to the empire after Santa Cruz for repairs and to receive new air groups.

9. Morison, *op. cit.*, pp. 233–34, 234 n. 7, n. 8.

10. CAS *Chokai, Kinugasa, Suzuya, Maya.* CLS *Isuzu, Tenryu.*

11. Tanaka, *op. cit.*, II, p. 820.

12. *Hiei* and *Kirishima* were reported as "two battleships or two heavy cruisers." Turner's estimate (furnished Callaghan) gave the Japanese two battleships.

13. Correspondence, Rear Admiral William W. Wilbourne, U.S.N. (ret.). Admiral Wilbourne, then a lieutenant commander, was gunnery officer of flagship *San Francisco.*

14. U. S. Navy destroyer doctrine at this time was well developed, but the torpedoes available were scandalously erratic and unreliable. Most ran too deep, and it can be argued that even had Callaghan positioned his destroyers in the van, and allowed them to execute a sudden attack and immediately withdraw (in accordance with doctrine) the results would have been negligible. Still, it would seem that he might well have taken the chance that a few fish would run true and hot.

15. In justice to Admiral Callaghan, it may be said that most senior naval officers did not, in those early days, appreciate the tremendous advantage conferred by radar on the side which possessed it. This was not entirely the fault of the admirals in combat zones. The Department then classified radar with the same stringency it later did the proximity (VT) fuse, and held information pertaining to naval search and fire control radar so closely that many of those who should have been thoroughly briefed on their capabilities and limitations had but a vague conception of what these were.

16. Morison, *op. cit.*, p. 239.

17. *Ibid.*, p. 242.

18. *Ibid.* The order to "Stand by" was given at 1:45 A.M.

19. *Ibid.*, p. 243.

20. *Ibid.*, p. 246.

21. I am indebted to Rear Admiral William W. Wilbourne, U.S.N. (ret.), for an account of his experiences in this battle.

The only authoritative published account by a participant is *The San Francisco Story*, Rear Admiral Bruce McCandless, U.S.N. (ret.). This article appeared in the *U.S. Naval Institute "Proceedings"* (Annapolis, Md.,

Nov. 1958). A statistical summary of the damage suffered by the ship and her crew is relevant.

1) She sustained 45 hits from Japanese guns (5-in. to 14-in.).

2) The crew fought 22 major fires, brought them under control, and finally extinguished them.

3) Eighty-six officers and men were killed and 106 seriously wounded of an on-board count of 1050.

If to these figures be added casualties sustained during the air battle of November 12, they read, respectively, 110 and 151, or 25 per cent of on-board count.

22. Morison's account of this battle is the only reliable one. Japanese sources are both scanty and incoherent. The version given here is but a pale reflection of Admiral Morison's detailed and masterful description of this frightful close-range encounter.

23. *Southeast Area Naval Operations*, p. 47.

24. Wilbourne correspondence, *op. cit.*

25. Correspondence, Bureau of Medicine and Surgery, Department of the Navy, Washington, D. C., does not support this figure. But the Bureau's records are both incomplete and incorrect. See Note 28 below.

26. Marshall, General of the Army George C. Arnold, General of the Air Force H. H.; King, Fleet Admiral Ernest J. *War Reports*, p. 537.

27. Hoover's message as given by Morison, *op. cit.*, p. 258. Halsey relieved Hoover of command. Later, he carefully reviewed the case and reversed the earlier judgment. In *Admiral Halsey's Story*, pp. 133–34, the admiral confesses he made "a grievous mistake": rescue operations "would almost certainly" have invited a second torpedo attack. And "at that critical stage, the loss of another ship—and possibly more—might jeopardize the whole campaign."

Rear Admiral McCandless (*The San Francisco Story*) witnessed the disintegration of *Juneau* from the bridge of *San Francisco*. The cruiser (he wrote) "didn't sink—she blew up with all the fury of an erupting volcano. There was a terrific thunderclap and a plume of white water that was blotted out by a huge brown hemisphere a thousand yards across, from within which came the sounds of more explosions. . . . When the dark cloud lifted from the water a minute or so later, we could see nothing of this fine 6000-ton cruiser or the 700 men she carried." (P. 51.)

28. The Chief of the Bureau of Medicine and Surgery stated (correspondence, June, 1962) that records show a loss of 377. As Morison has pointed out, (*op. cit.*, p. 258 note 2) the complement of *Juneau* was over 700. Such an apparent error, which the Bureau has never corrected, casts doubt on the accuracy of all Bureau of Medicine and Surgery casualty figures.

Rear Admiral F. P. Gilmore, Acting Surgeon General of the Navy, wrote (personal correspondence, 28 June 1962) that casualty data were not tabulated as of specific dates by the Bureau of Medicine and Surgery and therefore "figures for the night engagement of November 12–13 are not available."

The Bureau of Naval Personnel has compiled no figures for World War II battles.

CHAPTER 16

1. Tanaka, *op. cit.*, II, p. 821.
2. *The Army Air Forces in World War II.* Vol. IV, p. 59.
3. Sherrod, *op. cit.*, p. 115. Morison's figures, which are considerably larger, are incorrect. Morison, *op. cit.*, p. 263.
4. Tanaka, *op. cit.*, p. 821, says five. Morison says no losses were sustained in these early morning strikes, but that five American planes were shot down during the day.
5. It is impossible to reconcile conflicting claims for this day. Morison, *op. cit.*, is prone to give *Enterprise* pilots too great a share of credit. But there was enough for all participants.
6. Tanaka, *op. cit.*, p. 822.
7. *Ibid.*
8. *Southeast Area Naval Operations*, p. 49.
9. *Report of Night Actions, Task Force 64*, ONRL File 47371. The account is primarily based on Rear Admiral Lee's excellent narrative report. Of the four engaged destroyers, only *Gwin* made port. *Benham* was abandoned and sunk shortly before sunset, November 15.
10. *Ibid.* Comments, para. 7.
11. Tanaka, *op. cit.*, p. 824. At about this time *Kirishima*'s captain gave orders to scuttle. With steering gone, *Kirishima* was as helpless as *Hiei* had been.
12. *Southeast Area Naval Operations*, p. 49.
13. Morison, *op. cit.*, gives 17 *Enterprise* planes principal credit for destruction of the beached transports and goes on to state that the "star performance" of the day was staged by destroyer *Meade*, which "darted out of Tulagi harbor" to open fire "at a range of 12,500 yards." (!)

Meade would have been more suitably employed had she proceeded at once to pick up men floating in the water, many of whom were wounded and burned. The officers and crew of *Meade* certainly deserve commendation for the work of rescue, but so far as destruction of the transports was concerned, her activities contributed little.
14. Quoted extracts are from monitored Japanese language broadcasts. National Archives, Washington, D. C.
15. Tanaka, *op. cit.*, p. 824.
16. *New York Times*, Tuesday, Nov. 17, 1942.
17. *Ibid.*, Wed., Nov. 18, 1942.
18. *Ibid.*
19. Halsey, *op. cit.*, p. 130.

CHAPTER 17

1. *Southeast Area Operations Record.* Part IV (Revised). *Eighth Area Army Opns.* OCMH 8-5.1 AC 127, pp. 3, 4.

2. Imamura did not assume command in Rabaul until November 26. Prior to this date "ComGen 8th Area Army received his orders at Imperial General Headquarters in Tokyo, made necessary preparations, left Tokyo on Nov. 20, and arrived by plane in Rabaul on Nov. 22. On his way out to Rabaul, he contacted Admiral Yamamoto, Commander of the Combined Fleet on Truk Island." (Miyazaki correspondence.)

3. The short title for Guadalcanal, "KA," is pronounced in Japanese exactly as is the ideograph "KA" meaning "hunger." This coincidence did not, at the time, escape Generals Hyakutake, Kawaguchi, and Miyazaki, or, indeed, thousands of other Japanese who fought there.

4. *Daikaishi Dai Hyakugojikyo-go* (Imperial GHQ Navy Directive No. 159 of November 18, 1942).

5. Actually, the 21st Independent Mixed Brigade (Major Gen. Tsuyuo Yamagata) had been assigned to O/B of 17th Army on 28 October. The 51st Division (in South China) had been assigned a week earlier, but Lieut. Gen. Hidemitsu Nakano had as yet received no shipping to lift his command.

6. To be activated at Rabaul 27 November, under command of Lieut. Gen. Giichi Itahana, at a strength of 54 light bombers, 84 fighters, and nine reconnaissance planes. The air groups assigned were at the time in the Dutch Indies, Malaya, and South China.

7. Carlson had earlier served as an observer with the Chinese Communist Eighth Route Army, and had adopted this expression, "Work Cooperatively" or "Work Together," from them. Carlson also introduced his concept of the "Combat Group" squad organization to the Marine Corps. In each group he placed an automatic rifle. This triangular organization endowed the squad with unprecedented tactical flexibility. As later modified by the 1st Raiders, the squad was expanded to three 4-man "fire teams" plus the squad leader. This latter organization quickly became standard in the Marine Corps.

8. Carlson's patrol actions reduced enemy strength by some 450, at a cost of 34 casualties (17 KIA). The story of the Second Raiders' march in the jungle is told in detail by Captain Herbert L. Merillat, U.S.M.C.R., in *The Island* (Boston: Houghton Mifflin Co., 1944).

9. *Seventeenth Army Operations*, Vol. II, p. 51. Includes naval personnel.

10. *Ibid.*, Vol. I, p. 122.

11. Miller, *op. cit.*, p. 204.

12. *Ibid.*, p. 205.

13. The Japanese 90-mm. battalion mortar was an extremely accurate and effective weapon which outranged the American 81 mm. Within a radius of ten yards of burst, the concussive effect of its thin-walled high-explosive shell was tremendous—indeed, on occasion, lethal. Japanese mortar crews were proficient; they usually managed to locate good positions for their observers, and shifted mortars frequently. U. S. mortars could not reach them, and when artillery fire was called on their presumed firing

areas the Japanese 90s invariably responded with an accurate concentration on American front lines and then displaced. The immediate impression —that our own artillery was falling short—produced precisely the reaction anticipated: anguished pleas: "Cease firing own troops." Marines and soldiers had to be exposed to this trick many times before they realized exactly what was happening.

14. *Follow Me! The Story of the Second Marine Division in World War II,* Johnson, Richard W. (New York: Random House, 1948), p. 166.

15. *Eighth Area Operations,* p. 14.

16. *First MarDiv Final Report,* Annex T (Medical), pp. 5-7.

CHAPTER 18

1. Morison, *op. cit.,* p. 294.

2. Tanaka, *op. cit.,* II, p. 825.

3. *Ibid.*

4. *Ibid.*

5. *Ibid.*

6. Morison, *op. cit.,* p. 306.

7. *Minneapolis, New Orleans* and *Northampton* each carried nine 8-inch guns; *Pensacola,* ten. *Honolulu* carried fifteen 6-inch. The five cruisers were armed with a total of thirty-two 5-inch guns.

8. "The Navy's marksmanship that night was abominable." (Morison, *op. cit.,* p. 313.)

9. *Ibid.*

10. As of the date of its departure, casualty figures for the First Marine Division Reinforced show that 152 officers and 1,186 enlisted men were killed and missing in action, and died of their wounds. An additional 275 officers and 3,625 enlisted were evacuated, wounded or ill. Of this total many were malarial. Hospital records show 5,749 admissions to sick list for malaria (First Marine Division only). Of these, over 3,200 cases were diagnosed in November. *First Mardiv Final Report,* Annex X (Numerical Summary of Casualties).

11. Merillat, *op. cit.*

12. Organizations which comprised the First Marine Division, reinforced, in the Solomon Islands Area 7 August to 9 December 1942, during the period for which the Presidential Unit Citation was awarded. As given by Blakeney, Jane. *Heroes, U. S. Marine Corps 1861–1955, Armed Forces Awards, Flags, Reference Book.* (Washington, D. C.: Privately printed, 1957.)

MARINE UNITS

First Marines
Second Marines
Fifth Marines
Seventh Marines
Eighth Marines, Reinforced
Tenth Marines
Eleventh Marines

First Special Weapons Battalion
First Tank Battalion
Second Tank Battalion
First Parachute Battalion
First Marine Raider Battalion, IMAC
Second Marine Raider Battalion

Seventeenth Marines (Engineer)
Eighteenth Marines (Engineer)
First Engineer Battalion, Division Special Troops
Second Engineer Battalion
Division Headquarters Battalion
First Service Battalion
Second Service Battalion
First Medical Battalion
Second Medical Battalion
First Amphibian Tractor Battalion
Second Amphibian Tractor Battalion

First Aviation Engineer Battalion, FMF
Third Barrage Balloon Squadron, IMAC
Third Defense Battalion, FMF
Fourteenth Defense Battalion, FMF
155-mm. Howitzer Battalion
Antiaircraft Group, IMAC
Marine Corps Unit #290-A. Sixth U. S. Naval Construction Battalion and U.S.S. Jamestown YP's 239, 346 and 284

NAVY UNITS

Cub One, U. S. Navy
Motor Torpedo Boat Squadron—2
Motor Torpedo Boat Squadron—3

ARMY UNIT

Americal Division

MARINE AVIATION UNITS

Headquarters Squadron
FMAW Headquarters Squadron
MAG 14 Service Squadron
MAG 14 Headquarters Squadron
MAG 23 Service Squadron
MAG 23 VMF-112, Marine Fighting Squadron, MAG 11
VMF-121, Marine Fighting Squadron, MAG 14
VMF-122, Marine Fighting Squadron, MAG 11
VMSB-131, Marine Scout Bombing Squadron, MAG 14
VMSB-132, Marine Scout Bombing Squadron, MAG 11
VMSB-141, Marine Scout Bombing Squadron, MAG 14
VMSB-142, Marine Scout Bombing Squadron, MAG 11

VMF-212, Marine Fighting Squadron, MAG 23
VMF-223, Marine Fighting Squadron, MAG 23
VMF-224, Marine Fighting Squadron, MAG 23
VMSB-231, Marine Scout Bombing Squadron, MAG 23
VMSB-232, Marine Scout Bombing Squadron, MAG 23
Headquarters Squadron, MAG 11
Headquarters Squadron, MAG 25
Service Squadron, MAG 25
VMJ-152, Marine Utility Squadron, MAG 25
VMD-154, Marine Photographic Squadron, FMAW
VMO-251, Marine Observation Squadron
VMJ-253, Marine Utility Squadron, MAG 25

NAVY AVIATION UNITS

VS-3, Scouting Squadron
VS-4, Scouting Squadron
VS-5, Scouting Squadron
VB-5, Bombing Squadron
VF-5, Fighting Squadron
VB-6, Bombing Squadron
FTU-6, Field Torpedo Unit
VT-8, Torpedo Unit

VS-10, Scouting Squadron
VB-10, Bombing Squadron
VF-10, Fighting Squadron
VT-10, Torpedo Squadron
VS-54, Scouting Squadron
VS-55, Scouting Squadron
VS-71, Scouting Squadron
VF-72, Fighting Squadron

ARMY AVIATION UNITS

5th Bombardment Group (Heavy)
11th Bombardment Group (Heavy)
13th Troop Carrier Squadron
67th Fighter Squadron (SE)
68th Fighter Squadron (SE)

70th Bombardment Squadron (Medium)
339th Fighter Squadron (TE)
347th Fighter Group, Headquarters

CHAPTER 19

1. *8th Marines, Report of Operations, Guadalcanal,* Historical Branch, G-3 Div. Hq., U.S.M.C. #A 24-1, gives 78 KIA, 140 WIA for the period, a total of 218. Even today it is impossible to reconcile casualty figures given in various official documents and in secondary but presumably reliable sources. For example, *First MarDiv Final Report,* Annex X (Numerical Summary of Casualties in Units of First Marine Division, Reinforced) shows, for Eighth Marines (to December 10, inclusive) 56 KIA plus 11 MIA (presumed dead), with 207 "evacuated." As wounded and ill were lumped together under this heading, it is of little value for casualty analysis. Richard W. Johnson, in the unofficial history of the Second Marine Division, *Follow Me,* gives Eighth Marine casualty figures that differ, not only from those cited in the regiment's official report, but from those given in Annex X to the Division report. Machine records tabulations at Marine Corps Headquarters differ from all three authorities cited above.

2. *First MarDiv Final Report,* Annex N (Intelligence), p. 16. Some elements of the Volinavua garrison had landed a month previously at Aola Bay, and were now suffering from the usual afflictions, dysentery and malaria.

3. A handful of selected pilots of Smith's Marine Air Group 25 had been taught celestial navigation in the spring of 1942 by Captain P. V. H. Weems, U.S.N. (ret.) at his own expense. These pilots returned from his cram session at Annapolis to San Diego to teach others. When Smith's first squadron left the West Coast for New Caledonia in August, there was a fully qualified aerial navigator in each transport. (Correspondence, Lt. Gen. Louis Woods, U.S.M.C. (ret.)) Only one SCAT plane was lost by faulty navigation.

4. *First MarDiv Final Report,* Annex T ("Medical").

5. Marine aviators made special efforts to keep the native scouts and constabulary supplied with assorted patterns of cotton cloth and supplies of black tobacco twists. These men—and the loyal villagers—had picked up dozens of Marine and Navy flyers from the water, hidden them from the Japanese, nursed them if wounded or ill, and eventually returned them to Guadalcanal by canoe, schooner, or motorboat. No one ever offered natives a money reward, but they gratefully accepted cloth and tobacco.

6. The selection by those who served on Guadalcanal of MacArthur as whipping boy is not altogether explicable. There was no way MacArthur could have given any substantial assistance to Guadalcanal. He had problems in his own area. In terms of logistic support, he was at the very end of the line; the vast river of war material that was to flow to him later was at this time no more than a trickle.

7. As early as January 1942 the Bureau of Aeronautics (Navy Department) had urgently recommended a night fighter program for the Marine Corps. But "when the authorization emerged in March from the office of the Marine Corps' Commandant . . . the night fighter program seemed something for future generations. . . ." (Sherrod, *op. cit.*, p. 159.) Due to the efforts of Majors E. Colston Dyer and Frank H. Schwable, the Commandant finally agreed to speed the program. But it was almost a full year (1 November 1943) before a Marine pilot made the first night interception in the South Pacific. (See Chapter 11, Sherrod, *op. cit.* "Enter the Night Fighters," pp. 158-169.)

Brigadier General Colston Dyer, U.S.M.C. (retired), has provided the following information in respect to this program:

"Regarding the night fighters, Sherrod is completely accurate. I first learned of night fighters and their operations at a radar and fighter controller school in England in 1941. On my return home, I managed to get a few squadrons put into Force Tabs—1945 was the best I could do—and placed orders for ground control equipment.

"Sometime early in 1943, Admiral Halsey let out a bellow for night fighters, and E. J. King wanted to know what we were doing. Force Tabs were changed right quick! . . .

"But we couldn't have used night fighters until we had the ground control equipment, proper VHF radio, aircraft intercept radar, etc., not to mention trained people to operate and maintain. . . . It was a matter of first things first." (Dyer correspondence.)

8. *Southeast Area Naval Operations*, p. 54.

9. Awarded the American Legion of Merit for his exceptional services and now an honorary member of the First Marine Division Association and Edson's Raiders Association. After a distinguished career in the Colonial Service, Clemens retired (1960) to become a rancher in Australia.

10. Now (November, 1962) High Commissioner of the British Solomon Islands and stationed on Guadalcanal.

11. This was not the only barbarism committed by the Japanese on Guadalcanal. Happily, those responsible for such outrages were apparently later killed in action or died of wounds. Such actions were neither ordered by Lt. Gen. Hyakutake or by his Chief of Staff, Lt. Gen. Miyazaki. Both were honorable men and neither would have condoned such behavior had he known of it. Both these generals emerged from World War II with personal reputations completely unsullied.

12. A landing was finally made on the south coast, but achieved no important tactical result, as by that time the offensive along the north coast had reached Esperance.

13. *Unit Journal, 132nd Infantry Regt.* 300-INF (132)—0.7. No. 23628 National Archives, Alexandria, Va.

14. *Ibid.*

15. *Ibid.*

16. *Ibid.*

17. Account based on *Report, 132nd Infantry (Americal Division)* 300-INF (132)—0.3, No. 23417. The "Gifu" was named by the Japanese manning it after a prefecture in the island of Honshu. Actually, the extent of

the "Gifu" position was finally determined by scouts of the 2nd Battalion, Thirty-fifth Infantry, 25th Division.

18. *Unit Journal, op. cit.*

CHAPTER 20

1. Imoto correspondence.
2. *Ibid.*
3. *Imperial GHQ Army High Command Record*, p. 76.
4. *Ibid.*, p. 77.
5. *Imperial GHQ Navy Staff Section Directive No. 184*, Jan. 4, 1943.
6. *Southeast Area Naval Operations*, p. 59.
7. *Ibid.*
8. *Eighth Area Army Operations*, p. 17.
9. Actually, Major General C. Barney Vogel, U.S.M.C., informed Marston that these arrangements had been made by a higher headquarters. Vogel had some time before been designated to command a new headquarters in Nouméa, the First Marine Amphibious Corps (IMAC). This corps headquarters was administrative only. All Marine elements in SoPac were under operational control of Admiral Halsey. Vogel's action irritated General Holcomb and was, needless to say, a great disappointment to Major General Marston, who stated that he would be happy to waive all questions of rank and serve in command of his division under General Patch.
10. Robert Sherrod's phrase.
11. Miller, *op. cit.*, p. 254. But does not agree with the figure of 23,000 shown on strength graph, p. 51, *17th Army Opns*. This indicates that the Japanese had suffered almost 7,000 mortal casualties in combat and from illness since mid-November when their strength reports gave a figure of approximately 30,000. This is hard to accept, as there were no major engagements on land between that time and mid-January. On the other hand, if we take Shoji's casualties as a criterion, this may be correct. His force of 3000 had been reduced at Gavaga, by Carlson's Raiders, and by disease, to about 1000, of whom but a small proportion were fit for offensive operations.
12. Miller, *op. cit.*, p. 276. Captain Davis was later awarded the Medal of Honor.
13. *Seventeenth Army Operations*, p. 150.
14. Miller, *op. cit.*, p. 293, and p. 293 n., says that Colonel Oka, the regimental commander (whose headquarters were in the jungles bordering the upper Matanikau) was "reported to have deserted his troops about 14 January." Actually, Colonel Oka was ordered to withdraw to new positions at this time. When he did so, the regimental color bearer did not accompany him, and was killed. Later, the colonel learned that the regimental color had been left and went personally to retrieve it. He did so, and as he returned with the color, he was killed on the coastal track during an air attack. He was posthumously promoted to major general, as Colonel Ichiki had also been. (Miyazaki correspondence.)
15. Rear Admiral Morison was apparently unaware that this change of

command had been effected, as he has Tanaka in command of this run. Morison, *op. cit.*, p. 339.

16. Cited by Morison, *op. cit.*, pp. 368–369.

17. One Marine pilot, one Navy pilot, and five Air Force pilots later passed this score. The phrase "in combat" is an essential qualifier here, as the Air Force credited a pilot with a "kill" when he destroyed an enemy plane on the ground. The Navy and Marine Corps gave credit only for enemy planes destroyed in air combat. (Sherrod, *op. cit.*, p. 121, nn. 23, 24.) Foss was awarded the Medal of Honor and is now (November 1962) Commissioner of the American Football League. He has observed several times that this job causes him more trouble than Japanese pilots did.

18. The account of delivery of the orders to evacuate was provided me by Lieutenant General Kumao Imoto (retired), who delivered them, and to whom I am greatly indebted.

19. These quotations, and those in the preceding four paragraphs, are drawn from General Imoto's letters.

CHAPTER 21

1. *Seventeenth Army Operations*, Vol. II, p. 16.

2. 74 KIA, 226 WIA. Miller, *op. cit.*, p. 335.

3. Second Marine Division casualties: 278 KIA and MIA; 932 wounded. Almost 50 per cent were sustained by the Second Marines. Johnston, *op. cit.*, p. 81. *First MarDiv Final Report*, Annex X.

4. As previously noted, Tanaka had been relieved as Commander, Reinforcement Force, and on December 29, 1942, returned to Japan for a period of recuperation.

5. Miyazaki correspondence. These figures are drawn (General Miyazaki writes) from the most reliable existing records available to him in Japan.

6. Not all, however, in naval battles. The figure includes seventeen combat transports, of which sixteen were Japanese. Morison, *op. cit.*, p. 372, does not include transports, but lists two battleships, three carriers, twelve cruisers, twenty-five destroyers and six submarines. The submarines were all Japanese.

7. Kawaguchi, *op. cit.* Tanaka, *op. cit.*, p. 831, says "well over one hundred planes." This is obviously a misprint. Japanese official records show they lost 69 at Santa Cruz alone. Other Japanese sources give plane losses *in the first three days* (August 7, 8, 9) as from 25 to 30. Kawaguchi gives 893 for the campaign, a figure which presumably includes planes lost operationally as well as in actual combat.

INDEX

Aaron Ward, 198, 199
Abe, Vice Adm. Hiroaki, 192
Adachi, Lt. Gen. Hatazo, 210
Agnew, Lt. Cmdr. Dwight M., 170
Ahrens, Pfc. John, 47
Air forces, Japanese, 12, 16, 52, 211
  Fourth Naval Air Group, 12
  Eleventh Air Fleet, 18, 44, 70, 107, 117
  25th Air Flotilla, 42–43
  See also Plane losses, Japanese
Air forces, U. S., 18, 30, 51
  11th Bombardment Group, 30
  Marine Air Group 23, 33
  67th Fighter Squadron, 97
  Marine Fighter Squadron 212, 10, 33, 157
  Marine Fighter Squadron. 223, 83
  Marine Fighter Squadron 224, 98
  Marine Scout Bombing Squadron 132, 189
  Marine Scout Bombing Squadron 231, 98
  Marine Scout Bombing Squadron 232, 83
  See also Plane losses, U. S.
Akatsuki, 198
Akizuke, 172
Alhena, 98
Alligator Creek, 45
Amatsukaze, 198
Amphibious operations, doctrine of, 54

Anderson, 178
Aoba, 61, 63, 150, 151
Aoba Detachment, 79, 108
Aola, 16, 145, 186–187, 219
Aotea Quay, 28, 32
Argonne, 162, 163
Arnold, Gen. H. H., 25, 131, 137, 138, 180
Arthur, Col. John M., 182, 190
Asagiri, 94
Astoria, 40, 59, 61
Atago, 175, 203
Atlanta, 193, 196, 198
Auckland, 9, 10, 25, 33, 72
Australia, 34, 58, 59, 67
Australia, 7, 8, 11, 14, 19, 27, 32, 33, 55, 64, 245
Ayabe, Maj. Gen., 233

Bailey, Maj. Kenneth D., 119, 135
Balesuna River, 212
Ballard, 135, 136, 137
Banta, Sergeant Major Sheffield, 120
Barton, 198, 199
Battle of the Coral Sea, 17
Bauer, Maj. Harold W., 10, 157
Bellatrix, 108
Bemis, Lt. Col. John, 115
Benham, 203
Bergner, Sgt. O. S., 53
Bismarck Archipelago, 11, 12, 14
Blue, 60, 63
Blue Beach, 45–46
Boise, 149, 150